The Reminiscences of
Admiral Alfred G. Ward,
U. S. Navy (Retired)

U. S. Naval Institute
Annapolis, Maryland
1972

Preface

This manuscript is the result of a series of eleven tape-recorded interviews with Admiral Alfred G. Ward, U. S. Navy (Retired. The interviews were all conducted in his office at the Severn School, Severna Park, Maryland during the period from August, 1970 to December, 1971. Admiral Ward is currently headmaster of the Severn School. The interviews were conducted by John T. Mason, Jr. for the Oral History Office in the U. S. Naval Institute.

Only minor emendations and corrections have been made to the transcript by Admiral Ward, and the reader is asked therefore to bear in mind that he is reading a transcript of the spoken word rather than the written word.

Attached to the MS are the following documents:

a. Copy of letter from the Hon. Douglas MacArthur II, U. S. Ambassador to Japan, September 1, 1959.

b. Copy of Unclassified dispatch from ComSeventhFlt, November 8, 1959.

c. Copy of Citation for Distinguished Service Medal.

d. Copy of Citation for Gold Star in lieu of the Second Distinguished Service Medal.

e. Copy of Admiral Ward's address to the Committee of One Hundred of Miami Beach, Florida, on February 16, 1963.

f. Copy of Address given by Admiral Ward at a Reserve Officers' Association dinner, Oklahoma City, Oklahoma on March 18, 1967.

g. Copy of address given by Admiral Ward at a Chamber of Commerce Luncheon in Seattle, Washington, on May 19, 1967.

h. Remarks made by Admiral Ward on the occasion of his assuming duties as Headmaster of the Severn School, Severna Park, Maryland on September 21, 1968.

DECLARATION OF TRUST

The undersigned does hereby appoint and designate as his (her) Trustee herein, the Secretary-Treasurer and Publisher of the United States Naval Institute to perform and discharge the following duties, powers, and privileges in connection with the possession and use of a certain taped interview between the undersigned and the Oral History Department of the United States Naval Institute.

1. Classification of Transcript.

    (X)a. If classified <u>OPEN</u>, the transcript(s) may be read or the recording(s) audited by the qualified personnel upon presentation of proper credentials, as determined by the Secretary-Treasurer of the U. S. Naval Institute.

    ( )b. If classified <u>PERMISSION REQUIRED TO CITE OR QUOTE</u>, the user will be required to obtain permission in writing from the interviewee prior to quoting or citing from either the transcript(s) or the recording(s).

    ( )c. If classified <u>PERMISSION REQUIRED</u>, permission must be obtained in writing from the interviewee before the transcribed interview(s) can be examined or the tape recording(s) audited.

    ( )d. If classified <u>CLOSED</u>, the transcribed interview(s) and the tape recording(s) will be sealed until a time specified by the interviewee. This may be until the death of the interviewee or for any specified number of years.

2. It is expressly understood that in giving this authorization, I am in no way precluded from placing such restrictions as I may desire upon use of the interview at any time during my lifetime, nor does this authorization in any way affect my rights to the copyright of my literary expressions that may be contained in the interview.

Witness my hand and seal this __28__ day of __January__ 19__72__

Alfred G. Ward

I hereby accept and consent to the foregoing Declaration of Trust and the powers therein conferred upon me as Trustee:

R. E. Bowser Jr.

BIOGRAPHY OF ADMIRAL ALFRED G. WARD, U.S. NAVY
U.S. REPRESENTATIVE, NATO MILITARY COMMITTEE

Alfred Gustave Ward was born in Mobile, Alabama, November 29, 1908, son of Mrs. C. T. Hamilton and the late B. E. Ward. He graduated from the U.S. Naval Academy and was commissioned Ensign, U.S. Navy, June 2, 1932. He graduated from Massachusetts Institute of Technology with a Master of Science Degree in electrical engineering in June 1940. He graduated from the Naval War College in 1954. He was promoted to Rear Admiral on August 1, 1957; to Vice Admiral on August 1, 1961 and to Admiral on March 27, 1965.

Prior to and during World War II, Admiral Ward served afloat in battleships, cruisers, and destroyers. Following World War II, prior to selection to flag rank, Admiral Ward served in various destroyer command and staff billets. Since promotion to flag rank Admiral Ward has held significant command and planning assignments including assignment as Deputy Chief of Naval Operations for Plans and Policy and Deputy Chief of Naval Operations for Fleet Operations and Readiness. His most historic assignment was as Commander, U.S. Second Fleet. In this assignment he commanded United States forces which enforced the Cuban quarantine in October of 1962. Admiral Ward has been awarded the Bronze Star Medal and subsequently a Gold Star in lieu of a second award for duty in World War II on board the USS North Carolina. He was awarded the Legion of Merit for duty as Commander, United States Second Fleet during the Cuban quarantine operations. He has been award the Distinguished Service Medal for duty as Deputy Chief of Naval Operations fo Plans and Policy and Deputy Chief of Naval Operations for Fleet Operations. I addition to these awards, Admiral Ward has the American Defense Service Med American Campaign Medal; Asiatic-Pacific Campaign Medal; World War II Victory Medal; Navy Occupation Service Medal; Asia Clasp; China Service Meda and National Defense Service Medal.

Admiral Ward assumed his present duty as United States Representative to the NATO Military Committee in April, 1965.

Revised 1 Jul 68

1 July 1968

ADMIRAL ALFRED G. WARD, UNITED STATES NAVY
CHRONOLOGICAL LISTING OF ASSIGNMENTS

Jun 1932 – Jun 1937	USS NORTHAMPTON
Jun 1937 – Jun 1938	USS PERRY
Jun 1940 – Apr 1941	Navy Yard, New York, N. Y.
Apr 1941 – May 1944	USS NORTH CAROLINA
Jun 1944 – 1945	Naval Gun Factory, Navy Yard, Washington, D. C.
Jul 1946 – Oct 1947	USS HOLLISTER - Commanding Officer
Oct 1947 – Dec 1948	Staff, Commander Destroyer Force U.S. Pacific Fleet
Dec 1948 – Oct 1950	Naval Gun Factory, Production Officer Washington, D. C.
Oct 1950 – Jul 1951	Commander, Destroyer Division ONE HUNDRED TWO
Jul 1951 – Aug 1953	Staff, Commander Destroyer Force U.S. Atlantic Fleet - Asst Chief of Staff for Operations and Plans
Aug 1953 – Mar 1954	Naval War College, Newport, Rhode Island, Instruction
Mar 1954 – Aug 1956	Office Chief of Naval Operations, Navy Department, Washington, D. C. Strategic Plans Division
Aug 1956 – Feb 1957	Commander, Amphibious Squadron EIGHT
Feb 1957 – Jun 1959	Deputy Chief of Staff (Operations & Plans) to Commander in Chief, U.S. Atlantic Fleet
Jun 1959 – Jun 1960	Commander Cruiser Division ONE
Jun 1960 – Aug 1961	Asst Chief of Naval Operations (Fleet Operations), Navy Department

ADMIRAL ALFRED G. WARD, UNITED STATES NAVY
CHRONOLOGICAL LISTING OF ASSIGNMENTS - CONTINUED

Aug 1961 - Oct 1962	Commander, Amphibious Force, Atlantic
Oct 1962 - Aug 1963	Commander SECOND FLEET and Commander Strike Fleet, Atlantic
Aug 1963 - Jul 1964	Deputy Chief of Naval Operations (Plans and Policy)
Jul 1964 - Mar 1965	Deputy Chief of Naval Operations (Fleet Operations and Readiness)
Apr 1965 - Sep 1967	United States Representative to the NATO Military Committee, Washington, D. C.
Sep 1967 - Jul 1968	United States Representative to the NATO Military Committee, Brussels, Belgium

EXPERIENCE HIGHLIGHTS CAREER Alfred G. WARD

1965 - 1968

United States Representative to the Military Committee of NATO. Report directly to the Chairman, U.S. Joint Chiefs of Staff but also principal military advisor to U.S. Ambassador Harlan Cleveland, U.S. Representative to the North Atlantic Council. Attend NATO Council meetings as Advisor to Secretary of Defense Clark Clifford and occasionally to Secretary Dean Rusk.

Formulate or participate in formulation of policies and national positions on politico-military subjects for approval by highest governmental authorities, then attempt to get multinational concurrence in such policies and finally am charged with execution of some aspects of decisions reached.

Spend about one week in each month in Washington conferring with military and civilian leaders, with most of the remainder of time spent in Brussels.

At request of the Department of State have given lectures to Chapters of the Council on Foreign Relations in Seattle, Portland (Oregon), San Francisco, Detroit, Milwaukee and Miami Beach. Participated in seminars at the New York headquarters of the Council on Foreign Relations and at the American Assembly of Columbia University.

In addition, have the administrative responsibilities of the head of a sizeable organization.

1963-1965

Deputy Chief of Naval Operations. Prepared actions for and assisted the Chief of the Navy in his capacity as a member of the Joint Chiefs of Staff. With the help of some eight subordinate Admirals and about 200 other staff officers controlled the overall organization of the fleets and naval activities. Reviewed and supported in direct testimony before Congressional committees the Navy's requirements for new ships, equipment and weapons systems.

1961-1962
   Commander United States Second Fleet, consisting of all major combatant units except submarines in the Atlantic. In command of naval units enforcing the quarantine of Cuba. Prepared quarantine plans for approval by the JCS and President Kennedy and executed those plans.

1961-1962
   Commander Amphibious Forces, U.S. Atlantic Fleet, with more than 50 ships. As in other important billets, majority of effort devoted to organization and personnel administration; this assignment offered opportunities to work with underwater swimmers and commando type personnel; supervised and participated to some extent in their training in the Caribbean.

1958-1959
   In command of a Naval Task Force, as a Cruiser Division Commander, toured the Western Pacific, met and conferred with Chiefs of State and senior political and military leaders of Japan, Republic of China, Philippines and Vietnam.

1945-1947
   Production Officer, U.S. Naval Gun Factory. Manufactured naval guns, weapons, optics and associated equipment with more than 5,000 civilian employees in the production department. Further, coordinated this production with large Westinghouse satellite plants. Duties included personnel management, labor relations, planning and all phases of large factory production.

World War II
   Gunnery officer battleship USS NORTH CAROLINA operating in the Pacific. Was in commissioning crew of this ship and took an active part in completing her electronics and fire control installations.

EDUCATION: Master of Science Degree in Electrical Engineering
Massachusetts Institute of Technology, 1940
(Due to small classes and work in challenging new fields, became not only student but also personal friend of such outstanding scientists and educators as Dr. Stark Draper, Dr. Harold Hagen, Dr. Gordon Brown and Dr. Ralph Bennett.

Bachelor of Science Degree
United States Naval Academy, 1932

U.S. Naval War College, 1954
Strategy, Tactics and International Relations

Interview #1 with Admiral Alfred G. Ward, USN (ret.)

Severn School, Severna Park, Md.   August 19, 1970

Subject: Biography   by John T. Mason

Mr. Mason: Admiral, it's a delight to be with you this afternoon. I've been looking forward to this series with you on your very distinguished Navy career. Would you begin, Sir, in the proper and acceptable manner by telling me the date of your birth, where you were born, and something about your family background and your early education?

Admiral Ward: Dr. Mason, let me express my appreciation to you for taking an interest in people such as Alfred G. Ward and the people with whom he worked in his years in the Navy. I was born in Mobile, Alabama, in 1908, November 29. I was a son of a family that was quite prominent in Mobile, my great-grandfather having been given a grant by the King of England of a great tract of what is now the city of Mobile. My grandparents didn't carry this heritage forward in the best manner. My mother was married to one of the local men there, and when he died when I was age six, my mother had to go to work, which was unusual in those days, and I was left without the funds necessary to complete my education as we would have liked to have done.

Q: Had the family holdings been in a plantation?

Ward #1 - 2

Ward: It was land which later became part of the city and as the city gradually expanded this land was sold off. I went to the local high school in Mobile, which, by starting at age five and having only eleven years of school, I finished at a fairly early age. After completing high school, I went to work for two years on a road construction job in southern Alabama and northern Florida

Q: That was a very fortunate development, wasn't it?

Ward: It certainly was.

Q: You give indication of having been a bit precocious, maybe, and maybe had to give yourself time to grow up physically.

Ward: Rather than use the word precocious, I think I would say immature. I was just a little boy. I was small in stature. I didn't start to grow to be a fairly sizable, or at least a medium size person until after graduating from high school. These two years made a great difference in my future. This experience gave me self reliance, as a result of getting out and working for myself in a rather tough environment; mostly rough people were building roads then.

Q: Was your mother pleased with this development, or was she disappointed that you didn't go on directly?

Ward: I think my mother accepted the fact that she could not afford to send me directly and this was probably a good thing. I finally awakened to the realization that if I was to get a college education, I would need some kind of help and therefore I chose to come to the Naval Academy. I think my mother was proud but she was certainly not very happy about losing her older son.

Q: As an educator, in the second phase of your careers, you might comment on this development -- the fact you went out and worked in the world and it's suggested pretty often by educators that maybe this would be a good policy all along the line.

Ward: It certainly would be good for many individuals. It's fairly hard to generalize, in that in my present school we have some seniors who are completely capable of going to a college and getting the maximum benefits from the education and from the associations that they make in college. I would say that for these individuals, moving right on to the next level of education is desirable. On the other hand, we get a few who are not mature enough to accept, and absorb, the benefits that are offered to them, and I certainly was in this category. For me it was desirable that I stay out of school.

Q: How did you achieve your appointment to the Naval Academy?

Ward: I joined the Navy as an enlisted man but I never served

Ward #1 - 4

in the Navy other than in preparatory school for Annapolis. That was at Norfolk.

Q: Tell me about that system of having preparatory schools. I understand there were two, were there?

Ward: Yes. I believe the principal one was the one in Norfolk but there was one on the West Coast also. As you know, now there is only the one at Bainbridge, Maryland. These boys at Bainbridge today are getting a real good preparatory school education, as we did.

Q: Somewhat better, I would judge, than what was given by the famous Bobby Werntz and his cram methods.

Ward: Yes, much better than Bobby Werntz. As you know, the Werntz school had rather limited supervision, as I understand it. The education was good enough to get many boys in, but the whole outlook of the school was not particularly good. That's the reason for the founding of this Severn School. Mr. Teel, who was one of the teachers at the Werntz school, did not like what he saw at that school and felt that there should be a better school, a better organized school, a better supervised school with supervision of conduct as well as academics. Therefore he founded the Severn School to fill this apparent void. For many years the Severn School was almost exclusively preparatory for the Naval Academy and was essentially all boarding.

Q: When you were at the school in Norfolk, how long a period was this, and how many were in your preparatory class?

Ward: About a hundred of us from the naval service as enlisted men were actually admitted to the Academy that year.

Q: This is by Presidential appointment?

Ward: It is by law, passed by Congress and approved by the President.

Q: That comprised a fairly large proportion of your incoming class.

Ward: We entered the Academy about seven hundred and fifty and about four hundred graduated.

Q: Tell me about your years at the Academy, your achievements.

Ward: I gained some maturity when I arrived. This was a completely new experience for a youngster who had never been out of the Alabama/northern Florida area. For example, I had never seen snow before in my life. It was not only new from this point of view, but it was new being associated with boys from all over the United States and quite a broadening experience. I thoroughly enjoyed my time. Unlike some of the men who had gone to college and felt that they were repeating much of what they had had before, when being forced to take freshman subjects, I did not feel this way. Everything was new, bright and shiny, and I thoroughly enjoyed my time. I was not a leader in my first few years there, in that I was learning to get along with other people. I was learning to fit in the mold. I stood well in my class. I think in my freshman class I stood four in my class and several hundred of them had had some college experience.

Q: Obviously you had adequate background and preparation for what was offered.

Ward: I was helped a great deal by the school in Norfolk in refreshing me in algebra and geometry. I had a good background for a boy from the Deep South.

Q: Was the school in Norfolk manned entirely by naval officers?

Ward: Yes, it was. They were not particularly trained or adapted to this, but they imparted in us enough knowledge so that with the help of other boys, we had no problems. I have many friends from that group who have served well in the Navy with great distinction. Many of them have made the rank of rear admiral.

I found my place at the Naval Academy. I was designated as a battalion commander, the third ranking midshipman, during my senior year. I was editor of THE LUCKY BAG, the annual. I had a very rewarding experience during my Naval Academy days. I went out to the Fleet on graduation and was very enthusiastic.

Q: Tell me about your summer experiences, the cruises. Sometimes they prove to be awfully valuable.

Ward: They were valuable in my case, by virtue of seeing parts of the world that I had read about and never seen. It completely opened new vistas. On my first cruise we went to Europe, the second cruise was a summer cruise outside the United States. I played some lacrosse and got a little bit into the athletic program. I managed the varsity lacrosse team.

Q: Well, that gave you administrative experience.

Ward: Yes, and I think my experience on THE LUCKY BAG also helped.

Q: That's pretty strenuous, isn't it? THE LUCKY BAG editor?

Ward: Yes. I was one of the few midshipmen in those days, I guess, who had the privilege of working after hours. After the

Ward #1 - 8 -

bell had sounded, ~~so that~~ everyone else had to be in bed. Because of the heavy work load I was carrying, I was allowed to stay up as late as necessary in order to get this work done.

Q: And also I imagine, because you had such good standing in your class scholastically.

Ward: I'm sure that helped.

Q: A weak student wouldn't have had that privilege.

Ward: My class standing suffered a little bit as a result of this but not very much.

Q: What did you excell in in the courses at the Academy?

Ward: Mathematics and sciences. There was Some indication of this in high school in that I never had any trouble ~~whatsoever~~ with any math or science. My standings in those subjects were particularly good.

Q: What did you think of the courses as a whole, the education that was provided by the Academy, in retrospect?

Ward: At the time I thought it was very good. I was learning a great deal in basic math and basic sciences. In retrospect, I think much of the instruction was stereotyped. For example (I'm sure you've heard this from other people) our course in ordnance engineering was more a memory of procedures of manufacturing of weapons or manufacturing of gun powder and did not go into the principles involved and therefore was not conducive to a broad understanding on which you could grow in knowledge in these areas. Fortunately, this no longer exists --this short coming has been observed by many people and has been eliminated. Right now I think the course at the Naval Academy is superb. I've talked to midshipmen, I've talked to instructors over there and I think it's a very wonderful course. I recommend it to some of my best students in this school.

Q: At the time, how was it anticipated that a young fellow would achieve the broad understanding which he didn't receive in the course material? By actual experience aboard ship?

Ward: The whole subject of education was undergoing a change in those days, with the Naval Academy, in my opinion, lagging a little behind some of the colleges that had more modern approach, a more imaginative approach. These short comings did not exist for any appreciable time after I finished school.

Q: Who was superintendant when you were there.

Ward: Admiral Tommy Hart was one of my superintendants, We

later became a senator. I liked Admiral Hart very much. I still like him, he's a wonderful man. I love him, I think he's great.

Q: He had certain objectives in educating young men at the Academy, didn't he?

Ward: Yes, he did. He wanted to instill in the men a feeling of integrity, honesty, and I think he did. I think the whole academic program was weak, as we see it from hindsight, but the Superintendent was limited in the type of instructors he had. He'd been given officers from the fleet, who had gone through this type of an education and were not prepared to change it greatly.

Q: He once told me that he really strove to develop a boy as a leader and his second objective was to make him into a gentleman.

Ward: I would concur with this. I think he did his best in these two areas. He had some real good people in basic mathematics, some in engineering, electrical engineering -- the lessons were well thought out. It was only in the areas in which you learn by rote, particularly in ordnance and also in seamanship and the navigation department in which you learn the way to navigate as of that time, but you did not learn the principles which led to a look into the future and made it easier for you to adapt to some of the new systems which came in a few years later.

Q: As you say, things were in a state of change in the educational world and that type of instruction represented an old fashioned view.

Ward: Let me make one other comment on Admiral Hart because I love the old gentleman, too, I learned a great deal from him but even a man with his breadth of knowledge and his understanding of people can guess wrong. I would like to tell you one of the areas in which he guessed wrong. He was a speaker at our graduation (the year before I think the President of the United States spoke to the graduating class), but Admiral Hart spoke to us and he predicted that he had seen the Navy rise and fall, and that he thought that we, the graduates, would find the going real tough, that the future of the Navy was not at all bright. The events in the world proved him to be wrong. As soon as we had gotten out, the way the world was going necessitated our country to start building up a Navy and being prepared for events of the future.

Q: Of course, at the moment, that was in 1932, we were at a kind of a NADIR. The depression was just getting over and it was pretty rough going. Congress was tough on appropriations, too. Graduating in 1932 with a limited Navy and no early prospects being developed appreciably, what kind of assignment did you get? What were your prospects immediately?

Ward: Fortunately, by virtue of having been a battalion commander, and pretty well up in the hierarchy of the midshipmen class, and standing well in my class, I was given a very good assignment on one of our new cruisers and moved right into an area in which there were good people and the performance standards were high, and in which it was possible to grow with the Navy, as the Navy grew. I spent five years in this first ship, the NORTHAMPTON, a new cruiser, mostly in the gunnery department.

Q: Who was her skipper at that time?

Ward: We had several, of course, and very good skippers.

Q: This is so terribly important for a youngster getting out to have good leadership.

Ward: The friends with whom I was to work later, and you have named them, Admiral Hooper, Admiral Mustin, and Admiral Rivero had quite similar beginnings as officers in the Navy, all going to the fire control or gunnery work, with most of us in cruisers. We worked together frequently, even before our post graduate days, and we have worked together since.

Q: What are some of your outstanding recollections of that period of duty on the NORTHAMPTON? What kind of work was she called upon to do?

Ward: This was a fairly quiet period between the depression and the build-up in preparing for World War II. It was a very exciting, very interesting period. We were based in the Los Angeles area. As a young bachelor there, making a hundred and twenty dollars a month, I was wealthy.

Q: Was this minus the fifteen percent?

Ward: Yes. Minus the fifteen percent. We were welcomed at the big parties that were given by the movie people and it was a very exciting personal life. It was a very exciting professional life in that we were working with top people in the military service, working hard and learning how to get the most out of our ship's equipment.

I left the NORTHAMPTON and went down to join one of the old four stack destroyers for a year before going to post graduate school. This too was a very interesting period.

Q: Is that something you asked for?

Ward: Yes, I did. Moving from a destroyer to a cruiser was a standard pattern in those days -- moving from either a cruiser or a battleship to a destroyer was fairly standard procedure. I happened to find a good one in that I had a man named Charley Wellborn, who later became a vice admiral, as skipper and he ran a magnificent ship, so it was very interesting for me.

Ward #1 - 14 -

Q: What was your particular duty on the destroyer?

Ward: I was a communication officer at first and then a man of all trades.

Q: That's one of the virtues of serving on a destroyer, isn't it?

Ward: Yes. Everybody does everything.

Q: What was her complement?

Ward: I think we had about seventy men on board.

Q: This was limited because of the circumstances in the Navy at that time?

Ward: Partly, but also she was a small ship, too. I should add quickly that just prior to leaving the NORTHAMPTON in 1937, I was married. This came about by virtue of the ship, NORTHAMPTON, going up to Bremerton, Washington, for overhaul on two occasions and I met my wife in the Bremerton area.

Q: You had more leisure time at that point.

Ward: Yes, during shipyard overhaul you had time to climb the mountains and see the beauties of the Puget Sound area.

Q: What duties did you have with the ship during refitting?

Ward: We were overhauling our fire control equipment, particularly our computers that we had in those days, and this requires fairly close supervision by ship's people.

Q: This meant then that you were working with naval architects?

Ward: Yes. Shipyard people, naval architects.

Q: That, I suppose, is an example of where a man gets this broader background and understanding that you referred to before. You had a year on the destroyer and then you went to postgraduate school?

Ward: That's right.

Q: Which was, indeed, a recognition of a man's ability, wasn't it?

Ward: Yes. There was some selectivity with people who did the best job, particularly in gunnery, getting the assignments in the fire control area. Even in those days, while we didn't call them computers, we were working with this type of technology. Here again, the four of us, Hooper, Mustin, Rivero, and Ward, came together in the first group in this fire control effort.

Q: It must have been vastly stimulating.

Ward: It was hard work.

Q: That's a lesson that I expect you didn't have to really learn though, that to achieve you had to work.

Ward: That's right. But I found that after a year of post graduate work in Annapolis and going up to M.I.T. I never studied as hard in my life before. The amount of work that was poured on us was almost unbelievable and much more than any other students in that great university were attempting.

Q: Tell me first about the first phase of that at the Naval Academy.

Ward: We had some theoretical courses. We had a mathematics instructor named Professor Bramble, who was one of the really outstanding mathematicians and one who was capable of imparting his knowledge and of teaching the subject as well as any other whom I have ever worked under. Dr. Bramble was successful in teaching us some Heavisides Operational Calculus and in preparing us for some of the LaPlace transformations that we would get in the future at M.I.T.

Q: He knew what was being undertaken at M.I.T. so he was preparing you for it?

Ward: I'm sure he was preparing us for the additional education we would get there. I'm sure, also, that he was aware generally of what would be required of us. But I believe no one at Annapolis realized the level, particularly in theoretical math, which would be thrown at us when we arrived, nor did we. The course that we were faced with was much harder, as I indicated, than other people were taking and actually was so hard it was eased in the next few years.

Q: At the Naval Academy, what kind of living quarters did you have? What kind of opportunity for relaxation and that sort of thing? This is important when a man is working so hard.

Ward: As I mentioned we were married, and our first child was born during this period. We rented a small home in the vicinity. Even in those days there were reasonable rates. I remember we paid thirty dollars a month for a furnished house in the Annapolis area.

Q: So you were enjoying real family life as a background to all this studying.

Ward: Yes, and getting together on a social basis maybe one night a week, usually on a Saturday night, with our friends.

Q: Was the Navy Department keeping close tabs on you as you progressed in p.g. school?

Ward: Yes, they were. And particularly so because we were beginning to get into a critical international era. President Franklin Roosevelt had just decided to let the British have some of our destroyers and the Germans were becoming more and more war-like, tensi were rising and many of our students at post graduate school were pulled out of school and put back to work in a greatly expanded Navy The expansion was so severe that people were becoming important and as each individual became more needed at sea, it was only the fortunate few who were taking the toughest and most advanced work that were permitted to remain in the post graduate program.

Q: The men were separated from the boys in this case.

Ward: It was a question of using the talent, I believe, to the maximum benefit. I think one reason they did not pull out those who were taking this advanced course was the fact that it was recognized that some of the new equipment that was going into the battleships that were then on the drawing boards, and into the attack carriers that were then being considered and being tuilt, would require the maximum efforts of all engineers to get the equipment built and then it would require some expertise in operating those complicated equipments.

Q: It would appear some real wisdom stood back of the policy and the decisions that were being made.

Ward: I think it was fortunate for the nation that we had the flexibility to keep some of this work going on at a time when we were expanding very, very much, and it certainly benefitted us -- those of us who were permitted to carry on the theoretical work as well as the practical work.

Q: It benefitted you personally but it also benefitted the Navy in a larger sense. Having completed one year at the Academy, you went immediately to M.I.T. Would you dwell on that period in some detail if you can?

Ward: We were a small group of four naval officers with three other students with us -- one was a Chinese young man and the other two were brilliant young men who were getting their doctorates, but they did not take all the load that we were trying to handle. These others concentrated in the field of the just beginning computer technology.

Q: Did they come from various university backgrounds?

Ward: Yes. One of them had been at M.I.T. for his undergraduate work and was getting his doctorate, and the other two were from other universities. One was from the University of Chicago. All of us were introduced to these new developments in computer technology and electronics in the fire control area for servo-mechanisms of which you spoke. We were knocking on the threshold of knowledge in those days, with the help of some brilliant instructors, just tremendous people.

Q: Who were some of these men?

Ward: Dr. Gordon Brown, Dr. Stark Draper. Dr. Draper is one of the finest engineers I've ever known. He is a man for whom the Draper Laboratory at M.I.T. has been named and is now, once again, in charge of that great laboratory. Dr. Stark Draper, working with Mustin and Rivero to a great extent, and to a lesser extent with Hooper and myself, developed the gyro-sight which made it possible to put machine guns on a moving target much more effectively than it had ever been done before. I think that Dr. Draper's brilliance and Lloyd Mustin's ability as an engineer made possible this development for the Sperry Corporation. Hooper and myself were working on servo-mechanisms and again working at the threshold of knowledge in this area.

Q: You pursued this direction by choice?

Ward: It was more-or-less choice but with the help of the

excellent, superb instructors and professors that we had in those days. These were the smartest brains in the United States, I guess --brilliant people. Dr. Harold Hazen, the head of the department gave us great encouragement, and Gordon Brown worked directly with us. We worked actually in Gordon's office with the experimentation that we were doing in this field.

Q: Tell me about servo-mechanisms. What kind of objective did you think you had in mind that you would achieve?

Ward: As you know, a servo-mechanism is a device which takes a small signal, say a very light touch of the finger, in order to move a tremendous mass of equipment and make it perform in a manner in which you want that equipment to perform. You can put a program into it which will cause it to go through certain cycles of motion or to perform certain tasks which you have assigned to it. This had been done hydraulically before. Doing it electronically was anew in the technology of those days.

Q: But it's directly responsible for what has been developed lately in the space program, isn't it?

Ward: Oh yes. Many servo-mechanisms are used in all modern engineering devices.

Q: Tell me more about your efforts there.

Ward: I guess I should talk about a subject called LaPlace Transformations a bit. This was a mathematics used only in Bell Labs, at the time, on which books had not yet been written. We were faced with using some of these advanced theoretical studies in the practical applications of the devices in which we were experimenting. With the help of some of these great minds, we were able to do things at that time which had not been done before. Also new was the computer that was being developed there.

Q: At what stage of development were they then?

Ward: The micronization had not been effected so these computers were huge big beasts that used electronics and vacuum tubes. Some of the math which is now being used was just being worked out at that time and was a fore-runner of what IBM and others later developed into a tremendous industry, and one that's a boon to mankind.

Q: Did you have some realization of what this was going to develop into?

Ward: I confess that I did not foresse the tremendous advances that were coming but it was thrilling to see what was being done at that time. You'd go into one of these large rooms filled with vacuum tubes and you could see the work being done. Previously, it had to be done laboriously by hand, slow, with a brain controlling a pencil, and these devices were doing it in a fraction of the time and therefore were making it possible for developments to move at a much faster pace.

Stark Draper, again, while he was not directly associated with this effort, was using the results of these efforts in the experimentation and the developments that he was making in aircraft instruments.

Q: Your imaginations must have been stimulated no end by an introduction to this. Did you as four young men involved, and friends, have frequent bull sessions when you shared your ideas and your experiences from day to day?

Ward: Yes. As a matter of fact, in many of our classes we were completely informal so we not only had bull sessions on the technical aspects among ourselves, but we were able to work directly with many of our instructors and our professors. Gordon Brown, for instance, as a professor in the servo-mechanism laboratories, was a personal friend as well as an advisor. We felt free to work and to discuss with him, in an informal manner, not as a student teacher relationship but as an advisor and one from whom we could learn. Oddly enough in those days I had an instructor named Al Hall, who is currently the vice president of engineering at Martin-Marietta. He was our instructor in the electrical laboratories while we were doing some of our experimentation. Al has been a close friend through the days. He's currently the chairman of the Board of the Severn School.

Q: And putting his talents to work in a very constructive way, I would say.

Ward: He's responsible for my presence here.

Q: Radar was also, relatively speaking, in its infancy, wasn't it?

Ward: Yes, it was.

Q: What introduction did you have to it then?

Ward: I did not have any at M.I.T. I believe that when I was at M.I.T. this work in the practical aspects was not being done there. This was being done down on the banks of the Potomac at the naval laboratories there. It was so secret that we did not know of its existence until after leaving M.I.T. and finding these equipments on board our ships which we would be operating. The same principles were used but the practical application was unknown to us during the time we were at M.I.T.

Q: Was there any obvious overt cross-fertilization when you were at M.I.T. with ideas generated in Britain?

Ward #1 - 25

Ward: No, not to my knowledge. I'm sure that the professors there kept up, as all M.I.T. people do, with the professional literature of the day. I have no knowledge of any cross-fertilization between the British scientists and American scientists. I do know that Dr. Draper was a frequent visitor to the British area and I do know that he had some personal conversations with the British on the advances in some technical fields.

Q: Now a personal aspect of your sojourn there -- I understand that you were told very definitely when you went that it would not be possible to get a degree in master of science, that the time was not right for that, but you did it anyway. Tell me how this was done?

Ward: We worked hard. I think that the professors who were our instructors, who did help us a great deal, could observe that we were really hard working people. They knew some of the limitations we faced when we arrived there with some of the background not as good as with other students who were with us in the class. They observed that we were making a tremendous effort and did exceed the accomplishments of most of the other students who were working with us. The heavy load we had together, with the fact we were doing creditably in the subjects that were being assigned to us probably resulted in the decision to give us degrees. Ed Hooper and I were both made honorary members of the Sigma Xi, honorary fraternity, which is the Phi Beta Kappa of the engineering world.

Q: What was the reaction in the Navy Department to your achievements up there?

Ward: I think it was one of gratification that they had permitted us to go ahead and complete the program. I'm sure it was felt that this had been worthwhile, if for no other reason than the fact that the Draper (or the Mark XIV) sight which was done by Sperry Corporation revolutionized machine gun warfare in those days. This development was made possible by some of the efforts by Mustin and Rivero and Dr. Draper and the engineers of the Sperry Corporation.

Q: Once you had actually finished your period at M.I.T., your classwork, experiments, and so forth, did you not then go on a tour of various factories, or naval bases?

Ward: We were supposed to have gone on a tour, and we started such a tour, but our tour was cut short by world events so that normal tours which should have taken a year were called off. We were put on different working assignments where we could produce results.

Q: What did you see in that truncated tour?

Ward: We went down to Dahlgren, Virginia, where there is a proving ground. Some computer work was just being introduced. We worked there, in Dahlgren, in some of the experimentations in gunnery that were being conducted at that time. We stopped at the Washington Navy Yard gun factory and observed and assisted in the development of some of the work there being done in optics as well as gunnery. Very soon thereafter we were split up and went to places where we could contribute in the production of ships and ship's equipment. For example, I went to the New York Navy Yard for about six months, with the understanding that at the end of that time I would go aboard a brand new battleship which was the first of the new series of battleships, the NORTH CAROLINA, and serve in that great ship.

Q: What was it intended that you would accomplish at the New York Shipyard?

Ward: To help in the final construction and check out the materials and equipments that were going into the battleship, NORTH CAROLINA, and that I would serve and work with these equipments in battle, which I did. The radars were new, the optics were new, the gun directors were new, the computers were new--all these developments knocking on the threshold of knowledge in those days.

Ward #1 - 28 -

Q: And you, fresh out of M.I.T., knew more about these embryonic installations than most anybody else.

Ward: It was a very enlightening and a very interesting period in which we were working. Because of the background, I was able to help in detecting some of the errors that engineers had made, not serious errors but inadvertent errors and mistakes. We followed the work with the workmen, being able to check out and see if the equipments were performing in the manner in which they should be, and if not, get in and work with the engineers to correct the errors.

Q: This is where you were first introduced to radar?

Ward: Yes.

Q: How did you react to that revelation?

Ward: I must admit it was a very exciting development. We did not actually get radar antennae until after the ship had sailed from the New York Yard. We were getting the equipment that was going down into the middle of the ship, some of the electronic equipment, and after leaving the yard, we were given the antennae. And all of this, of course, for security reasons. No one except the British and ourselves knew that there was such a thing as radar, and it was only after we had gone to sea that we were able to get and work with the equipments. Ours was one of the first. It was a great big old thing, but it was good. It was so effective during the battle down in the Guadalcanal area, the carrier battles, that we were able to detect the incoming Japanese aircraft with this tremendous old bed spring type of a radar that we had. It had ranges that were just phenomenal. We would inform the task force commander and he was able to get the fighters that were on the deck of the carrier off in time to make the interceptions and save many ships from being sunk.

Q: When it first was installed on the NORTH CAROLINA, was there some knowledgeable radar person there to help with it, to indoctrinate you people who were going to operate it?

Ward: Yes, we had some engineers who came aboard and described the equipment to us, who gave us some information on maintenance of these equipments. But these engineers did not stay with us.

Q: Where had they learned?

Ward: On the banks of the Potomac.

Q: At that point was there any sharing with the British knowledge?

Ward: I could not comment on this, I don't know.

Q: What about some of the other new installations on the NORTH CAROLINA? You didn't know about all of them?

Ward: No, we didn't. We had better devices for communications, the cryptology devices were better. I did know, and was the expert on the gunnery and particularly fire control. I went aboard as the fire control officer and two years later was the gunnery officer of the ship.

Q: Where had the cryptology devices been developed?

Ward: Again, I'm not an expert in this so I should not comment on it. My specialty was gunnery.

Q: With these new devices being installed on a brand new battleship, you might comment on the security measures which were enforced while she was still in the ship yard.

Ward: They were quite severe. Some of the areas were blocked off. We had Marines guarding our equipments down in the fire control room. In the fire control area and combat information center (which in the NORTH CAROLINA was down in the middle of the ship) access was highly limited. No one was permitted there who did not have a reason to be there, and, again, the topside equipment, the equipment that was visible, was not put aboard until after we had sailed from Norfolk.

Q: It was installed at sea, was it?

Ward: Much of it was installed at sea. The big bed spring was put aboard at Norfolk harbor but access to the entire area was limited.

Q: What about the enlisted men on board ship? Was there a heavy screening on everybody in personnel?

Ward: Yes, there was. Speaking of personnel, this was a time just before the war when the Navy was being greatly expanded. I had never seen such educated, devoted, alert, intelligent young men as were coming into the ship. Most of them were coming straight out of high school and they were top-notch boys. Many of them would have gone to college under normal circumstances, but because of the war came into the Navy to serve in these critical times. Many of them, as soon as the war was over, went back and finished college courses. Many of them were promoted during the war to officer status from enlisted status. We had no serious personnel problems and I was greatly impressed with the caliber of people we were getting.

Q: I'm glad to hear you comment on that. Red Whiting told me about recruitment and emphasized this also. I gather that there was something of a contrast between the men who came at this period and those who were drafted later.

Ward: I still maintain contact with many of these fine youngsters. One of them, for example, is editor of Petroleum magazine. He has done some great work in the oil industry and is now working in New York as an editor. We have a reunion every year, usually in the California area.

Q: This was really an ideal assignment then for you with your prior background, wasn't it?

Ward: I think the others could say the same thing. Ed Hooper went to a battleship, the second new battleship WASHINGTON, and Rivero and Mustin both went to cruisers, and all had very interesting tours.

Q: And in each case, I suppose, the very newest installations were put on these vessels.

Ward: Yes. This was a new Navy, new equipments, exciting times.

Interview # 2 with Admiral Alfred G. Ward, USN (ret.)
Severn School, Severna Park, Md.   August 27, 1970
Subject: Biography   by John T. Mason, Jr.

Mr. Mason: It's good to see you this afternoon, Admiral. I've been looking forward to this second chapter in your oral biography. Last time when we concluded, you were in New York and involved in the fitting out of the new battleship NORTH CAROLINA. We talked about some of the new installations on the NORTH CAROLINA and the fact that some of them were installed at sea. You talked of the security precautions that were taken in New York because of all this equipment. Now you're ready to go forth to battle. I think the NORTH CAROLINA was assigned at that time to Task Force 39, was she not?

Admiral Ward: Yes, she was. We made a quick entry into the war because intelligence had indicated that the Japanese were ready to launch a new assault against our forces in the Pacific which they did in the Battle of Midway, made a valiant effort to be present for the Battle of Midway. We went in company with an attack carrier, the HORNET, through the Canal and made a mad rush to get out in order to participate in this battle. Unfortunately, the HORNET made it but the NORTH CAROLINA did not. I believe it was determined that the presence of the NORTH CAROLINA was not vital for this particular action, but the presence of the HORNET was vital, and therefore she rushed ahead of us and did participate in the battle.

Q: She had greater speed, anyway, didn't she?

Ward: She had greater speed and she was much more needed for this air battle that was forthcoming. It didn't take us long to follow, though, and we were present at the beginning of the battles of Guadalcanal, followed the progress of our own forces to the north and took part in all of the following engagements.

Q: Then I am mistaken, and apparently Morison is not exactly correct either, because he gives the impression that the NORTH CAROLINA together with the WASHINGTON was given temporary duty with the home fleet of the Royal Navy because of the need for Royal Navy warships in the Indian Ocean.

Ward: This is not true. The WASHINGTON did have such an assignment but not the NORTH CAROLINA. The NORTH CAROLINA went directly to the Pacific. We were present at the initial battles of Guadalcanal; we sat there off the coast for some seventy days in support of our forces on that island and participating in some of the battles that took part at that time.

Q: One more question, based on Morison again. He said the NORTH CAROLINA had passed through the Panama Canal on the tenth of June in '42. Where had you been in the interim?

Ward: We were training in Chesapeake Bay and preparing for sailing, getting the equipment which we discussed earlier, our radar installations, and getting completed and doing our training, shakedown training.

Q: Were there any bugs apparent in that shake-down training?

Ward: There are always some bugs but none that were insurmountable. We had a very interesting time. It was unusual to do gunnery practice inside Chesapeake Bay but because of the danger of submarines, we did train within the Bay.

Q: You must have taken extra precautions as you went through the Caribbean enroute to the Canal because this was a time of heavy German submarine activity.

Ward: Yes. We went with HORNET and, of course, had a destroyer screen, wartime conditions.

Q: So we have you in the Pacific and we have you missing the Battle of Midway but getting in on the Guadalcanal fracas. Do you want to tell me something about that?

Ward: I suspect the most thrilling and certainly the most active battle we were in during those early days was an engagement called the Battle of Espiritu Santo. That was an air engagement between our two big carriers, the LEXINGTON and the SARATOGA, and the best of the Japanese carriers, who came down to challenge the air supremacy of the U.S. in that area at that time. This was about the same time as the nightly runs of the Japanese forces to bombard the American forces on Guadalcanal. During daylight, our air was over the islands and in command. The Japanese chose to challenge this command by means of an air strike. During that air strike, if I may mention a little of the detail because it shows something of the effectiveness of the new installations and new radars which were in the NORTH CAROLINA. We were the first to detect those aircraft. Because of some primitive arrangements it was hard to tell whether an aircraft was at one hundred miles or two hundred miles -- the scale only showed one hundred but by certain manipulations you can find out whether or not it was ten percent error, and if it was ten percent error you knew it was double the range, a hundred miles more than it showed on the screen. We did detect these aircraft at a hundred and eighty miles and were able to inform the Task Force commander of a coming threat so that he could have our aircraft airborne and ready to intercept the Japs. We were effective in getting our gun stations manned and ready for the Japanese. We shot down many aircraft with rising suns painted on them.

Q: That must have been a revelation to the Japanese. They were unfamiliar with radar, were they not?

Ward: Yes. They had none at all. We sent messages by radio and whether or not they were intercepted, I do not know. They launched at least an eighty aircraft strike against the Task Force. They were successful in getting a bomb in a carrier but the carrier was not lost. That was the ENTERPRISE.

Q: The NORTH CAROLINA was not damaged?

Ward: Not damaged at that time. The Task Force commander made an odd comment later. He stated that he glanced over during the middle of the battle and took a look at NORTH CAROLINA and thought that she was aflame, thought that she had been hit and was really in flames, and that probably her life was limited. Not so, because what he saw was the anti-aircraft guns firing at such a rapid rate that it appeared as though she were enveloped in flame.

Q: I read somewhere where the appearnace of the NORTH CAROLINA and the WASHINGTON in that area to join the other elements of the fleet was a great morale booster to men whose spirits were somewhat low.

Ward: Yes, I believe that would probably be true. They were the biggest things out there at that time. Together with the carriers they were the first line of our defense in the war with Japan. I spent about two years on this assignment. Soon after that at the battle of Espiritu Santo, a Japanese submarine was successful in getting a torpedo in the NORTH CAROLINA. We were making, as I remember, twenty-one knots at the time and when we were torpedoed we increased speed to twenty-four knots, which is unusual. It was a huge torpedo but the NORTH CAROLINA was built to take just such punishment.

Q: Was this in the area known as the Slot?

Ward: Yes, in that general area. The HORNET was also torpedoed in the same salvo. She was lost, unfortunately. The NORTH CAROLINA proceeded back to Pearl Harbor where we stayed about six weeks and had the holes repaired and went back on the line.

Q: Your damage control arrangements must have been pretty effective.

Ward: They were good. We had a well trained crew. I think I mentioned earlier that those men in that crew were among the finest I've ever served within my long time in the Navy. They were top-notch people. We had a good crew. We started off, as WASHINGTON did, with a large number of regular. They'd been in the regular Navy earlier, but very soon that proportion changed and officers were detached to take over commands of new destroyers in the tremendously expanded Navy. We ended up with people who did not have extensive training earlier, but it was still a splendid group.

Ward #2 - 39 -

Q: That put an added burden on the officers, did it not, with a crew that wasn't thoroughly trained?

Ward: Yes, it did put a burden. I think I mentioned earlier that during a period of about eight months, I went up from fire control officer, which is about fourth ranking officer in the department to the gunnery officer and remained gunnery officer the rest of my time on the ship, people above me were being detached and people below me were being detached.

Q: I read that when you went to Pearl for repairs, anti-aircraft guns were improved or changed, or something of this sort -- new installations. What was this predicated on?

Ward: This was primarily an air war at this time. The Japanese had, I think, decided that they would not try and challenge the surface forces in the Guadalcanal area. They later did in the Philippines, but they felt that this was not a worthwhile undertaking for them, so we were primarily in support of the carriers and the bombardments ashore. As a result of this we had a greatly increased anti-aircraft battery put aboard. We had some additional forty millimeters and we had a great number of the small machine guns put all around the deck. This was a comparative simple thing. They just bolted the guns to the deck.

Q: Did this reflect an entirely new concept of the use of

carriers and battleships in the conflict in the Pacific?

Ward: I would think so. It certainly was a far cry from what had gone on in previous wars in which the battleline of Great Britain, for example, faced the battleline of the Germans in World War I where surface action was predominant. Not so in World War II -- air war was predominant. It did make a change in warfare. I believe there is a general concensus that under the conditions that existed at that time, the support given air warfare by battleships, cruisers and destroyers was essential to success.

Q: During that refitting operation on Pearl, did you come in contact with Admiral Nimitz?

Ward: Yes. Admiral Nimitz visited the ship on several occasions, and I went to some of his staff briefings. He was a terrific man -- just wonderful.

Q: Can you recreate one of the staff briefings? How did he function?

Ward: In his own inimitable way he was in command of his staff and in command of everything that went on within the Fleet but he was a very gentle person. He was very fair. He was inquisitive; he asked many intelligent questions but he was always polite; a wonderful individual. He gained the respect and the admiration of every sailor in the Pacific Fleet.

Q: Did you have on board the NORTH CAROLINA a contingent of men to decode Japanese messages? Was this a part of your installation?

Ward: I believe not. I'm not knowledgeable, but I believe we had no linguist in the NORTH CAROLINA. I'm confident that such people were available to the Task Force commander.

Q: After your refitting, you went right back into the fray, didn't you?

Ward: We sure did. We were at Pearl Harbor only as brief a period as necessary and went right back out again.

Q: How did you react personally to battle of this sort?

Ward: My position was one of being in charge of what we now call combat information center as well as being fire control officer. In the first engagement I was aware of everything that was going on. We not only had a combat information center in our plotting room, which was the brains of the gunnery department, but also the computers which directed the firing of the guns so that we had

Ward #2 - 42 -

all the sensitive equipment necessary for detecting a target first and then hitting the target ~~available to~~ us. It was a very busy time; too busy to get much concerned about your own welfare. You had too much to do to get frightened.

Q: You weren't the flag ship, were you?

Ward: No.

Q: And yet your equipment, and so forth, gave you a knowledge perhaps superior to what some of the other ships in the Task Force had so there was a problem of communicating the information to them, too?

Ward. That's correct. We used voice radio. We had a simple system of encoding and decoding which was quick and reliable. Our voice transmissions were in a very simple code.

Q: Were you at that point a part of Admiral Willis Lee's fast battleship contingent?

Ward: Not at that time. That contingent did not form until after this phase of warfare had completed. During the Guadalcanal actions, the NORTH CAROLINA was the only battleship present. Later when WASHINGTON came out, and ALABAMA, and other battleships under Admiral Lee, then we had a battleship task force ~~under Admiral Lee~~

Ward #2 - 43 -

and we did take part, under Admiral Lee, in the battles in Kwajalein and the further battles that took part in the later campaigns.

Q: But in the Guadalcanal fracas you were part of a conglomerate Navy, were you not? Weren't there elements of the Royal Navy, Australian Navy, and so forth?

Ward: I don't believe so. We did have some elements of the Australian Navy there from time to time but in the battles of Cape Esperance and Esperitu Santo it was the two U. S. carriers, the NORTH CAROLINA, cruisers, and destroyers. I think Australia at that time was taking care of protection of the island of Australia because, as you may remember, it was not much before this that the big action in the Coral Sea in which Australians played a key role, took place.

Q: Yes, and the Japanese tide came as far as Port Moresby which was right next door, wasn't it, to the continent? Do you have any specific recollections of those engagements of Guadalcanal?

Ward: The principal recollection I have is this one I've mentioned of seeing for the first time enemy aircraft at the range of about a hundred and eighty miles. Having done our homework earlier, we could estimate quite accurately the altitude at which they were flying by means of fade charts, which under modern radar are no longer applicable, so I can speak of these without releasing secret information. Under the radars then existing, which were pretty simple in comparison to the complex machines we now have, the aircraft coming in would fade from the screen and during this period we received no reflection from the aircraft; then it would reappear, and by plotting out on curves ahead of time through many tedious hours, we could tell what range an aircraft at a certain altitude would fade and when it would reappear. So we were able to determine not only the range and bearing, but also the altitude. This made it possible for the Task Force commander to have much more information and be able to plan his counter action against the incoming raids by the Japanese much more effectively.

I believe that I did mention that we did take part in the bombardments.

Q: This was largely with the sixteen-inch guns, was it?

Ward: Yes. As a result of the battles in Tarawa in which we lost many marines, it was decided that any future action such as this, any future assault, we would really soften up the place with the big gun bombardment prior to making the assault landings. In Kwajalein,

USS NORTH CAROLINA went in the night before the bombardment. We went in alone with two destroyers. About every fifteen or twenty minutes during the night we let go with some salvos in order to keep the Japanese defensive troops awake, first; confused, second; and demoralized. Evidently they were because the next morning when the six big battleships line came in and really gave those islands a going over, every square yard was supposedly subject to some devastation. When the Marines went ashore they could find so very few people alive, even, and those were so terrified that they put up no resistance whatsoever. The effectiveness for the assault had taken place before the first man ever crossed the beach.

Q: And were those islands fortified in the same manner as Tarawa with pill boxes?

Ward: Yes, they had quite a few fortifications. They were not as well defended as Tarawa because there were not many trees or much land on these atolls for defense.

Q: By that time Halsey was in over-all command, was he not?

Ward: Yes. Admiral Halsey was in over-all command shortly after we first arrived in Guadalcanal. He had taken over from Admiral Ghormley. I had the privilege of going to his headquarters and visiting with him and his staff during breaks in the engagement on Guadalcanal.

Q: What was his state of mind at that time?

Ward: Admiral Halsey had a tremendous staff, very effective, lots of enthusiasm and high morale which had not existed earlier.

Q: That was built into his own personal make-up, wasn't it?

Ward: Yes, it was, and in the people he had working for him, too. I was offered a position with Admiral Hill, and wanted it very badly, but the Powers that Be decided that I was needed in the NORTH CAROLINA, so I stayed in the NORTH CAROLINA until detached after the really tough part of the war was over. When I left the NORTH CAROLINA it was inevitable that the Allies would be victorious -- it was just a question of when.

Q: Admiral Hill at that point when you were offered a job was still in charge of the MARYLAND and the COLORADO and the older battleships?

Ward: No, he had command of the amphibious forces.

Q: That was another phase of warfare which you wanted to get into?

Ward: Yes. I felt that I could have contributed something to that phase of warfare. I felt that the people in the NORTH CAROLINA were trained so that they didn't actually need me as badly at that time. I later joined the amphibious force and thoroughly enjoyed my tour.

Q: What kind of job did he offer you?

Ward: To be his flag secretary, not socially but to be a fighting aide.

Q: You could have served with no better man, I'm sure. Tell me a little bit about the Admiral Willis Lee fast fighter battleship contingent when you joined that.

Ward: He had a very effective organization. A man named Ray Thompson was with him. Lloyd Mustin had served with him and was to serve with him later. He had six first line battleships, the best in the world, all comparatively new, very powerful, very effective. I had a feeling that they were not used as fully as they should have been used. I had a feeling that maybe we could have been a little bit bolder in the use of these particular ships during that time. This is no criticism of Admiral Lee but rather on the way the campaigns developed.

Q: I suppose there was a hesitancy to be too reckless, and we had a limited number of ships.

Ward: I'm sure this is right.

Q: There was a criticism leveled at the use of the SARATOGA at one point in the Guadalcanal engagements in that she had been withdrawn ostensibly to refuel some destroyers but they thought perhaps the commanding officer was a little more timid that he might have been.

Ward: I heard some criticisms, too, on Admiral Ghormley; the fact that he kept the ships in the same general locations for many days in a row, and eventually one of the Japanese submarines did come into that area and hit two of our important ships.

Q: I think this, too, reflects a change of concept of naval battles, doesn't it?

Ward: Yes.

Q: Anything more on that period when you were on the NORTH CAROLINA? I think this was a terrific experience.

Ward # 2 - 49 -

Ward: I think that's about it. I'm more mindful of some later work.

Q: I see. Well, you left her in May of 1944.

Ward: Yes, and went to the naval gun factory to take over a job which a short time before had been held by a man named Arleigh Burke. We were in building and inspecting the anti-aircraft guns that were going on the ships that were then being built. I worked in that job for not quite two years, twenty months, in producing hardware for the Fleet. I didn't stay in the anti-aircraft gun business very long, but became the Progress Officer, which means the expediter for everything that was built at the naval gun factory. I not only had the chore and responsibility of the building of guns by the naval gun factory but also by civilian contractors. I coordinated the work that was done by the various Westinghouse Corporation plants with the naval gun factory's efforts. For a Commander, U. S. Navy, this was a fairly sizable personal responsibility.

Q: And made you a sort of a Peripatetic person didn't it? Didn't you have to travel a great deal?

Ward: Yes, I did. We traveled quite a bit to the various satellite plants that were in the gun business at that time.

Q: How many satellite plants were there roughly?

Ward: Actually we had three that were directly under our coordination. We didn't actually hire and fire people at these plants, but we did go out and assign work to them; we did check their performance; we did expedite work that had to be done; it was more of a management effort than it was a production effort in this coordination. At the gun factory, itself, it was a production effort.

Q: Did this involve you with Admiral Hussey and the Bureau of Ordnance quite extensively?

Ward: Quite extensively.

Q: Can you cite some illustrations of your joint cooperation?

Ward: In our meetings, which we held routinely at monthly intervals, and more frequently at times when certain work or coordination had to be done, we would have members of Admiral Hussey's staff present with us, and Admiral Blandy's staff. Admiral Hussey was personally knowledgeable of the work that was being done.

Q: He was knowledgeable of every element of ordnance?

Ward: He surely was. He was a fine gentleman.

Q: Since you were sort of in management, did it involve you in the Navy E, effort, the citations, and public relations?

Ward: Only to a very minor extent. We were to make nominations but not to participate in this effort. It was very minor. The war was over during this period, of course, and toward the end of my twenty months there, the effort was greatly decreased and, as a matter of fact, was drawn to a stand-still.

Q: How big a business was this in dollars and cents?

WARD: I better not guess on this one. It was big, though.

Q: This also, I would think, involved you in some sort of cooperation with Admiral Lee again when he was sent back to Washington with Lloyd Mustin to be ComDevFor.

Ward: That's right. He came back and established a staff up in Casco Bay, with headquarters on the Great Diamond Island, to try and develop systems and procedures and methods of defeating the kami-kaze attacks that were being launched against our ships by Japanese. I was actually assigned temporary duty on his staff while I was attached to the naval gun factory and helped with this effort.

Ward # 2 - 52 -

I was greatly surprised one day to find orders to proceed to Casco Bay immediately and report to Admiral Willis Lee and was up there part of the summer.

Q: Before you came back to the States, had you experienced any kamikaze attacks?

Ward: No.

Q: That was before they began, wasn't it? But still you brought to the whole problem a know-how -- you had been in the Fleet and this was one of the valuable parts of Admiral Lee's contribution, wasn't it?

Ward: It certainly was. And he had some really expert people, such as Lloyd Mustin, helping on this problem.

Q: Do you know the origin of this idea, setting up this division in the department, ComDevFor? Whose concept was this?

Ward: I don't know. It was a very good one, though. It became later the Operational Development Force and has done a tremendous job.

Q: Admiral, since you came fresh from the battle fleet, did

Ward # 2 - 53 -

you contribute something to the operations and the developments in the naval gun factory because of your own fertile brain, your own imaginative powers?

Ward: I wish I could say yes to that question, but I'm afraid I cannot. The war was about over and the time of changing in the development of guns was about over, also. We were busy in getting the guns for the ships that were just being completed at that time. I think that probably the experience in the war was the greatest value as a morale booster; going around and talking to the people at the Westinghouse plant as well as to our own people in the gun factory, explaining to them the effectiveness of the weapons which they had completed and the fact of our superiority in naval warfare; the fact that we had not lost ships; we had not lost the number of men normally expected to have been lost in a great war such as this. This success is attributed in large part to the total efforts of everyone in the United States, particularly those that were participating directly in such things as gun manufacturing and development. I believe that this effort was probably a more valuable effort than any improvements in the designs. I actually didn't get into this phase at this time.

Q: You were then, in yourself a big Navy E.

Ward: It was a very wonderful time for me because, as I said, you could see that the war was nearing its end and that we would

Ward # 2 - 54 -

be victorious. To realize that we had accomplished the purposes which we had set out to accomplish made some compensation for the Japanese victory at Pearl Harbor.

Q: Was this an attitude which was growing and increasing at this stage in the war or had it been evident in these industrial plants from Pearl Harbor on?

Ward: I think this was new. For example, when I would talk to some of these people, it was a new thought for them. Some of these contractor representatives and some of the workmen had not heard this part of the story before. Many of them had gone to work and worked for their country at a certain time of the day and got off at a certain time and didn't realize what effectiveness their work had been in contributing to victory.

Q: Did this growing attitude in the time you were involved then lessen any labor problems that might have shown forth?

Ward: I don't believe we had any major labor problems right then. Certainly there were no strikes and there seemed to be a feeling of trying to do what they could to aid the war effort. We had not problem with labor in the naval gun factory, for example. We had some great artisans, some tremendous technicians, people who were putting their effort into it. At a later time, particularly with the contractual people, after the war, we did have trouble, but not in these days.

Q: This great staff at the naval gun factory had been assembled under Civil Service, was it?

Ward: Yes.

Q: Where did they come from?

Ward: As you know the Navy Yard in Washington is a very, very old place and these people had gravitated there. Many of them had been there for many, many years and were some of the best technicians in the world in their particular fields. For example, we had a foundry man there who could make steel as well as anyone in the world could do it. They were tremendous people.

Q: Almost people with latent talents that came to the fore.

Ward: Yes. They were just expert. They had grown up there, had worked there twenty, thirty, forty years. The gun factory itself was more an experimental laboratory until the war came and then, of course, it went into full production. It built all of the big guns that were built for years. Of course, during the period of the 1920s there were no guns built, or very few guns built. Beginning about 1935 we started a real building program.

Q: You were there until after the war had come to a close, were you not?

Ward: That's right.

Q: This entailed toning things down, cutting down, did it?

Ward: Yes. There were some reductions before I left but the real big reductions came after I left. They were still ending the shipbuilding program. The war was over and I went to command of a destroyer.

Q: Was this something you were seeking?

Ward: Very much so.

Q: This was the HOLLISTER?

Ward: Yes. She was a new destroyer, had been in operation only for a short time.

Q: She had not had any battle experience?

Ward #2 - 57 -

Ward: No, she had not had any battle experience. She was finished after the war was over and had been under a previous commanding officer for a short time and I was ordered to take command.

Q: Where did you join her?

Ward: In San Diego.

Q: And what was your duty then?

Ward: We had a very interesting time. As a matter of fact, a most interesting time. We worked there in San Diego for awhile with training the crews of other destroyers since many of them didn't have enough people to get underway. My ship was fortunate in that we did get underway every day, and we did go out and were able to train crews of other destroyers that were immobile because of lack of people.

Q: Was this "bring the boys home" --

Ward: "Bring the boys home" idea, yes. After this period of a few months then we went out on the patrols off Korea and around Japan. The HOLLISTER was one of the first U.S. destroyers in many ports in Japan. My orders were to show the United States flag, and to report every night my position. I could go almost anywhere I wanted but was expected to visit the various odd ports where Americans had not previously been.

Q: You were a CinC yourself, were you not?

Ward: Yes. It was a most interesting time.

Q: How were you received in these various ports?

Ward: Very well. The reception varied with ports. In Tokyo when an American walked down the street, the Japanese would get off the street and not interfere with his progress. Not so in Nagasaki. In Nagasaki the effect of the bomb was still felt. We were treated with respect but the people were not subservient. I was met by the mayor and was given good treatment and was taken on tours of the bomb area and tours of the sites of the area and was treated well. We enjoyed these trips very much. I received some odd orders once. My cruiser division commander in Tokyo sent me orders to go up in a bay called Kachibama Wan and go as far as I could into this bay and anchor and spend the night and then come back out the next day, to let these people in that part of Japan see an American flag. I later told a Japanese admiral that I'd taken my twenty-two hundred ton destroyer into the bay and he said I must have been mistkane, that it was not possible to get a twenty-two hundred ton destroyer into this bay, that it had never been done in history. I told him he didn't know his history very well because I had done it. I was frightened to death because it was a big bay -- not as big as the Chesapeake Bay but a big bay in back of Nagasaki.

Q: But shallow?

Ward: It has a very narrow entrance and unless you go in in slack water, the current rushing through between these big rocks makes it almost impossible to manage. You lose control of your ship in whirlpools. Of course, we had no tidal current, predictions, no charts, no nothing. I had no knowledge of whirlpools or anything else other than the map says this is Kachibama Wan and I was told to go into it. We went in and it was quite a harrowing experience. I learned enough going in to send some people out in a small boat and measure the tides to find out what time of day I could go out with a little more security than when I went in. The helmsman was quite excited and he would say, "Captain, the rudder is hard right and the ship is swinging left rapidly and I can't stop it!

Q: Sounds worse than . . .

Ward: Right now there's a big bridge over this entrance and it's very interesting to watch the swirling waters underneath this bridge. They do have a cruising passenger boat that goes through this place but this small passenger boat stays close to one side of the channel where the water is comparatively calm. A destroyer with her deeper draft could not get that close to the edge of the entrance.

Q: Was the commander of the destroyer flotilla not aware of this either?

Ward: I'm sure he was not.

Q: Why was it so essential to show the flag in this area?

Ward: I think it was important. This is an important part of Japan. It was a resort area between Sasebo and Nagasaki and is the gateway into the resort areas up the mountainside. The whole operation was successful, was effective.

Q: Did the people show real surprise at a war vessel coming in there?

Ward: Yes, they did. I went in to this village with its beautiful hotels. I took the only boat we had, with the American flag flying, into the dock and was met by the mayor and a delegation, and was invited up to a magnificent hotel. I went in with my staff, up to a room that was quite apparent something exceptional, up on the top floor. I've never seen such lavish, gorgeous furniture in my life; some of it Western style. Through an interpreter, a United States Navy lieutenant who could speak Japanese fluently, it developed that this was the suite reserved for the emperor and that no one used it other than the emperor. This had been reserved for him in this hotel for ever, I guess. A beautiful spot.

Q: You were something of a deputy to the conquering emperor.

Ward: I was the representative of power at that time.

Q: Did you have contact with General MacArthur during this period in Japan?

Ward: Not personally, on official business. I went to receptions in his home several times. I worked with members of his staff quite closely. Quite frequently members of his staff would ride my ship into rarely visited areas, so we did have some contact. I had no personal business with him, but did have with his staff.

Q: When you went to Nagasaki, did you visit some of the hospitals and see some of the victims of the atomic bomb?

Ward: Yes, I did. I met an American surgeon there at that time who, I guess, was the senior surgeon working with the people who had been subjected to radiation. He took me through the hospital and showed me some of the effects of the bombing.

Q: That must have been rather jolting, wasn't it?

Ward: Yes. He not only worked with the Japanese doctors but he had a team of specialists that were making a thorough study of the effects of the bomb on people and things. It was a rather large organization.

Q: We hadn't yet begun to build a hospital there, or anything. Didn't we do that later?

Ward: This was a Japanese hospital in which I went, but we did have some housing in a compound for this team of specialists doing this investigation. The senior military officer in Nagasaki was an Army officer. I was there at the time of the first election and it was really interesting. The mayor called the American lieutenant colonel and told him that the election was over, the ballots were completed, and he could come in and count the ballots to determine who had won the election. The lieutenant colonel explained in some detail that this was not an American election but a Japanese election, and the Japanese should count the votes and determine who elected and the United States government would support whomever the Japanese elected to govern the city. But there were many such odd t going on.

They had a big parade and it was very much pro-U.S. They showed some floats of kamikaze, and people being killed and said, in effect, this is what the previous Japanese administration has done to us. Then they showed a float of a liberty ship off-loading wheat and said this is what our conquerors have done for us.

Q: A curious about face, wasn't it?

Ward: I have been in Nagasaki many times. I have many friends in the city I admire the Japanese as a whole, and am particularly fond of the people down in Nagasaki.

Q: Why are they different from others?

Ward: They are proud people. I think the bomb itself caused some of this reaction. They never were as fully subservient as were Japanese in some of the other areas of the country. I'm not enough of a psychiatrist to know why the great devastation in a city of the size of Nagasaki would cause this result, but it happened.

Q: You say you were also in some of the Korean ports?

Ward: Yes. We were on patrol off Korea in our destroyer.

Again, almost with no orders except to stop the smuggling between Korea and the communist part of China, that part of China that had gone Communist, the northern part. A sampan, or small sailboat, could take rice from Korea to northern China, and bring back chemicals, or dyes, or machinery, machine tools, from nothern China to Korea, and on this one trip a man and his son could make a fortune that would last him the rest of his life. So there was a great incentive to smuggle rice out of Korea. It was to the disadvantage of the Koreans and the United States, who was trying to support the Koreans, to have the rice smuggled out of there because there was just about enough rice there for Koreans. If it were smuggled out, then it would be our responsibility to bring in wheat or some other staple to feed the starving Koreans. So our job was to try and stop the smuggling. We operated off Korea for a period of many months as a patrol to stop this smuggling and also to try and stop other nations, the northern Chinese and other people from going into Korea.

Q: How effective were you in preventing this traffic?

Ward: Very effective. Those Koreans are very stern people. If we caught a boat, we put an inspection party of Koreans aboard, and we had Koreans aboard our ship at all time. If they found some of these prohibited articles, they would get on board the craft and take it into port to court. If they were found guilty in court, they were thrown into prison for an indefinite period and subject to very rough treatment. You've never seen such barbaric treatment for a prisoner in your life. At least I never have. So it was very stiff stern punishment for any violators.

I was fortunate in having Korean midshipmen, rather than the Korean sailors, bluejackets, in my ship. The other ships all had Korean sailors. So I had considerably above the normal level of intelligence and education.

Q: And does education make a difference in terms of this brutality?

Ward: I doubt it. There were not many middle class Koreans in those days. Of course, there are now. There were a few people at the top and then coolies, because the Japanese had been the middle class people, the administrators, bosses for several generations. The Koreans had not developed the straw bosses and middle class people.

Q: Did you get down to Formosa, also, and Taiwan?

Ward: Yes we did. I went all over the whole area and I went quite thoroughly around Japan.

Q: Up into the northernmost part?

Ward: Yes.

Q: Did you have brushes with the Russians up there?

Ward: No, I never did. We went into the northern ports, though, into the Hokkaido ports. We went in and visited Gen. Swing who was the commanding general of the 11th Airborne Division in Sapporo, Hokkaido and saw his operations. It was a very interesting two years following the war, seeing the gradual recoupment going on in Japan and in Korea.

Q: It must have been rather rapid, was it?

Ward: It was rapid. The Japanese, as you know, are very hard working people.

Q: Was it in part due to our own efforts and the MacArthur set-up in Japan?

Ward: It helped them a great deal but I think the recovery was inevitable with an industrious people of that type. They had nothing. They had not enough to eat and they pulled themselves up by the bootstraps, and we helped them a great deal.

Q: I suppose the factor was that they retained their system of government and didn't have complete upheaval in that area.

Ward: That's correct. They had some wonderful people there,

people such as Admiral Namura.

Q: Did you know him in Washington before?

Ward: No, I didn't. I met him out there. I met Admiral Hoshina there. Hoshina was also had been in the United States quite a bit but was in the high command in Japan throughout most of the war. He was not personally responsible for any of the major decisions, but he was a staff officer in the high command. When I was there, he was a member of The Diet. He was "the Mr. Carl Vinson" of the Japanese Diet. I've been friends with him through the years.

Q: Well, I understand that the Japanese navy echelons were somewhat different anyway from the Japanese army. Did you have contact with army officers?

Ward: Yes, but not to the extent that I did with the Navy. I traveled with the navy in those days in a destroyer and later as a cruiser division commander. In my tours of Japan I would invariably invite a Japanese admiral to go with me wherever I went, and this paid dividends. We were much more effective in our liaison with the Japanese, in meeting right kinds of Japanese and in our effectiveness in making friends and trying to coordinate common efforts. After the war, most of these Japanese officers were penniless.

They had no means of livelihood but they were resilient and resourceful. Many of them were making pieces of art and selling them for enough money to buy rice.

Q: Did you see something of the devastation of their industrial plants?

Ward: Yes, particularly in Nagasaki and Hiroshima where the two bombs fell, but also in other places. Nagoya and Tokyo were badly damaged, as was Yokohama.

Q: Well, that was a fortuitous kind of tour of duty, wasn't it?

Interview # 3 with Admiral Alfred G. Ward, USN (ret.)
Severn School, Severna Park, Md.   August 31, 1970
Subject: Biography   by John T. Mason, Jr.

Mr. Mason: Admiral, this morning we begin the third chapter of this interesting story of your naval career. Last time you had been on assignment on the USS HOLLISTER in Japanese waters. You concluded that story, I believe, and then were on the staff of commander, Destroyer Force.

Admiral Ward: This was Admiral "Spike" Fahrion who had command of the destroyers in the Pacific. He brought me in to be his gunnery officer and his athletic officer. Because of the times and the shortage of men after the war, very few of these destroyers could get under way and he had quite a demoralized force. He chose to try and do something about morale by having a strong sports program and he decided that he would have a championship destroyer football team, and he did. He pulled me in to form such a team. I had the benefit of some of the outstanding football talent in the Navy at that time with three or four college All-Americans in the officer ranks, and some of the biggest and toughest bluejackets in the destroyers. I had unlimited authority to pull anyone I wanted from any ship to play football.

Q: That was a marvelous assignment. Who were some of these All-American players?

Ward: Don Whitmire was probably the outstanding one. He had an interesting story. He played for the University of Alabama. The coach at Navy was "cussing" because he couldn't get qualified people. Rip Miller, even in those days was effective, said, "You pick one man that you want and I'll get him." So the coach took the pictures of that year's all-Americans and found this sophomore from the University of Alabama who had made All-American in his first year of college ball. The Navy coach decided he was the biggest and the ugliest looking man in the book, so he said, "I want him." Whitmire tells this story on himself. Sure enough, Rip went down and got young Whitmire. He came up and was all-American at Navy for his remaining two years of eligibility. We had others. We had an officer who had not gone to the Naval Academy but had attended LSU, named Graham, who had been on an All-American list. We had an officer named Bo Coppedge on that team, currently the Director of Athletics at the Naval Academy. Bill Busick, a football great at the Naval Academy, was on the team and a real star. We played not only service football but we also played college ball. We played and defeated Brigham Young University, for example. We played the college freshmen at the University of California. We had a good team.

Q: Where were you based, largely?

Ward: In San Diego. Our games at Foreman Field in San Diego outdrew any other event in that city. We became a real value not only to the destroyer force but also to the city. Spike Fahrion was successful in improving morale in his force.

Q: Were there other sports as well as football?

Ward: Yes, we did have other sports. We had a Fleet championship baseball team. And we had a crew in the whaleboats. But primarily football and baseball.

Q: Well, that was a divergence. What else is notable about that tour of duty?

Ward: It was a very pleasant tour under very pleasant circumstances. We had come through the war and it gave me, as a person, and my family, a chance to unwind and actually enjoy life. I also had some satisfaction out of being able to operate the destroyer, HOLLISTER, as I mentioned in our previous session.

Q: Did the fact that you had a highly developed sports program help recruitment?

Ward: I believe it may have helped, but actually we were not much in the recruiting business at that time.

Q: But you were feeling the effects of a lack of people.

Ward: Yes. But our numbers after the war had dropped considerably. The budget, of course, had dropped after the war so, as

Ward #3 - 72 -

I recall, there was not at that time a tremendous recruiting program in effect. Certainly we did not participate directly in a recruiting program.

Q: It just occurred to me that it might well have been an incentive for young men.

Ward: I think so. We were decommissioning many ships -- putting them in the reserve mothball fleet.

Q: After that tour of duty which was for only a little more than a year, you then came back for a second assignment at the naval gun factory. It must have been one of your favorite spots. Did you ask for this?

Ward: I was ordered to the Bureau of Ordnance but when I arrived in the Bureau, the organization had changed. At that time my previous boss, Spike Fahrion, had returned to Washington to the Naval Gun Factory, so he saw to it that I was diverted down to the Gun Factory.

Q: What were your specific duties on this occasion?

Ward: I was the Production Officer with more than five thousand men in my department, most of whom were elderly. The average age was around fifty with some being up in their sixties, but splendid artisans.

Q: Civil Service people?

Ward: Yes.

Q: What were you concentrating on particularly in production?

Ward: We were still making a few guns but had gone more into the ancillary equipments. We had a very big optical shop. The gun factory, too, at that time, was beginning to phase down in its operation.

Q: Was there any feed-in from the experiences of the war?

Ward: Yes, and from my previous experience there, too, at the gun factory. It was a fairly logical assignment. The only thing unusual about it was that at that time I was still a Commander and this had been a very senior Captain's job through the years.

Q: That must have spoken well for your previous assignment there.

Ward: The background helped, I'm sure.

Q: Again that was an assignment that allowed you to be with your family.

Ward: Yes. I was in a house as a Commander which is now

Ward # 3 - 74 -

occupied by my friend, Lloyd Mustin, who is a Vice Admiral.

Q: At the Navy Yard?

Ward: At the Navy Yard.

Q: How was living at the Navy Yard? It seems rather a crowded place.

Ward: It's very pleasant living inside the wall. As you know, it's not the nicest part of Washington outside the wall. In those days we were not afraid to walk outside the wall. Now it's on the dangerous side to go out in that part of the city, particularly at night.

Q: Who was head of Bureau of Ordnance in that day? Was Stroop there then?

Ward: If I had a guess I would say that George Hussey was still there.

Q: Then you went on to another assignment with destroyers?

Ward: Yes. I had a division in Newport. I was promoted to the rank of Captain soon after arriving in the destroyer division. We operated out of Newport and had a very delightful tour in the

Mediterranean with two successive captains in the flag ship. The second captain is now Vice Admiral "Squidge" Lee. This was his first command. The only thing unusual about that is that I developed a program which was then unique. I believe it's been repeated since. Any time I would go into a new port I would invariably call, regardless of seniority or rank between myself and the military man ashore, on the senior military man, the senior political man, and the senior churchman. I found that this was tremendously helpful. I had complete cooperation from the police in the event any of the people got into mischief. We had very cordial relations between the Italians, the Turks, the Greeks; wherever we went we were well received. I also tried to give small parties, informal type buffet suppers in the small quarters in the destroyers for at least the senior military people and their top aides and families.

Q: Was your family based on shore anywhere near?

Ward: No. They stayed in the States. We were moving quite rapidly from port to port, showing the flag. We, at that time, had an interesting visit up to Salonica, which in biblical days was Thessalonica where St. Paul had one of his first churches. We were there at the time of the 1900th anniversary of St. Paul's founding of this mission in Thessalonica and had a great celebration.

Q: This is under the aegis of the Greek Orthodox Metropolitan?

Ward: Yes. I attended the service there. The Archbishop had warned me that it would take all day with the men standing on one side of the church and the women standing on the other side of the church. I showed up in my white uniform with my aide and my top people and we were escorted to the front part of the church by the men who were standing. Pretty soon one of the Bishop's assistants brought some folding chairs down. Later in the service he sent one of his assistants out and asked me to come behind the altar. He had a bottle of brandy, which he broke open and we enjoyed.

Q: I'd think some respite of that sort would be necessary.

Ward: He had been educated at the Episcopal Theological Seminary in Philadelphia. He was a tremendous churchman and was number two in the Greek Church at the time. These were rather typical experiences during cruising in the fleet in those days. We were well received by everyone. We had our men indoctrinated that they were ambassadors of good will so that we had very little discipline problem. If a man seemed to have been drinking too much or in any manner not a good representative, other men who were trained or indoctrinated would take him back to the ship. So it was a very well conducted crew.

Q: This is quite an achievement. How did you accomplish that?

Ward: It not only happened in my ships but throughout the Fleet in those days. Admiral "Cat" Brown, who was the Fleet Commander, had done a terrific job with all ships, but the morale, particularly in the destroyers was superb. "Cat" Brown, himself, was a character and was an excellent representative of the United States because of his attitude toward the peoples in the countries bordering the Mediterranean, many of whom just loved the old gentleman.

Q: Did you have occasion to call at the Vatican?

Ward: No, I did not get up to Rome at that time. We were in sea ports, of course, and it was sometimes difficult to leave the ship for any period of time. We had a pretty busy schedule both in training and working at sea with the Italians and the Greeks, the Spanish occasionally, and the British. We had a very busy schedule.

Q: Did the events in the Far East have any repercussion on you in the Mediterranean?

Ward: No. It was a different world.

Q: Then you mounted another rung in the ladder, did you not?

Ward: Again I joined my friend Spike Fahrion in the Destroyer Force Atlantic headquarters.

Q: You must have been a very effective duo, the two of you.

Ward: Well, I certainly admire Admiral Fahrion. He was real tough on many people but I found that if you worked hard and you did your job, he would permit you to do that job without any interference and with only occasional guidance. It was a very pleasant relationship that I had with Admiral Fahrion. Many people were afraid of him. He was a tough task master for those people who did not measure up to what he demanded. I was his operations officer at that time and had a thoroughly enjoyable tour. He had given up his great emphasis at that time on athletics because we had a force to run. His interest and primary concern had shifted to having a group of well run, highly expert, destroyermen.

Q: Were there any particular assignments? This was '51 - '53.

Ward: Here again, I worked very closely with the operational development force and this was nautral as a result of our improved sonar equipments and our improved radar equipments. Everything about the Navy was becoming more complex, more difficult to maintain and required more expertise in the care and the operations of these complicated machines and equipment.

Q: Was it difficult for you to keep abreast of these developments? You had the background.

Ward: Yes, and we had some good people too. We had quite a few contractor representatives who would accompany new equipment when it was being installed on the ships and would give us some training and knowledge. It was a practical p.g. course. We had the basic fundamentals but this was a practical course in operating those particular equipments. We had some real expert young men working on them. Newport was a very pleasant place to be -- the home of the destroyers. We had destroyer schools in the various phases of destroyer life.

My time away from home limited somewhat a family but we had a daughter born when I was a captain.

Q: That made how many children?

Ward: Three. I think my wife is the oldest mother in the record of naval hospital in Newport

Q: Well, you liked Newport so well that you stayed on.

Ward: Yes. I was transferred and went to the War College. It was at the end of my tour in destroyers. It was time for people in my category to go to the Naval War College so it was natural for me to stay there. We bought a home there and were in Newport for four years. I enjoyed the time at War College but it was a time of relaxation and getting away from the strain of day to day operations with people and things.

Ward #3 - 80 -

Q: The Korean War had been concluded and there was nothing on the horizon, except the cold war?

Ward: That is correct. A very pleasant time. My record was good enough there to land me a job in the Pentagon in the Strategic Plans Division, which is one of the key divisions in the office of the Chief of Naval Operations. It was a very challenging assignment. Admiral Arleigh Burke was the CNO. Admiral Bob Dennison had Op-60 with his assistant being Admiral Wallace Beakley. These, of course, were top-notch people, with Burke being at the peak of his career, Dennison going on from that job and becoming Commander in Chief of the Atlantic Fleet and NATO Commander, Atlantic; Wallace Beakley going on to become a vice admiral and Fleet Commander in the Pacific. Just terrific people working on the difficult problems of national importance.

Q: For instance, what did you concentrate on?

Ward: We were working on many of the NATO problems and many of the great problems that were facing the world in those days. Of course, Burke was fighting to get a modern Navy, and was fighting successfully. I was in a political military sphere and was in the State Department quite a bit.

I recall one incident when Admiral Dennison assigned to me a study that he wanted on what to do about the Tachen Islands, the small Islands off the coast of Vietnam, which were uninhabited but which were being visited frequently by Chinese Communist groups. There was some fear that the Communists would colonize the islands.

Both China and the Philippines claimed ownership. I never heard of the Tachen Islands until this assignment. He called me at nine o'clock in the morning and he wanted the study out by three in the afternoon, so we went to work on it. Around two, I took a piece of paper up to Admiral Dennison, who didn't look at it but sent me up to Admiral Burke. Admiral Burke read it and did not like it and just gave me the devil. He gave me some ideas, told me to go back and re-write it and have it back in twenty minutes. So I took it back up there and he again didn't like it, so he dictated some modifications to it, again bawled me out and then said, "Now, young man, you take this piece of paper over and you go in to the Secretary of State, Mr. John Foster Dulles', office and you hand it to him, and don't give it to anyone else, and I will stay here until you return." I was successful in getting the paper to Mr. John Foster Dulles. Secretary Dulles liked the paper and immediately dictated the dispatch recommended in the paper, with only minor modifications. This message of instructions went out to his ambassador in Vietnam and to the ambassadors in Taiwan and in the Philippines outlining action the United States would take with regard to this threat on the Tachens by the Communist Chinese. I went back to Admiral Burke and he smiled and said, "I figured you'd get in. That's the reason I sent you."

Q: After two lacings down.

Ward: He was kind to me. It was during that tour that I was being selected to be an admiral, two years ahead of anyone else.

Q: Was Tom Gates Secretary of the Navy?

Ward: Yes.

Q: This was the day of John Foster Dulles and his so-called brinkmanship policy so it must have been rather exciting.

Ward: It was. Our relationships with State were very good. I would go to State and find out what their positions were on some of these issues and would develop a position for Admiral Burke to take as one of the members of the Joint Chiefs of Staff. So it was a very busy time. I was in Admiral Burke's office much of the time. I worked closely with Admiral Dennison and frequently went with Admiral Burke to the meetings with the Joint Chiefs. This training, of course, stood me in good stead for later assignments in this same field in Washington and in Europe.

Q: With your perspective of future assignments that developed, and with this particular one, was there any evidence of greater concern with the military because the president happened to be a military person? Was there a more favorable climate prevailing?

Ward: I don't know whether or not this had a direct bearing. I doubt it because, as you know, President Eisenhower, as a President, worked through a staff much more than other presidents. He did not take the direct personal involvement in day to day happenings that President Johnson did, and President Kennedy did, or President Truman. He worked through this staff and much of the work was done by his staff. I would rather doubt that the fact that he had been a military man had much bearing on the military in those days.

Q: Did you have any White House contact?

Ward: Not with President Eisenhower. I did later with President Kennedy. President Eisenhower was somewhat non-approachable by anyone other than top people, and this happened not only to the military. At Columbia University, for example, it was very difficult for a Head of the Department to get in to see the President.

Q: When he was at Columbia, I was told by his Chief of Staff, so to speak, that he was away fifty percent of the time because he was on Federal assignments of various kinds.

You say the two years you spent in Op 60 were key years for you?

Ward: They certainly were because I had done well as a sailor but I had not had any sensitive duties in the heart of the government. Here, as a captain, I was injected into a key position in the organization of the Chief of Naval Operations. After being there a very short time I was made Head of this part of the political work in the Strategic Plans Division and worked pretty much directly for Admirals Dennison, Beakley, and Burke. I worked in their offices much of the time. For example, if a Joint Chiefs of Staff meeting were coming up in the afternoon, I would be briefing Admiral Burke along with the other members of the staff. There would be as many as twenty people for a briefing for Admiral Burke before he would go down to the "tank", but I fell heir to maybe half of those subjects that were being briefed. So it was an important position -- it was, of course, three down in the echelon of command, but the positions the Navy would take were formulated as a result of those briefings. I got known and I knew things which I otherwise would not have had known.

Q: Admiral, how closely did you work with the intelligence agencies in this partiaular assignment?

Ward: I did not work directly with the CIA or DIA. I did work very closely with the Navy people in intelligence. If something transcended the scope of naval intelligence, the close liaison between Op-60 and Op-90 people, that is the strategic plans and intelligence people within the office of the CNO, made it possible for me to go to the Navy people and get answers from them. They did most of the intelligence work themselves -- the naval intelligence people. I later became quite closely cooperative with CIA and DIA when I was Op-06, which is a principal support of CNO for his position as a member of the Joint Chiefs of Staff.

Q: In this particular assignment working with ONI did you see the developing need for what Secretary McNamara later set up as the Defense Department Intelligence Agency?

Ward: I think the Defense Intelligence Agency was a good thing in that it certainly coordinated the efforts of many different people in the intelligence field. It reduced somewhat duplication. There is still some duplication.

Q: I suppose a certain amount of that duplicating is absolutely necessary.

Ward: Yes, I would agree.

Q: How closely did you work with your opposite number in the Army and the Air Force?

Ward: Very closely.

Q: Did you have joint assignments that you had to work on with them in preparation for the Joint Chiefs of Staff?

Ward: Frequently, yes. Frequently we would get together as staff elements between the three or four services, occasionally the Marines, but Army, Navy, and Air Force invariably would get together before meetings of the Chiefs and find out if we could resolve a problem at our level and many problems were resolved at our level without ever going to the Chiefs. If we didn't resolve some of the minor problems, they would be kicked up to the Dennison level and these Deputies would have formal meetings trying to resolve issues, with the Chiefs getting those real tough problems of great national interest and importance.

Q: How much time did Admiral Burke have to spend as a member of the Joint Chiefs.

Ward: Quite a lot. If I would give a rough estimate I would say about forty percent of his time was directly involved with matters of Joint Chief interest with some additional time indirectly involved.

Q: It becomes difficult to wear two hats, doesn't it?

Ward: It does, but it's important because he's representing the Navy, not only in working on national problems, but also in getting support for the Navy from the Defense Department and from the White House and the government.

Q: When you worked on problems in preparation for the Joint Chiefs of Staff you developed them from a Navy point of view. You didn't attempt to be eclectic in the approach to the problem, did you?

Ward: No, you're correct. It was from a Navy point of view. Quite a few problems were not directly naval problems but they all had some effect on all the military services so we would present our problem for Admiral Burke's representation at the Joint Chief's meeting from the Navy point of view.

Q: Did you have anything that had to do with Quemoy-Matsu? This was about that period.

Ward: Yes, we sure did. We had many, many issues that were concerned with Quemoy and Matsu. Issues such as whether or not United States forces should patrol the Formosa Straits between Taiwan and Quemoy and Matsu, or whether we should withdraw to the north and let the Chinese handle these problems. Issues whether or not in the event of an attack whether or not our destroyers and our ships should bombard the zones in Quemoy and Matsu under the gunfire control of people on the shore; whether or not we would permit our advisors to go to those islands and stay there, and incidentally we did for a long time have advisors on Qemoy and Matsu. We were directly involved over an extended period of time. There was some talk whether or not it was the worth the effort to maintain this presence that close to the mainland.

Q: It certainly was debated in the Senate. Was this not also the period of the Burmuda Conference when President Eisenhower met with Churchill?

Ward: I don't recall.

Q: And followed it with his speech before the United Nations on the peaceful use of Atomic power. That didn't come into the Navy realm?

There nothing else you want to add to that period?

Ward: I guess the most important thing from a personal point of view I'd like to add to that period is the fact that I was selected for rear admiral while on this assignment and to my great surprise because there was only one officer in the class ahead of me, in the class of '31, who was on the selection list. Admiral Burke called me in and used some language which is not printable but he commiserated with me in the fact that I had the toughest job in the Navy because I was the youngest admiral selected to date and was quite junior. Having people older than I and heretofore senior to me working for me would be a real challenge. He talked to me as a father would for several hours. He gave me advice and counsel on how to handle some of the problems that were bound to come up for a man faced with this situation.

Q: Be specific will you? What kind of problems would come up under such a set of circumstances?

Ward: Well, for example I went down to the Atlantic Fleet still as a captain wearing captain's stripes, and worked with people who were much senior to me on the captain's list, years and years senior to me, but I was their boss. I had to give them orders and they were wise enough to accept me as their boss. Any resentment that was present was certainly not shown. It was a very difficult circumstance in which to be placed, particularly so since Admiral Wright had two hats at that time -- he was not only Commander in Chief of the Atlantic Fleet but he was also the NATO commander and because of the sensitivites between the U.S. and British regarding control of NATO, he wisely determined that his more important job at that time was the NATO command. He spent most of his time on NATO matters and running the NATO end of the fleet in order to maintain his position and keep the command for the United States. I found myself doing things that were unusual even for a junior rear admiral, by virtue of filling a vacuum that had to be filled.

Q: Yet when one thinks of the business world or the education world, the same kind of problem doesn't exist. Age isn't really a factor there in a man's promotion, or anything else.

Ward: That's right, it isn't. It would be like a department head going over the vice president to the president, but if the department head were going to be the senior vice president next week he would start functioning ahead of time.

Q: If this puts a man in a difficult position, why does the Navy go ahead and reach down and select a man for admiral when these are built-in difficulties?

Ward: This is a good question and it has an answer which is logical in that I was the first deep selection -- the first time that any Board had gone down this deep to get a person far down the line. Now this is accepted. You don't now have the same feeling that you have to be taken in line. You get the best people regardless of their age or seniority. This has now become a matter of custom so it's no longer quite the impact that it was when it was first attempted under Secretary Gates. There is another answer too, in that not only is it accepted but some of the younger men have pretty broad experience now. Officers are now frequently selected early for promotion all the way up the line, which was not true then.

Q: This is indicative of an evolving Navy, isn't it?

Ward: It certainly is.

Q: A Navy that is specializing in so many areas. Was it your vest technical knowledge and experience which induced them to reach down for you?

Ward #3 - 91 -

Ward: No, I don't think so. I think it was the fact that I had some training in the political military field as well as having the technical training. I think it was a broad knowledge rather than any specific knowledge and the fact that I was willing to go out and work and actually make decisions without always going up and asking for guidance and directions.

Q: Was Admiral Burke particularly opposed to this or apprehensive, or what?

Ward: No, I think he was not opposed. If he had been opposed, it never would have happened. I don't believe he was apprehensive either. He just wanted me to know that I was going to have, or I might have a rough time in performing the duties of admiral under the conditions that existed in those days. He had a somewhat similar experience in that he had been selected the CNO, the Head of the Navy, over about half the admirals in the Navy who were senior to him. I think he was highlighting possible danger spots and making suggestions on how best to get around some of these without confrontations with people who were older and more senior.

Q: Had the Naval War College course prepared you in any way for the involvement in political affairs?

Ward: Yes, it of course helped. It's a regular political military course that's given there. It was of considerable help.

Beakley and Dennison were wonderful admirals. They were also tremendous in helping me do my job.

Q: Dennison was thoroughly indoctrinated in that aspect of naval planning, wasn't he?

Ward: Yes, very much.

Q: He had served as aide to the President -- much more than an aide, actually. You mentioned Gates. Did you have direct association with him?

Ward: Not too much, I had some. I was closer with later Secretaries, but had some with Secretary Gates. Secretary Gates is the man, I understand, in his precept to the selection board directed that they recognize younger people who could be moved up into command responsibilities. Of course, the Secretaries now also require this.

Q: They then give a set of directives to the Board, do they?

Ward: Yes. The Navy was the last of the services to break with the old tradition of seniority. The Air Force had young generals long before Curt LeMay was a general at age twenty-eight, I believe.

Q: That was a different ball park, wasn't it?

Ward: Yes. The Army had younger generals long before the Navy.

Q: After the Strategic Plans Division in August of '56 you became commander of the Amphibious Squadron 8. Tell me about that.

Ward: This was a natural follow-up in my selection. I had not had command of a cruiser or a destroyer squadron. I had not had what is know as a deep draft command, a big command. An amphibious squadron is such a command. After my selection it undoubtedly would have been a year before I would have actually worn admiral stripes because there were that many admirals ahead of me to fill the vacancies. Again Spike Fahrion came to the fore. He was then Commander Amphibious Force, and he asked Admiral Burke if he could have my services as a squadron commander even though I had never been in the amphibious forces before. Admiral Burke evidently thought that this experience was good for a young embryo admiral and he acceded to the request with the understanding that Admiral Fahrion would not request that I be there longer than six months. So I was Commander Amphibious Squadron 8 for about six months. I didn't do much amphibious operations though, because my first assignment was to take command of a task force that was sailing for the Arctic to re-supply the dew line. My flag ship was an icebreaker. I had for the first time in my life, and only time, duties involving aircraft, so I had pilot's orders.

I went up into the ice. I had never seen ice at sea before in my life, and had a marvelous time. We had many, many problems but no problems that a sailor hadn't had before except for the ice. The ice just made these problems come more frequently. They were more serious because if something went wrong you could get in trouble in a hurry. It was a very interesting experience. We had ships of the United States Navy, some with Army crews on board. Army stevedores and Army boat crews handled the cargo. We had ships in the Canadian Navy, icebreaking. We had Canadian merchantmen, we had United States merchantmen operated by MSTS, and we had some merchantmen operated by charter that were not under MSTS. It was a conglomerate force that we took up into the Fox Basin area. We had no charts. We went in areas some of which had never been sailed before. One of my captains was a man named Pullen, who commanded a Canadian ice breaker and his grandfather had gone through that same area a hundred years before by sail. It took his grandfather two years to get through. It took us some thirty hours to make the same passage.

Q: We had some effective ice breakers?

Ward: Yes, very. Coast Guard, U. S. Navy, and Canadian ice breakers. The materials we carried up were to equip the radar station on the Dew Line, north of the Arctic Circle. The building materials, diesel oil necessary to keep them going, some food but not much food because the food was generally flown in in big cargo aircraft. The heavy construction equipment had to be taken in by sea.

Q: Did you stay during the period that these were being constructed?

Ward: No, we were there for a period of about two months. Just long enough to get the material in, land it on the shore, and get out. The core of the fleet, that is the ice breakers, stayed up there about two months. The merchant ships would come and go. We frequently had to escort them in through the ice and back out again.

Q: Did you have a scientific team on board? Did you have any special projects in that area?

Ward: Yes, we did. We had some civilians who were doctors of science who did some of this work. Some of them specialized in geology, others oceanography. They would take samples of the waters, very deep water, of the salinity and from these were able to determine the best areas for navigating and help us out a great deal. It was a very interesting sidelight. It was not of any great tremendous importance to the nation at that time but it gave me an interest in this field, oceanography. During that same period under the amphibious force, I did load out an amphibious squadron force and sail it to the Mediterranean but I was not personally involved in it for any length of time. We did conduct many exercises for which I was commander of the forces, off Vieques for example. At the end of six months, almost on schedule, I was detached to go to work for Admiral Jerauld Wright, on his staff.

Q: Since you mentioned Vieques, the island is of great importance to the Navy. Do you think it continues to be in light of all the controversy about it today?

Ward: Oh yes. I think it is. It's a valuable place for both Marine and Navy to train. As you probably have read, the numbers of natives who live on the island are very small. The politicians, both in Washington and in San Juan, support getting this island back again. I think at one time they were down to seventeen families. I believe there are several more now but it's a very small number of people.

Q: I read somewhere that the Navy considered this a rather unique island that they couldn't achieve anywhere else-in the facilities they have there.

Ward: It's a tremendous asset to amphibious operations and to the Marines because the Marines have a temporary base there. Usually a considerable percentage of the Fleet Marine Force, people from Camp LeJeune in North Carolina, are in Vieques training. They can use their tanks and part of their weapons. They can have the off-shore bombardment from ships, with the troops on the shore participating, and make regular over the beach type landings under simulated combat conditions which cannot be done anywhere else that I know of.

Q: That substantiates the point I read about. Why then do officials in Washington advocate that we abandon our naval facilities there within a reasonable period of time?

Ward: It's politics, of course. They get some political mileage out of it because people in Massachusetts, who don't know anything about it think the Navy is removing large numbers of people from this area, which is really not true. The natives down there get some benefit from having these Marines there. They sell their langouste and they sell their produce. It is true that the island is a beautiful island and it would make a very nice place for an island paradise and I suspect inevitably that civilization will demand that this be used for the enjoyment of man more than it is being currently used. I suspect that it is true that when this island is opened up, some promoters will make a great deal of money from the island.

Q: What aspect of oceanography intrigued you as a result of your Arctic trip?

Ward: I think there are several facets of it. One is the ice formations up there and the rather peculiar way in which the wind affects the ice and the dangers of a storm in the presence of ice. Another thing that's unusual is that the fish are different there than they are anywhere else I've ever been. You get a cross between salmon and trout that are just wonderful eating fish, just delicious. Why would salmon cross with trout? I don't know but I've had many discussions with some of the learned men who were in the force conerning matters of nature just mentioned.

Q: Would isolation be one of their theories?

Ward: Yes. And seeing the animals, too. Silver foxes that come up and eat garbage in the camps, for example. Polar bears that would crawl into the well deck of your ship if you give them an opportunity, after food and hand-outs.

Q: Was there any knowledge gained from the scientific observations? Any knowledge gained from the expedition, itself, which might be useful in the problems of the Northwest Passage nowadays?

Ward: I'm sure there was. As a matter of fact, during the time I was there, a ship did use the Northwest Passage leaving from Alaska and coming across the north of Canada and into some of these channels and into the Fox Basin. We had to help one of them out with an ice breaker at one time. I'm sure some knowledge was gained and will continue to be gained.

Q: Our development of ice breakers was, in large part, responsible, or the result of building of ice breakers for the Russians in World War II?

Ward: I don't know. I believe the Coast Guard had ice breakers well before that. There's some question whether the Navy should be in the ice breaker business. The Canadians have turned their ice breakers over to what they call a Transportation Corps --not military at all.

Q: A civilian outfit?

Ward: Yes. We are turning many of ours over to the Coast Guard or a MSTS type operation.

Q: Whats the advantage to that? Is it somewhat similar to salvage where private concerns function more readily?

Ward: Yes. It's a basic question of whether or not you want military to operate service ships or have civilians operate them. The feeling in Canada is that only ships with guns and aircraft and war implements should be operated by military people and they have gone to civilian operation for anything that is not directly connected with combat. We are leaning in this direction for MSTS operations. I find no fault with this.

Interview # 4 with Admiral Alfred G. Ward, USN (ret.)
Severn School, Severna Park, Maryland   Sept. 4, 1970
Subject: Biography   by John T. Mason, Jr.

Mr. Mason: Last time when we broke up, Sir, you had just recieved your assignment as Deputy Chief of Staff for Operations and Plans to the Commander in Chief, U.S. Atlantic Fleet, Admiral Wright.

Admiral Ward: Yes. He's a wonderful man and as I mentioned, it was a tremendous assignment for a freshly caught admiral who was not even yet wearing admiral stripes, just wearing captain's stripes, a really tremendous challenge. A challenge because as I mentioned, Admiral Wright was heavily involved with the NATO part of his responsibilities and the Deputy was one of the type people that if it didn't fly, he didn't want to hear about it. So I found myself running the Fleet. It was a real interesting and challenging assignment. We had as second Fleet command at that time a man named Bob Pirie.

Q: Did he have his beard in those days?

Ward: He had his beard. I would give Pirie some orders and Pirie wouldn't like them so he would come running to Admiral Wright and Wright would adjudicate the situation. I had great respect, great admiration, and still do, for both Admiral Wright and Admiral Pirie.

Q: What are Admiral Wright's outstanding characteristics as you assess them?

Ward: He was a tremendously powerful leader, an effective, inspirational type leader. He was thorough in everything he did. He was a terrific speaker but not so when he became Commander in Chief of the Atlantic Fleet. He had been a poor speaker but he developed into one of the finest speakers I've ever heard. He could get up before a television audience and be told that he had fourteen minutes to make a talk and during those fourteen minutes, Admiral Wright would start by saying, "I have twelve points to make." And he would make those twelve points without looking at a single note and as the clok struck the fourteen minutes, he would have completed his talk. He was just tremendous. He worked hard at it but he was good.

Q: This must indicate a great awareness of things, of what was going on around him.

Ward: He had a very broad background, as you may remember. He had been a White House aide and he'd been working in the Pentagon/head of government area arena for a long time. He was and is a very fine gentleman. He was successful later as an Ambassador to Tapei for many years until he and Madam Chiang Kaichek decided maybe he had had it long enough.

Q: Be specific about some of your duties in this job if

you will.

Ward: The biggest duty, I guess, was to control the operations of the Fleet by making out schedules. We would have routine conferences with all the type commanders and the operational commanders and would make out the schedules for each of the ships. Most of the ships were fairly short handed but had adequate numbers of people to operate. It was still touch and go on some of the ships as how strenuous you could make their assignments. I believe that this was probably the area that was the most challenging. We also, at this time, had work with the Operational Development Force, which we talked of earlier. This Force was under the command of the Atlantic Fleet. Many innovations in hardware and techniques, procedures, were introduced. There was no limit to the spheres of interest and the various activities which were involved in running a very large number of ships such as the Atlantic Fleet.

Admiral Wright was unique in another way in that he let a young man such as I was (not young but a comparatively junior young man) have such responsibility. About once a month he would call me in and he would say, "What have you been doing with the Fleet this month?"

Q: As you say, he wore the NATO hat, too, and this involved him in western Europe much of the time.

Ward: Yes. He spent a great deal of time in Paris at the NATO headquarters. He visited the NATO countries frequently. He observed the observations of the navies of other NATO nations in his capacity of command of the NATO fleet. He was very much interested and felt it was necessary for him to have this interest because of the desire of other nations to take this assignment and he felt it was vital that the United States hold it.

Q: Did you get involved at all in the NATO aspect of the job?

Ward: Yes, peripherally. I was not on his NATO staff. Admiral Wright would tell me that I ran the fleet. But the largest element of the NATO fleet was the Atlantic Fleet of the United States. Our ships were involved frequently in NATO exercises, working with the ships of other navies on both sides of the Atlantic.

Q: How did that work out? I mean this joint operation idea.

Ward: Very, very well. We had no significant difficulties at all

Q: Was it largely with Royal Navy units?

Ward: Royal Navy, Canadian Navy, Dutch units frequently, destroyer types from Holland, a few Belgian mine sweepers and small craft. The French were quite active at that time. The French had a small navy but very effective, well trained.

Q: What would a joint operation involve or comprise?

Ward: A small joint operation would be an anti-submarine warfare exercise in which two or three or four United States submarines, some nuclear, some non-nuclear, would go down and make attacks on a combined surface fleet, with destroyers of the Dutch and French and British navies joining the U. S. Navy units in trying to detect and simulate attacks on these subs. We also had frequent air exercises with the Royal Navy units with the carriers from the Royal Navy and the carriers from the U. S. Navy operating together and actually interchanging aircraft. An aircraft from the Royal Navy carrier would take off from his home carrier and land on a U. S. carrier and they'd be based there for several days and serviced, repaired, maintained during this period -- just these type of operations.

Q: How did the Royal Navy carriers compare with our fleet?

Ward: They were very good. As you know the Royal Navy had the first carriers. They innovated this method of warfare. They did not have the capacity that our own carriers had; that is, our carriers would carry more aircraft. Our aircraft was generally of a more effective design, could fly higher, faster, more bomb load. But the British carriers were good; they were very proficient in their operations.

Q: Where were you actually based? In Norfolk?

Ward: Yes.

Q: Did this then mean that you reported to Washington occasionally to congressional committees—that sort of thing?

Ward: Yes, I did. By virtue of both his U.S. hat and his NATO hat, Admiral Wright was called before congressional committees on many occasions and invariably he would take me as back up man. I would help him prepare his charts and his presentations. Frequently the questions asked by the committee would be referred to me because I had the detailed information that was needed to answer some of the questions.

Q: The fact that the President at the time had been involved with NATO, did this mean that there was a greater cognizance of such things in Washington?

Ward: I don't believe so. I believe that Washington was well aware of our NATO commitments and approved the commitments, but I believe the fact that the President had relationships probably was not of any great impact.

Q: From the point of view of your personal story, can you recall any of your appearances in Washington before committees, or what have you?

Ward: I think that the ones that I would recall were fairly detailed and the question of characteristics of Navy units would not be particularly pertinent.

Q: What else in terms of this assignment had any bearing on your personal history?

Ward: I suspect one of the greatest things is the fact that I became better known by virtue of having this particular assignment at that particular time. The influence that I had on the Fleet operations was significant and because of this many people whom I had not known before worked closely with me and I worked with them. I think that this was probably the most greatest single effect of the assignment.

Q: Your technical background and understanding -- how was it brought to bear on the problems of the Fleet?

Ward: I would think that it was probably less of an impact in running the Fleet than in previous assignments but it did have some effect. For example, the second fleet at that time was very strongly oriented toward electronic warfare. The second fleet commander particularly was involved, as was the Operation Development Force. This was the single technical development that was foremost during those months and years.

Q: You as the deputy and the acting head of the Fleet, did you make inspection trips to various naval ~~vessels~~ ships and how did you conduct such --?

Ward: Yes, I did. Primarily not so much for inspection but for my own information. Frequently I would go down to Charleston and ride a destroyer on an anti-submarine warfare operation, or on an electronic mission operation, just to improve my own knowledge and keep up to date. I'd like to correct the statement that I was acting commander of the Fleet which is not quite true. Admiral Wright was always there if you needed him.

Q: The aircraft carrier was, of course, ~~was~~ of immense importance in the operations of the Fleet. You must have been present at some of their sorties, and so forth. What about the psychological aspect of the operation of a carrier, the tremendous power, the great noise, and so forth? What bearing does this have on the personnel?

Ward: You have to get used to it, as anyone does working under different conditions. It doesn't take long for a man to sleep under a catapult, which makes tremendous noise when an aircraft is launched. A man after a few nights will sleep through it without any interuption of his sleep or rest.

Q: One of our young chaps at the Institute, not too long

Ward #4 - 109 -

ago, was invited to go on board a carrier during some of their exercises and he came back with a great question in his mind. He felt that the sense of power was so overwhelming, the noise was so overbearing, he thought this must generate in the personnel, the officer personnel and even the enlisted, a deeply ingrained sense of the conquering hero, the invincible. Could you comment on that?

Ward: I will admit and concur with the first statement that the noise is overwhelming. The movement, the tremendous power of the aircraft --standing on the flight deck you do get a sense pf something that is almost beyond comprehension and you don't understand how all these things can be happening at one time. But a man gets accustomed to anything and certainly the poeple on the flight deck and below deck in the carrier have learned their lessons well, their precision is unbelievable, and it becomes a routine which becomes a method of living. I had much more contact with the carrier Navy when I had command of a second fleet later and actually had my flag in a carrier a great deal of the time.

Q: Drawing on that experience, but focusing on this, does it do something to your thinking? Does it give you the feeling that we, as a military force, are invincible?

Ward: No, I don't believe that. I think, again, it becomes a way of living to which most of the people who have been in this business a long time, become accustomed. You do get a feeling of great power available to the nation and to the commander of the fleet and to the people operating these ships. It's an exhilarating experience but I don't believe it's one of invincibility. You are always aware that two torpedoes could destroy the whole thing. Therefore you must maintain your guard, not only against outside but against internal problems that could arise. The big fires, for example, that have done such damage to a few of our ships are always uppermost in your mind.

Q: I expect that it was routine to have VIPs aboard. I mean political figures, and so forth.

Ward: That's right, it was.

Q: Do you recall some of those?

Ward: Yes, I do. See the picture of President Kennedy with the Shah of Iran, the commandant of the Marine Corps and me. We were with some fifty foreign ambassadors. The President had been out over night in one of our carriers conducting an air fire power demonstration and had just come ashore to see a Marine landing at the beach. It was not unusual to have delegations such as this -- chiefs of State of other nations watching and seeing the might, the power of the Atlantic Fleet.

Q: What precautionary measures are taken when such individuals come? How much are they shown other than the fire power?

Ward: Depends on the person, of course, a man like the Shah of Iran would be permitted to see anything that we have on board the ship. He would not have the technical competence to learn some of the electronic secrets but anything he wanted to see would be shown to him.

Q: Quite in contrast with a visiting Russian notable?

Ward: Yes. Even a U.S. citizen who would have special competence would not be permitted to see the internal workings of, for example, our coding systems.

Q: Since you had considerable experience with morale problems, and so forth, what about the situation in the Fleet at that time when you were deputy chief?

Ward: The morale was good but even in those days we operated the Fleet more than had been normal before that time except in war. Today it's even worse.

Q: Why is this development?

Ward: It's because of the heavy international commitments of our government; the fact that we keep so many of our ships deployed away from home. The Vietnamese war is part of the problem; the fact that we're trying to maintain a large segment of the Atlantic Fleet in the Mediterranean to counter the Soviet threat in the Mediterranean and yet still want to show our flag in other parts of the world. We have a few units in the Indian Ocean, but not enough to make significant influence felt. These pressures for more evidence of American power outside of our own country result in a requirement that we have ships in various places in the world and we don't have adequate numbers of ships to keep that number in and have still a one and three rotation overseas for fleet units. For example, where you would have thirty-three percent of your time away from home ports, another thirty percent of the time training out of home ports, and thirty percent of the time where people could be with their families. That's the ideal situation but we don't have it.

Q: So it works a hardship then?

Ward: It's a hardship and this is part of the reason for our failure to keep the good people in the Navy. They just want to be with their families more than is possible for them to be under current world conditions.

Q: The conditions are not such that they accept it as a real challenge, demanding sacrifice.

Ward: That's right. A man expects to be away during war time.

I think I mentioned I had been away about two years without coming home during the war, but this causes no resentment whatsoever. We were out fighting for our country and realized that this was necessary. Today it's hard for a man to be away from home for a year when he knows that other people aren't putting forth such sacrifices; he just refuses to do so and leaves the service.

Q: As deputy in the Atlantic Fleet, what measures did you take to counter that?

Ward: I did the best I could, that's for sure. I was frequently at odds with the Fleet commander who wanted to get his units out and train his units at sea. I'd do all I could to keep them in as much as I could. We'd train on electronic training devices which permitted simulation and were fairly successful in this effort, both in anti-submarine warfare and training of radar men, combat information center people.

Q: This could be done while you were based in port?

Ward: Yes, through electronic synthetic training devices.

Q: But the Fleet commanders thought that it should be done actually at sea?

Ward: Yes, and with absolute right in this contention too,

because it was necessary to go to sea. You can't do it all by synthetic devices but you can do a great deal.

Q: This device of yours so to speak, was instrumental in keeping morale high?

Ward: Morale was not as low as it would have been if they were out more as they are today. Morale in the Fleet is not as good now as it was in those days.

Q: Did you resort to increased athletic programs, and so forth, as you had in the past?

Ward: We did have an athletic program but it was not anything near as intensive or as thorough as it was in the days immediately after the war when my friend made an all out effort.

Q: This period when you served with the Atlantic Fleet was one of not too great prosperity in this country as I remember. There was a slight depression, was there not?

Ward: Yes.

Q: I would think this would have encouraged more men to have been willing to serve in the Fleet.

Ward: We were short of people but I think we had about all the people we could pay on our budget.

Q: Did this mean you had to fight for increased appropriations?

Ward: I think a military man is usually fighting for increased appropriations except during times of war.

Q: The Mediterranean units were a part of the Atlantic Fleet, were they?

Ward: That's correct. The units in the Mediterranean served there on rotation. Usually four months or six months at a time; the destroyers and submarines usually four months and the carriers six months at a time.

Q: This took you into the Mediterranean then frequently?

Ward: No. The Atlantic Fleet provided the ships and they were Atlantic Fleet units but the command was under a Sixth Fleet commander who was not a component of the Atlantic Fleet.

Q: He was an independent operator?

Ward: Yes. Operations were controlled by the European command while the units themselves were supported, trained, owned by the

Atlantic Fleet.

Q: During that time, were you bothered by the inquisitive Russian Navy units that now we see operating?

Ward: No. In those days the Soviets rarely entered the Mediterranean. They stayed pretty close to home in the Black Sea and up in the North Sea; the Southern Fleet in the Black Sea and the Northern Fleet close to Murmansk. This period was before the period in which the Soviets began world wide operations.

Q: So it wasn't something you could anticipate -- the present day developments, their actions in the Mediterranean?

Ward: I think it was inevitable that this would come. They were beginning to build up their fleet at that time. They did have a few submarines operating away from home ports but not at any great distance.

Q: There were some in the Atlantic, weren't there?

Ward: Yes.

Q: Did you keep watch over them?

Ward: No. Most of these were pretty far up north of Scotland

and in that area. They were not the far flung operations that we see today.

Q: What about the Russian fishing trawlers that were equipped with electronic devices, and so forth.

Ward: They, too, had not become the world wide operations that they are now. They did have some but they didn't keep them off our coast at that time. They did not have them in the Mediterranean in any number. It was a period before the great expansion of the Soviet fleet made possible the current operational patterns of today.

Q: Were there any incidents involving single units of the Atlantic Fleet which are worth mentioning during this period?

Ward: This was the period during which some of our nuclear submarines were making history, the first of the nuclear submarines was the NAUTILUS. We also began to operate in the Antarctic.

Q: For what reason?

Ward: The exploration of the South Pole and that area. It was in connection with the governmental effort.

Q: Operations Deep Freeze?

Ward: Yes.

Q: Did you get down that far yourself?

Ward: No.

Q: What cognizance did you have actually of that?

Ward: Our Fleet units were the ones ~~actually~~ who did the work.

Q: These were the operations that Admiral Dufek was involved in?

Ward: Yes -- He ~~who~~ was part of the Atlantic Fleet.'

Q: On these Deep Freeze operations, because they are of considerable interest in scientific areas, what provisions did you have to make for them other than just assigning units?

Ward: Well, Admiral George Dufek was pretty much operating without too much guidance. As you know, the Seabees were quite effective in these operations also, ~~and~~ these units would train up in the Newport, Rhode Island area during the off season and then would get aboard Admiral Dufek's units for the trip down to the South Pole area to Deep Freeze. We actually controlled the Seabees who were participating in the unit but George Dufek was the man in direct command. He did much of it himself without the need of any help.

Q: But you were aware always of the objectives of each mission, were you not?

Ward: Oh yes, surely.

Q: What were these objectives largely?

Ward: It was primarily scientific. The National Science Foundation would set forth the missions and the tests to be accomplished. Admiral Dufek had a hat, that is he was responsible to the National Science Foundation for the accomplishment of the work that they wanted done.

Q: As I remember the international geophysical year fell within this period when you served. This operation, of course, did involve other governments too, didn't it? The Deep Freeze.

Ward: Other governments did participate but to a very limited extent. Some of the South American nations would send an observer down occasionally. It was primarily a U. S. operation.

Q: Did you get involved with South American navies?

Ward: Not to any great extent, no. Occasionally we would participate in an American defense exercise in the Caribbean but this participation was limited.

Q: This was under the authorization of OAS?

Ward: Yes and the Inter-American Defense Board.

Q: Did this involve problems different from those involved in cooperation with European navies?

Ward: I believe so, in that European navies were further advanced, were more capable of participating on an equal basis with us. We did at that time begin operating a destroyer in South American waters with the South American navies. This participation with South America actually increased with annual combined training operations. Lloyd Mustin took a force down there and trained for a period of several months.

Q: What was the purpose of a single unit first, and then a force?

Ward: It was primarily to give the South Americans some benefit of our experience and our training in combat, particularly, in anti-submarine warfare. The great help that the South American navies can give to the free world effort is in anti-submarine warfare. We have no units operating south of the equator as a normal routine. This whole body of water, the south Atlantic, would be threatened by Soviet submarines in the event of a global conflict and we would depend on the South American navies to try and meet that threat. Some of these navies are pretty good, too.

Q: What kind of units do they operate in the submarine warfare?

Ward: They have destroyer types. They would like to have submarines and a few of them do have submarines but they are not very good submarines. Chile did have a big cruiser. I believe that that ship has been phased out now and they've gotten into small units which are really more effective and more useful.

Q: Are they mostly former units of the U. S. Navy?

Ward: Mostly, but not all. The cruiser, as I remember, was British built. Some of those navies are building their own ships, or buying them from us; having them built in the United States. Brazil, for example, had some very modern, very fine ships.

Q: They were no longer satisfied with second hand units. Was President Eisenhower a visitor to the Fleet at any time during this period?

Ward: Not to my knowledge, no.

Q: When he went abroad, and I think this was the time of some of his extensive travels, were units of the Fleet assigned as a protective measure?

Ward: On several occasions he would go down to an island off the southern coast of Florida and invariably we would have a cruiser stationed just off the coast of that island not only for safety, but also for support. The President frequently would come out and sleep aboard the ship, use the ship as a base, go fishing from the ship.

Q: These were recreational times for him?

Ward: Yes.

Q: This whole tour of duty certainly gave you a very broad experience.

Ward: It was a very interesting period for me and I believe that I had about as much responsibility in that period as I did later with more rank.

Q: This was due to Admiral Wright and his ability to assess people.

Ward: His ability to delegate authority, which many people don't have.

Interview No. 5 with Admiral Alfred G. Ward, U.S. Navy (Retired)

Place: His office at Severn School, Severna Park, Maryland

Date: Tuesday morning, 9 March 1971

Subject: Biography

By: John T. Mason, Jr.

Q: Admiral, last time when we broke off you had been talking about your assignment as deputy to the commander-in-chief of the Atlantic Fleet, Admiral Wright. Today, I think you're going to tell me about one of the happy phases of your career which was as commander of Cruiser Division 1 and your assignment in the Far East.

Adm. W.: Indeed it was a happy occasion. I had the privilege of getting command of this Cruiser Division at a most interesting time in world history and thoroughly enjoyed it. The flagship was en route to the Western Pacific at the time I joined her. Serpel Patrick, a rear admiral, had command of the division, and I relieved him in Honolulu in Hawaii just prior to her sailing for the Western Pacific.

We had an unusual tour in that once again I had freedom to do just as I wished and traveled around the Japanese islands and in other areas in the Western Pacific, showing the flag, making friends for the United States.

Q: That was your commission, was it, to show the flag?

Adm. W.: That was my commission.

Q: Well, give me some of the details of showing the flag.

Adm. W.: We first went into Japanese ports. We went in to Hiroshima, where the bomb had caused great havoc, just at cherry blossom time and, believe me, those cherry blossoms are magnificent. We saw cherry blossoms in Hiroshima, we saw cherry blossoms in Sasebo, Toyama, and all the way up into Hokkaido. This is a happy time for the Japanese, it's a time for holidays. The Japanese families move as families on foot out into the hillsides and the mountainsides and have picnics and grand celebrations.

Once again I had the fortune of having Japanese senior officers on board the flagship with me, and this made it very easy to make friends.

Q: How did you arrange for that?

Adm. W.: At that time, we had MacArthur as our ambassador - Douglas II - and he was interested in improving relations with the Japanese at all levels and I had no difficulty at all in selling him the idea that I should have Japanese nationals riding aboard the ship with me in order to be more effective in our position of being ambassadors of good will.

Q: Incidentally, before you went out, were you briefed by the State Department, or was there any contact there?

Adm. W.: No. None at all. I was briefed thoroughly on arrival by Ambassador MacArthur and his State Department representatives. We changed our honored guests between ports. We had various senior admirals of the Japanese Navy, with the exception of Orhara, who was the chief of the Navy at that time, and as a result had a different experience gained from the knowledge of different individuals.

I had a man named Takai with me whom I discovered in Nagasaki. Takai had an unusual background in that he had spent most of the war in Singapore in a Japanese prison. He was a Japanese national but was suspected of leaning against the Japanese administration and had been sent to Singapore to go to school at the home of his brother. On arrival, he showed some of his antagonism to Japanese tactics and was put under custody for the rest of the war.

Q: He was a civilian?

Adm. W.: Yes, a Japanese civilian.

Q: Well, they treated him rather kindly, didn't they?

Adm. W.: He was a young lad. He was in his teens. They permitted him to go to school but they kept him under surveillance, and as a result, at the end of the war, knowing the Japanese language and not being a member of the ruling party, he was hired by the Americans in Tokyo and was later sent to Nagasaki, where he was head of one of the American libraries.

Q: He was a rare kind of Japanese, wasn't he?

Adm. W.: He was rare, and he was a very welcome sight when I met him. He traveled with me wherever I went with the ambassador's permission. I had to make many speeches and would take the position on my knees in a circle among the Japanese men. I was later criticized for this, but not very much, by people who are not very smart in my opinion.

Q: You mean not being dignified and in Western style?

Adm. W.: I mean not carrying out the Western views of living completely, but adapting to the Japanese-type culture whenever I felt it was desirable to do so. For example, I slept on the floor on mats in hotels in preference to being in a Western bed. Sat at Japanese tables.

Q: You must be very agile!

Adm. W.: I was younger in those days. When I would be called on to make a speech, Takai and myself would go up into the center of the area, on the floor, kneeling, and I would tell Takai to tell them that I enjoyed being with them. Takai would translate that and ten minutes later he ended his speech, or my speech, and I would invariably ask him, "What did I say?" and he would tell me what I said and it was good.

Again, we had the privilege of going into unusual places, places where Americans did not frequent, and meeting some of the people who had not been with Americans and we were invariably well received, well treated, as honored guests.

Q: This was under the guidance of MacArthur's skill?

Adm. W.: Yes. The ambassador was well pleased with this tour and thought it was well worthwhile.

Q: It must have put something of a strain on you, however, to entertain all these VIP Japanese on board constantly.

Adm. W.: Not at all. I enjoyed it thoroughly. They were interesting people and, being high officials, they all spoke English. I had no problems-

Q: Did they as individuals and loyal Japanese have any latent animosity towards the Western Powers?

Adm. W.: No, not at all. You see, the war had been over several years at that time. There was no animosity. On the contrary, they appreciated our help in what they were trying to do to rebuild their small navy. We had Japanese destroyers accompany the cruiser.

Q: You were on the Toledo?

Adm. W.: The Toledo, and these Japanese destroyers were our escorts. We a United States submarine with us on the tour and the Japanese destroyers had the unusual experience of conducting antisubmarine warfare exercises. Of course, this was their mission, antisubmarine warfare, but they themselves had no submarines and this provided them an opportunity to do some most valuable training.

Q: Was our submarine an ordinary type or was it an atomic-powered one?

Adm. W.: No, it was an ordinary type. It was a fairly small one- but adequate for the job.

Ward #5 - 129

Q: Did you visit some of their ship yards?

Adm. W.: Yes. We went in to the big plants at Nagasaki which were just beginning to recover and were actually building some large merchant ships. They were building no warships at all. The Mitsubishi Shipyards in Japan, at Nagasaki, were very active at that time building ships not only for Japan but also for Western European nations and for the United States.

Q: Was this at the very beginning of their great economic expansion and upsurge?

Adm. W.: Yes. I would say it was early in their economic upsurge, quite early, but they had made great strides between the time that I was there in a destroyer and several years later when I came back in a cruiser. There was an amazing difference in attitudes, in economic standards, in their way of life. They had regained much of their pride as a nation and had made a great recovery.

Q: What do you think is largely the reason for regaining pride in such a short time and utilizing it to build their country in such a remarkable way?

Adm. W.: Again, they're a disciplined people, an industrious people. They had no way to go but up, and they chose to go to work and make the best of the situation. And they had great help from our leadership, beginning with MacArthur - General MacArthur - and then Ambassador MacArthur was very good as an ambassador.

Q: Would you comment on the political situation at that time?

There were obviously those on the radical fringe. Wasn't this shortly before President Eisenhower was unable to go?

Adm. W.: This was before the Eisenhower episode, but I did not observe any antagonism against the United States in my travels. On the contrary. I went in to a port called Sendai, a big city halfway between Tokyo and the northern tip of Honshu. In this port we had a guest who had been an admiral in the Navy and who was running for re-election to the Diet. He asked me to go with him on some of his tours trying to get votes.

Q: You were an asset!

Adm. W.: He asked me to not only go but to wear uniform and be on the platform with him and he attributes his second victory to the fact that he did have and was friendly with representatives of the United States government. I say his second victory because it was his second time. He had lost the election when he ran for the position as representative to the Diet but before new members were installed his opponent died, so they had another election and on the second go-around he was elected.

Q: And that's the time when you assisted him?

Adm. W.: I was with him during much of his campaigning.

Q: Did you have much contact with some of the political personalities in Japan during this tour?

Adm. W.: Very little other than military. I was with the military most of the time. That is, in Tokyo. Now, on my tour through other areas of Japan I invariably met with the mayors, with the governors, and have many pictures of being with governors in all of the provinces of Japan, including the northern provinces.

Q: On this tour, did you get up into the far north of Japan, that sensitive area where it borders on Russian control?

Adm. W.: No, I did not. We went in to Hokkaido and the ports around Hokkaido but we did not go north of Hokkaido.

Q: Was it verboten to you?

Adm. W.: I think so. I believe the question had been raised before with Ambassador MacArthur and he would have recommended against it. I think the State Department would have taken a dim view of causing a confrontation at that time.

Q: In addition to Japan, what other areas did you visit?

Adm. W.: We went down to Hong Kong on several visits during that tour. That's a magnificent place to relax and enjoy if you have the money to do so. We went in to Taiwan. We went in to Saigon, Vietnam, and we went in to the Philippines. We had a wonderful tour.

Q: Did you go to Korea?

Adm. W.: Yes. We went to Korea. We went to Pusan.

Q: Were you charged with any intelligence-gathering during this time?

Adm. W.: No, I had no specific directive to gather intelligence but it is standard operating procedure that when you go in to a foreign port and observe certain things you submit reports on those observations.

The most interesting one was in Saigon when I had the privilege of meeting frequently with President Diem.

Q: Tell me about him.

Adm. W.: In my opinion, he was magnificent. As you know, he was an aesthetic. He had been a Catholic priest at one time. He had a doctor's degree and had been a professor at a college. He was unmarried. He lived with his brother and sister-in-law, the famous Madame Nu. His life was one of strict personal discipline. He did not drink, he did not smoke, he never had a date. He lived for his people. He was successful in making one nation out of Vietnam, which had been a conglomeration of different groups prior to his arrival in Saigon. In South Vietnam there were three different Buddhist sects plus the Montagnards, each of which had its own army and its own leader, and only loosely controlled by Emperor Bai Dai. Diem changed all this. He eliminated the military power of the individual Buddhist sects and made one viable nation out of these separate and competing groups. He did this against unbelievable odds. To complicate his task there was a great influx of people from the north with many of the people, particularly the Catholics, trying to escape in order to avoid Communism, and, as you know, for a long time we refused to assist in any manner, but then we had the great operation in which

Admiral Sabin moved his entire amphibious group in to the port in northern Vietnam and carried hundreds of thousands of people down to the south.

Q: Largely Roman Catholics?

Adm. W.: Largely Roman Catholics, but not exclusively Roman Catholic.

Q: That element was an educated group, was it not?

Adm. W.: Quite a few of them were well educated. These people arrived in Saigon and Diem had a reception ready for them. He put them in barbed-wire enclosures, and fed them, clothed them, and within a few days would normally have them resettled on a plot of land somewhere out in the country with the proper tools to start their rice paddies or their farms or to engage in some small business enterprise. It was unbelievably successful.

Q: In your conversations with the President was there anything interesting that was revealed?

Adm. W.: Yes, some very interesting things. I don't believe I told you this before but I did not speak French well at that time.

Q: And that was his language?

Adm. W.: Yes, he spoke in French. His English was very poor, and Ambassador Dubrow, the U.S. Ambassador to Vietnam, was the interpreter at meetings attended only by the President, myself, and the Ambassador acting as interpreter. The President came aboard my ship one afternoon at four o'clock, and that afternoon we had scheduled a reception for the top leaders in Saigon at 6.00 p.m. and the President didn't leave until after the reception was supposed to have started. It was a long discussion and during our discussion the central them was that "Admiral, your ambassador is no good. Get me a new ambassador," with the Ambassador doing the interpreting!

Q: Embarrassing!

Adm. W.: Not at all. Ambassador handled it with equilibrium and composure. Of course, I knew the problem. It was not Ambassador Dubrow he was so mad about, it was the United States government in trying to tell him to move faster towards democracy, with the President claiming repeatedly that he was moving as fast as his people would permit, but they were not yet ready for full democracy as we had it in the United States, that he had to be tough in order to have a viable nation and that if he were not tough, if he did not carry out his policies, his nation would go to pieces.

You asked me if we had interesting discussions. They were interesting.

Q: This was the policy of our State Department, pressing for a democratic setup?

Adm. W.: That's correct.

Q: Did it seem a feasible policy at that time to you?

Adm. W.: Not to me, but I was not a State Department representative. I had great respect for President Diem.

Q: But this was a fairly general policy, as you understood it then, wasn't it?

Adm. W.: Oh, yes, it was general. We had you see, a military man there, a lieutenant general, "Hanging Sam Williams." I had a private meeting with General Williams, who told me that he had received instructions from the President to support Diem and that later he would get orders from the ambassador to take actions which he felt were not in support of Diem and he would tell the ambassador, "Ambassador, I cannot comply with those orders unless you get my orders from the President changed because they are in violation of my instructions from the President of the United States."

Q: That being President Eisenhower?

Adm. W.: Yes, and General Williams did not deviate from instructions received from the White House and, as a result, was eased out sometime later. I am confident that the instructions from the State Department were to work for United States policy to insist that President Diem move faster towards democracy. I am also confident that we withdrew our support from President Diem and it is my own personal belief that we let him get killed.

Q: Did you have conversations with the brother?

Adm. W.: No, I never met his brother.

Q: Did you meet Madame Nu?

Adm. W.: Yes, I met her but I did not have any conversations with her. I met many of the leading political figures at that time, including the mayor of Saigon and various governors, village chieftains.

Q: Are any of them in prominent places now?

Adm. W.: I don't know.

Q: What was the attitude of the British officials in Saigon at that time? Were they also in conflict with our State Department?

Adm. W.: I don't know that either. It's my belief that they were pretty much lightweights and they were just looking to see what went on. I believe that they took no leadership position.

I had other interesting experiences at that time. I met with the International Control Commission who were supposed to observe the line of demarcation between North Vietnam and South Vietnam and who did meet frequently.

Q: Were they under the aegis of the United Nations?

Adm. W.: Yes. I had several members of the International Control Commission ride my cruiser as it entered the harbor in the south and went upriver to Saigon, and got to know some of them quite well, particularly the Canadian member.

Q: Who else was represented besides Canada on the Commission?

Adm. W.: India and Poland. The secretary of the Commission was a colonel in the Vietnamese Army who was a wonderful man. Even in those days the Communists played rough. His wife missed him one night and woke the next morning to look out the front door and his head was on top of a pole in the front yard.

Q: What was the attitude of the members of the International Control Commission about the ultimate success of this division? Were they optimistic?

Adm. W.: Oh, I believe not, and I believe they felt that they were not doing the job that should have been done at that time. There were divisions, of course, between the Pole and the Canadian and the Indian, and they were fairly ineffective.

Q: Was there obvious bias in their points of view or did they work as a team?

Adm. W.: They did not work as a team. There was great bias in their points of view.

Q: In your opinion, can a conglomerate of that sort - an international conglomerate - work as a team ever?

Adm. W.: No, not if it means the destiny of a nation. I think they might work as a team in a scientific endeavor that has no military implications, but this was a hopeless situation.

Q: What was the attitude of President Diem towards this Commission? Did he express himself?

Adm. W.: No. I guess he felt they were ineffective and he had nothing to do with them.

This was a time in which there was no feuding going on between the north and the south. There was some action by the North Vietnamese trying peacefully to subvert some South Vietnamese people, and it wasn't all peaceful anyway, even in those days. You would find some action such as I've just described, murder of the secretary of the ICC. Quite frequently a village chieftain would be found missing, too, with pressures being brought to force the Communist views on some of these country people.

Q: There was a kind of infiltration, then, into the village areas?

Adm. W.: Yes, but not on the military side. I saw no military action at all, and I was permitted to travel more widely than Americans had been permitted to travel earlier. I went into a village which was the so-called capital or center of one of the Buddhist sects called Bau Dai, a magnificent temple, a religion that's not unlike the Catholic religion, with priests dressed in their white robes, as Catholic priests would be dressed, many of whom spoke in English, but an unusual combination of Buddhism and Catholicism or Christianity. They have lovely temples with the priests kneeling down in the center and the parishioners worshipping along the sides, with a big ball hanging down in the center of the church with a big replica of a human eye; with the priest explaining to us that the people felt that this was the spiritual eye that was observing them and their deeds.

Q: It's the same concept, then, as the Old Testament symbol of the eye of God?

Adm. W.: Yes. They had a pope who had been deposed by Diem because the pope demanded his own army, so Diem banished him and he was at that time living in Cambodia in exile. But his church was still going on. His army had been disbanded. One of their saints of the church was a fourteenth-century Vietnamese poet who I understand is studied today in many languages. Another one of their saints was Winston Churchill.

Q: How interesting.

Adm. W.: Franklin Roosevelt was a lesser saint, but most of their top saints were Vietnamese people.

Q: How did Churchill happen to achieve that status?

Adm. W.: I have no idea. I think he was a highly respected man.

Q: Did you observe the kind of poverty that has been described to us in the villages?

Adm. W.: No. As a matter of fact, I observed that the villages didn't have much. They were using caribou in the rice paddies to plough the fields. They didn't have many possessions but they appeared to be well fed. There was no evidence of any starvation at all of any kind. As you know, their country is a very rich country. At that time it was underpopulated - lots of land, lots of opportunities for growing the food they needed, magnificent rubber plantations which were being worked at that time.

Let me get back for just a moment to the Bai Dai. I asked one of the priests what percentage of people in that area were Bai Dai, and his reply was interesting. He said one hundred percent, that if they aren't Bai Dais they don't have a head on tomorrow.

Q: He was to make converts, then!

Adm. W.: Yes. The people, in my opinion, were not ready for democracy.

Q: Was there any evidence in those days of the widespread use of drugs as we read about it now and hear about it?

Adm. W.: No, I had no evidence of drugs. There were some bad things going on in South Vietnam. One of the Buddhist sects controlled the prostitution in the Saigon area and that is the way they financed their private army. Another Buddhist sect controlled the gambling along the river and got their funds for the support of their troops from that source. There was widespread gambling, widespread prostitution, but Diem was doing a yeoman job in eliminating this and had done so.

Q: He, through his strong faith, represented a different set of moral standards from what prevailed, I suppose.

Adm. W.: Oh, yes, that's right. The old corrupt emperor, Bao Dai, had been banished and Diem brought in a strong faith and Christian beliefs but was not antagonistic or repressive against people of other faiths.

Q: How did the Buddhists react to the Roman Catholics? Was there tension between the two?

Adm. W.: Not to my knowledge. I believe that there was good will between the two, and that it was a question of live and let live. There was some repression done by Nu in order to preserve peace in the area and I suspect he was ruthless in eliminating thefts and this had been widespread, particularly on the river, where bandits would go aboard a ship and diver it. He was tough and our government didn't like it. Of course, Diem claimed he had to be tough.

Q: Was there at that time any noticeable material support from the United States in terms of wherewithal? Were we aiding them?

Adm. W.: Yes, we were aiding them. We were aiding greatly, to the extent that our U.S. government paymasters would pay individual soldiers - Vietnamese soldiers - and they did this because they did not want to turn over the monies to the Vietnamese Government for the Vietnamese officers to pay their troops because of the fear that if they did, even if there were no graft, that we would accuse them of graft. So our people paid the individual soldiers rather than putting it through the Vietnamese system.

Q: Was this a source of irritation to President Diem?

Adm. W.: No, absolutely not. General Williams and his people, the military advisers, had the great respect of the President and political support.

Q: Graft, of course, is what we hear so much about now, black markets and so forth. This was then apparent?

Adm. W.: I didn't observe any graft. General Williams assured me that graft was much less than it had ever been in the history of Vietnam at that time. He would have been foolish to say there was no graft, and he did not say there was no graft. In the same manner, I would be foolish to say there's no dope in this school. I believe there's none, but I just could not say that, or I believe it's minimal and I believe that General Williams felt the same way, that he was successful in reducing any graft that existed.

Q: Do you think - this is just hypothetical - that if Diem had lived the picture would be vastly different from what it is now?

Adm. W.: I'm convinced of it.

Q: You think that ultimately he could have really gotten things in control?

Adm. W.: I think he was doing a magnificent job. I must add that I'm not an expert and people who have been there much longer than I know more about the problem than I do. I'm sounding off on my personal views based on limited observations.

Q: But much privileged views!

Adm. W.: Yes, privileged views and after discussions with people in positions of authority.

Q: Was there any evidence of the activities of the SEATO powers during your time there?

Adm. W.: No, not in Vietnam. SEATO was in existence, of course, and I participated in SEATO exercises.

Q: Tell me about them, will you?

Adm. W.: The ones I participated in were fairly simple ones. We worked with ships from China - that is, Formosa - and with ships from the Philippines, but they were all small exercises.

Q: Designed for what purpose?

Adm. W.: To train their ships, primarily in antisubmarine warfare and in bombardment.

Q: Tell me about your visit to the Philippines.

Adm. W.: That was fun. We were enjoying good relations with the Philippines at that time. The Huks had been eliminated, and our relations were excellent. I went into Subic Bay in the Toledo and met many old friends by virtue of its being a naval base and participated in some of the activities that were going on at that time. Rear Admiral Art Spring was in command of the base at Subic and the forces in that area, and he was magnificent. He and his wife circulated among the Philippine people, they were close friends with the Philippine people. I happened to be there on a religious holiday and he insisted that I dress up in my white dress uniform and accompany him to both the cemeteries with the flag flying on the car as we passed through the villages, and all the village kids yelling, "Hi, George, to Admiral Spring. It was a fun time.

Q: Did you go up to Manila?

Adm. W.: Yes, we did.

Q: For presidential, red-carpet treatment?

Adm. W.: No. I did not meet the president at that time, but I did go into Manila. We did go into Manila Bay and stay there for several days. The Philippines have some beautiful spots. There's a little town called Bagio up in the hillside. It's about a mile high. The climate is magnificent. The president had his summer palace there. A cottage was made available to me and my staff. The village is affluent in that even the people who work there make good wages. I had a Filipino working for me later who retired and is currently living in Bagio.

Q: It was a resort place, wasn't it, for international colony people?

Adm. W.: Yes. Beautiful golf course. As you're probably aware, a Philippine national who serves twenty years in the U. S. Navy can go back to a resort like Bagio and live in comfort for the rest of his life on his retired pay.

Q: Yes. Tell me about the Taiwan visit.

Adm. W.: This was about my third or fourth visit to Taiwan. My first one was that with Admiral Arleigh Burke by air just prior to Burke's becoming CNO and at that time we were billeted in the guest house in the center of Taipei which is a magnificent castle. On later trips, my ship would go in to one of the ports and invariably I would go overland to Taipei. Again, we had good relations with the Chinese, always do. At that time our relations were particularly good. The economy of Taiwan had started its upturn and the recovery had really been amazing.

Q: Can you contrast that with the Japanese recovery? Are they equally vigorous?

Adm. W.: No. The Japanese are much more industrious, much more capable, and their recovery has been much more astounding, I would say.

Q: Does the climate, perhaps, have anything to do with it?

Adm. W.: I think so. A warmer climate leads to some type of indolence sometimes. The Japanese are very industrious. The Chinese are no slouches. They've done a really good job with our help. As you know, we have provided them with small factories and the ability to make gunpowder, to make sugar, to make matches, and they have been industrious enough to make a success of their economy.

Q: Was there any noticeable improvement in the Chinese Navy in the interval between your visits?

Adm. W.: Yes, there was some improvement. I have respect for the Chinese Navy. One of the roughest bodies of water that I've ever been in are the Taiwan Straits. For months the seas are tremendous in those straits and even a seasoned sailor will get seasick and have to hold on day and night. The Chinese sail on those waters in smaller craft than I would want to be happy in.

Q: I would think that the straits would present something of a barrier, then, to invasion?

Adm. W.: It does in certain seasons of the year.

Q: The units of the Chinese Navy, are they all furnished by us? Or do they build any themselves?

Adm. W.: I don't believe they build any but I'm not sure they're all from the U.S. Navy. Their largest ships are destroyer types and small destroyers. They have nothing any larger than our old 2,100-ton destroyers, but they sail them well.

Q: What are they used for primarily?

Adm. W.: They're used for anti-invasion primarily. They are trained for stopping invasion and I suspect that the presence of these ships has, in fact, influenced the Communists against going on an invasion against Taiwan. They're used to bombard some of the offshore islands. They're used in support of Quemoy and Matsu, they patrol the straits constantly.

The admiral in command of the destroyer navy of Taiwan has a son in this school.

Q: In Severn School?

Adm. W.: Yes.

Q: Does this have any relationship to your visit out there?

Adm. W.: No. I met Admiral Tsou when he was the naval attache to the Chinese Embassy in Washington and his young son, Peter, was attending schools in the District of Columbia and came down to take a look at the school and stayed here when his Daddy went back to China. All four of Admiral Tsou's children are in schools in the United States. I rather doubt if any of them will ever return to live permanently in Taiwan. They're all brilliant.

Q: Any of them destined for naval careers?

Adm. W.: No. Unfortunately, they're not eligible for naval careers. Young Peter would love to be in the Navy, but he can't read and write Chinese. He speaks Chinese, but by virtue of spending most of his school life in the United States he's unable to read and write the language. And, of course, he's not eligible to be in the United States Navy because he's not a citizen.

Q: Your mission out there as commander of Cruiser Division 1, was this a part of the Seventh Fleet or was it independent of the Seventh Fleet? Was it entirely a diplomatic mission? What was your status?

Adm. W.: We were very definitely a part of the Seventh Fleet. Vice Admiral "Knappy" Kivette had the fleet at that time, and my friend Knappy gave me a pretty free rein and we've been close friends ever since and have been boosters for each other. We were part of the Seventh Fleet and would have been the principal bombardment agent with the greatest capability for bombardment of any of his ships, in the event of a bombardment. Had there been an invasion of Taiwan, we would have been in the front lines. The condition existing at that time made it possible for us to be ambassadors of good will and travel around because there was no conflict in the offing.

Q: The Quemoy business had calmed down then?

Adm. W.: Yes, and the Chinese Communists did not have the capability, at that time, to attack Taiwan.

Q: Were you in any way a target for the Chinese propaganda from the mainland during your visit there?

Adm. W.: Not to my knowledge. Not in the same manner that existed during World War II when Tokyo Rose would get on the radio daily. There was no evident propaganda effort on the part of the Chinese.

Q: Did you see any evidence of Russian Navy activity in that Far Eastern area when you were there?

Adm. W.: No, not of any significance. We would occasionally pass a Russian ship in the Japanese straits between Japan and Korea, but we had no direct contact with them at all.

Q: They weren't very numerous?

Adm. W.: That's right. They didn't come down at that time to the extent that they do now. They now maintain surveillance by small craft with all kinds of electronic equipment over much of the waters of the world, certainly in the Atlantic and in the Western Pacific. At that time this was not in existence.

Q: This represents quite a new phase in their naval development, then?

Adm. W.: Yes, and it's new within the last two to three years.

Q: Now, you were out there as a psrt of the Seventh Fleet for what, a period of a year?

Adm. W.: Yes. I went out in the Toledo for six months and I came back to the UNited States briefly - no, I didn't make it all the way back to the United States, I shifted from the Toledo to the Rochester and finished the tour in the Rochester. I was out there quite a while.

Q: And you found that one of the happy -

Adm. W.: Yes, it was a very happy experience. One of the happiest moments was the arrival back in Long Beach to meet my wife and daughter.

Q: Your picture indicates that fact. It was happy because it was not dedicated to preparations for warfare, it was dedicated to another cause. Was that the reason?

Adm. W.: That's right. We continued to train with the carriers from time to time, but we had a second mission and that was, as you have indicated, as ambassadors of good will, which made it possible for us to meet new and different people and handle new and different tasks that were challenging and interesting. And the troops responded, too, to this new environment. We had no problems of discipline on shore and they enjoyed seeing new places and new sights.

Q: Did you have an educational program of any sort in operation on your cruises?

Adm. W.: Yes, we had a college program which aimed at giving credit for work and we also had a high school program in which boys would study high school classes. It was more or less along the Calvert System lines.

Q: Did you have any special courses providing them with background knowledge of the various countries they were visiting?

Adm. W.: No, not courses. Prior to going in to a new port or a new country, we would put out a brochure, circulate a brochure to all the people on the ship, describing the port and describing the conditions that existed, and something of the people that they would meet.

Q: Any cautionary advice as to how they should act ashore?

Adm. W.: I don't remember but certainly if it had been indicated this would have been included. There were cautionary notes on going into Hong Kong, to avoid the border between Macao and Hong Kong, to stay clear of any entanglements. We had no discipline problems of any magnitude whatsoever.

Interview No. 6 with Admiral Alfred G. Ward, U.S. Navy (Retired)

Place: The Severn School, Severna Park, Maryland

Date: Wednesday morning, 31 March 1971

Subject: Biography

By: John T. Mason, Jr.

Q: Admiral, in reviewing the manuscript of Interview No. 4, I see that you talked, but very briefly about your period of graduate work at the Naval War College in 1953 and 1954. I wonder if you'd mind going back now and saying a little more about that time. Something about the course of study, perhaps, and the impact that it may have had on your thinking and the effect it had on your future operations.

Adm. W.: I'd be very happy to do this, Dr. Mason, because this was a period of great interest and it did have a strong impact on the career which I had that followed.

I think one thing that stands out in my mind with the greatest emphasis is the international relations flavor and the introduction for me into this field of political importance. We had, as you know, at that time and still have an ambassador on the staff of the College.

Q: A career man?

Adm. W.: Yes, a career ambassador.

Much of the curriculum is associated with international relations. Up until this time I had been a sailor and had been operating machinery and commanding troops - men on board the ships.

I had studied international relations at the Naval Academy, I had had some introduction to the importance of making friends and influencing people and foreign nations by virtue of my travels, but I had never studied it in the depth that we had at the Naval War College. The course there was oriented primarily towards military-political relationships. This course culminated in a final week of global strategy discussions, in which many important persons of all walks of life participated. I'll never forget that we had not only assistant secretaries of state but also top-level businessmen who made presentations and who helped us in our understanding of the factors that affected world history.

Q: This, of course, is an area that you got into almost immediately thereafter, isn't it?

Adm. W.: That's right.

Q: Was this intended, then, as a real preparation for you personally?

Adm. W.: I think this is a general preparation for people who have reached the rank of captain in the Navy, and most of us were fairly senior captains, with the realization that no longer would we be technicians but we would be in positions of influence, not only in military but also in the affairs of nations. Certainly this was true in my case.

I left the War College after making a good record there and was moved directly into one of the key positions in the Pentagon, which was in the political and military sphere.

Q: When you were at the War College, did you prepare a special study, a special paper, of any kind? If so, what was it?

Adm. W.: Yes, we did, and it was in the political-military field. Actually, my paper dealt with the Middle East, the problems of the Middle East. Each of the War College students was required to submit a thesis on some political-military subject.

Q: Yours was a very timely one, wasn't it?

Adm. W.: That's right.

Q: Did it deal with the economic problems mainly, or what?

Adm. W.: Economic and political. As much political as economic.

Q: Who was your Russian expert at the time?

Adm. W.: I don't know.

Q: Thank you very much. I'm always interested in the impact that a course at the Naval War College has upon a man. I assume that the course of study there was somewhat similar to the one at the National War College?

Adm. W.: Yes, it is. The one at the Naval War College is a little more oriented toward the Navy and naval influence throughout the world, but it is quite similar. We had almost exactly the same type of a program in that we would have lectures two or three times a week by people of almost world stature, people that are prominent in our government and also in foreign governments. These would be helpful in leading us in our thinking in areas of politics and international relations. We were required to prepare papers and to write studies on various problems that were affecting the world at that time.

Q: When these noted authorities in various fields came, did you have an opportunity to talk with them personally, in addition to listening to their lectures?

Adm. W.: Frequently we did. The procedure would normally be for the lecturer to talk for about forty minutes and then to open himself for questions for another thirty to forty minutes - questions from the floor. Following this period, Admiral Connolly, who was then the president of the War College would have a dinner or a luncheon in honor of the speaker and he would invariably invite some ten to twenty students to have luncheon with the speaker. At this luncheon again, we would have an opportunity to delve in greater depth into some of the thinking and reasoning behind the points made by the speaker.

Q: What was the composition of the student body when you were there? The graduates?

Adm. W.: Most of the senior War College students were captains in the Navy, and we had some Marine colonels. We had a junior class of lieutenant commanders and commanders.

Q: Did you have any outside people, like State Department people or any government - ?

Adm. W.: Yes, we had some exchange students. We had a few Army officers, a few Air Force officers, and we had a few State Department people.

Q: What about foreigners?

Adm. W.: We had no foreigners in our course because of the security classification. There were foreigners attending courses at the College, but none were actually in the senior course.

Q: Yes, the security aspect would make it difficult. Thank you for that little paragraph. Now we go on. Last time, you talked about the command of Cruiser Division 1 and it was a very interesting chapter. You came back in 1960, and in June of 1960 you were assigned to the Navy Department again as Assistant Chief of Naval Operations dealing with fleet operations. Will you tell me about that job?

Adm. W.: Yes. This is a job that's known as Fleet Operations and it required monitoring all fleet operations for the CNO. We were involved in preparing operating schedules and designating the strengths of the fleets that would be operating in various parts of the world and in actually monitoring all fleet operations. I had charge of the operations center for the CNO and had quite a staff of people working in that center. For example, we always had at least a senior Navy captain on duty, day and night, every day of the year, ready to answer questions that might be posed by any governmental authority or by any fleet authority.

It was a very demanding position, insofar as the day-to-day operations went, in that we had to know everything and be everything for the CNO as far as the fleet went.

Q: How many fleets were in being at that time?

Adm. W.: We had the normal fleets that are in being now: we had a fleet in the Atlantic, a fleet in the Pacific, with the Seventh Fleet operating in the distant part of the Pacific Ocean and the Sixth Fleet operating in the Mediterranean.

Q: And how many ships were included in the active fleets, then? Do you know?

Adm. W.: No, but it was up in the area of about 600 ships.

Q: Did your outfit have to be concerned with the fact that some of these ships were becoming obsolete?

Adm. W.: This was a period in which - some ten years ago, and most of the ships were ten years younger than they now are. We have not been building ships quite up to the rate that would keep them modern. Our ships were in good shape at that time.

Q: Because you were with fleet operations, did you get involved with refittings and repairs and that type of problem?

Adm. W.: Yes. Of course, we had to make sure that the schedules were balanced so that, while the details were handled by the fleet commanders - the Atlantic Fleet commander in Norfolk and the Pacific Fleet commander in Hawaii - we had over-all control, particularly as regards funding. We had to make sure that we were within the budget that Congress had approved. It was broad management.

Q: And did this involve you actually in budget-making, then?

Adm. W.: To some extent. The CNO had a separate section for budgeting. Frequently we would be called to go before the Congress to testify in order to get money.

Q: Did you have any interesting experiences there?

Adm. W.: Not as much as I did later when I moved up one echelon to Op-03, which is the deputy for fleet operations.

Q: What was the philosophy of Admiral Burke in respect to the active fleet?

Adm. W.: Admiral Burke was a fleet man. He liked the ships. He liked to control the ships. He never lost the significance of the 31-knot Burke. He was very active in every aspect of running the Navy. He spent quite a bit of time in the flag plotting room. I'll never forget one occasion at the time of the Bay of Pigs fiasco when he lived - literally lived - in the operations room.

Q: What proportion of fleet operations was dedicated to what we call showing the flag, being diplomatic, and that type of thing?

Adm. W.: That's a difficult question to answer, but I would think that the Seventh Fleet in the Western Pacific and the Sixth Fleet in the Mediterranean had as their primary purposes at that time showing the flag and making the power of the United States - military power of the UNited States - evident to the people in those areas.

Q: In planning for a given fleet, you, as director of this operation, had to take all of this into consideration, did you?

Adm. W.: Yes. We had to figure out operating schedules, the percentages of time that ships should be in port, and had to give guidance to the operating commanders-

Q: In order to do that in terms of diplomatic niceties and so forth and diplomatic imperatives, did you have to be involved with the State Department?

Adm. W.: I personally was not involved with the State Department at that time, but was directly involved at a later time. This particular job was more the mechanics of figuring out operating schedules and budgets so that we could keep a modern fleet going.

Q: But, in order to say a given number of ships will be in certain waters at a given time, if there was a diplomatic reason for them being there, you had to know this, did you not?

Adm. W.: Yes. Quite a few of these decisions emanated from the Joint Chiefs of Staff and from the State Department. Usually, these decisions would come down from the Joint Chiefs of Staff through the CNO, and then the CNO would actually control the operations of the various fleets.

Q: And in terms of the Atlantic Fleet, did you have to consider some of these little South American navies and be sure to include them in certain operations and exercises?

Adm. W.: We were involved with the South American navies. At this time we started the annual cruise. A small number of Atlantic

Fleet ships went down around South America in order to train with South American navies. This was not a major effort.

Q: No, but it was important in terms of relations.

Adm. W.: Yes.

Q: Because of Admiral Burke's great interest in the fleet as such you were attempting, I suppose, to reflect his ideas and his wishes?

Adm. W.: That's right. As you probably know, Admiral Burke controlled everything in the Navy, and he did a magnificent job. He had the job of CNO for some six years, the longest any individual had filled that job.

Q: Yes. This assignment of yours came at the very end of his CNO period. He was there from 1955 to 1961. Would you say something more about him as a naval officer.

Adm. W.: He's a very strong person. I just stated that he controlled every aspect of every operation. He was strong in his position as a member of the Joint Chiefs of Staff, he was strong in his position as the Chief of Naval Operations. He demanded excellence, he took personal interest and was personally involved in everything that went on. He worked very hard and long. He would be in his office at six o'clock and at night with a state dinner, maybe, coming up at seven he would shave in his automobile on the way to a party, and actually change his clothes while driving through the city of Washington. He was a hard-working, dedicated individual. He was sometimes hard to live with, but this is to be expected in a man of his character and his dedication.

Q: You mean "hard to live with" in that his expectations were always on a very high plane?

Adm. W. Yes.

Q: Hard to live up to.

Adm. W.: "Hard to live up to" is a better way of putting it.

Q: What kind of relationship did he maintain with President Eisenhower?

Adm. W.: He was influential, I think, with everyone in government. President Eisenhower, as we mentioned earlier I believe, was somewhat unapproachable, except on major decisions. Much of the work done at the White House was done by staff in those days. I suspect that Admiral Burke had as much influence with the President as almost any other individual.

Q: Just as a kind of a footnote and an observation on your part, was this a detriment that the President was not approachable with great regularity?

Adm. W.: I'm not really in a position to answer that. I never did have direct contact with the President.

Q: You just mentioned a few moments ago the Bay of Pigs. Will you tell me about that episode and your role in that?

Adm. W.: I first learned about an operation called Bay of Pigs the day before it happened, and I was supposedly in charge of everything that went on, at least monitoring everything that went on, in the fleet. We had no ships at all directly involved. We did have a helicopter antisubmarine warfare carrier operating south of Cuba, but this was sheer happenstance. The operation was controlled completely by CIA. I learned later that the Joint Chiefs of Staff had taken a look at a plan developed by CIA and had stated that it did have a chance of success. After this opinion expressed by the Joint Chiefs of Staff, I understand that the plan had many changes made before it was actually executed. It was a complete fiasco and on hindsight it could have been nothing else. The biggest error made was the fact that they thought that the people of Cuba would rise up against Castro and this did not happen.

Q: Why did they assume that?

Adm. W.: It's my understanding that this was a judgment from the people at CIA - agents who were on the island and the contacts that they had with people on the island.

Q: If, in retrospect, it was doomed from the beginning, why then did the Joint Chiefs offer some ray of hope that it might be successful?

Adm. W.: The plan was never actually executed as it was intended to be - the earlier versions of the plan that were reviewed by the Joint Chiefs. As you undoubtedly know, after this fiasco, Mr.

Bobby Kennedy headed a group which made an analysis of why the failure of the Bay of Pigs operation and, of course, was a member of that group. None of its findings were ever published or even released on a confidential basis.

Q: If the fleet was to be involved in the least way, why didn't they give adequate warning so that naval ships could be at least in the area?

Adm. W.: It was not intended that the fleet be involved or that any U.S. forces be involved. This was purely an operation by Cubans but under the leadership of a few - and I repeat few - CIA people, some of whom had some military experience. The most senior military man, I understand, at least as far as the Navy and Marine Corps were concerned was a lieutenant colonel and he stayed in Washington most of the time. I understand, too, that they did have a few Army personnel, U.S. Army personnel, who helped train some of the Cubans in mountain retreats in Central America prior to launching the operation.

It was unbelievable to me after I saw what this plan was. They tried to have an amphibious operation without any of the support which is normal in an amphibious operation. The people in Central America had six old military aircraft which were supposed to destroy the few aircraft that the Cubans had. They did plan to have a bombing raid on the Cuban fields but, I'm also told and I believed as a result of being present and listening to some of the messages, that this bombing raid was canceled by - and stopped, prevented - by a decision made by a man who was fairly low in the CIA organization as a result of pressures put on by some low-level State

Department people in the middle of the night. And, of course, President Kennedy not even being advised that the operation had been stopped. This in itself was enough to defeat the operation.

Q: In retrospect it looks a little bit like a fantasy, a graustarkian kind of thing that you read about in romantic tales or something.

Adm. W.: It was a poor plan poorly executed.

Q: If it involved an amphibious operation no matter how large, I would think Navy consultation would have been imperative.

Adm. W.: There was no consultation.

Q: Did Admiral Burke know about it in advance, or did he have only a day's warning, too?

Adm. W.: No, Admiral Burke had seen the plan several months earlier and was a participant in stating that it had a chance of success. Admiral Burke was not authorized to reveal it to anyone else in the Navy - the fact that such an operation was being contemplated.

Q: If the decision for canceling the bombing raid came at such a low level, why then wasn't all this revealed, because the White House more or less got the blame for canceling it, as I understand it?

Adm. W.: The decision was made in the White House war room, operations room, but not by people in authority. I mentioned that the President was not informed nor were the Joint Chiefs of Staff informed.

Q: Were there any repercussions as a result of that fact?

Adm. W.: Oh, I'm sure. I guess the major repercussion was what happened down at the Bay of Pigs in that most of the Cubans who were on the operation were actually killed. Because this bombing raid was stopped, the Cuban aircraft were not destroyed and they attacked these old rusty ships that were bringing the people in and actually sank the one ship that contained all of the ammunition to be used by the tanks that were to be landed, so that they had no ammunition. This, too, should never have happened. No amphibious commander in his right mind would put all of his ammunition in any one ship, but this happened at the Bay of Pigs.

Q: These ships were operated by Cuban personnel, were they?

Adm. W.: Some Cuban and some were hired American crews of merchantmen. They were old ships. Many of them had been pulled out of storage with a make-up crew put on board, no protection. Admiral Burke spent the night in the Pentagon that night, as did I, and I've never seen a man cry as hard as Admiral Burke did that night. We were able to listen to the voice communications going back and forth between the ships' captains and the people some few of whom had landed on the beach. It was unbelievable.

Q: It was just an exercise in frustration for you people.

Adm. W.: Absolutely. Frustration to be there and to hear people telling of the terrible things that were happening to the men who were trying to get off the ships, onto the beach and actually got on and the Cuban tanks came up and demolished the whole thing.

Ward #6 - 165

Q: Were you able also to listen in on communications from - was it the White House?

Adm. W.: No. As a matter of fact, I don't believe there was any communication during the course of the actual operation from the White House.

Q: That was a sad episode. It may have led to a bigger event later on. It may have been an encouragement for that. What else happened during that period when you were in charge of fleet arrangements?

Adm. W.: I don't believe anything of major significance. I had that assignment for only a little over a year.

Q: Yes, June 1960 to August 1961.

Adm. W.: Our submarine force was being greatly expanded at that time.

Q: Talk a little about that, will you?

Adm. W.: All right. Nuclear power was the big thing and during this period the nuclear-power submarines were beginning to come off the line and it was a very exciting development. It revolutionized submarine warfare.

Q: It made it possible for submarines to travel great distances under water? This was prior to the Russian development in that area?

Adm. W.: Yes, we were ahead of the Russians in nuclear power. If

I recall correctly, there were no known nuclear-powered ships in the Russian Navy at that time. We were well ahead of them. They caught up. They've put a great deal more effort and more resources in their ship program in the last ten years than have we.

Q: Well, at that point, what was the great thrust in shipbuilding in our Navy? It was submarines, wasn't it, or was it aircraft carriers. attack carriers?

Adm. W.: We had some surface ships being constructed and have always had a few in each year since the war, but the major thrust was on nuclear submarines and the major amount of money was being spent on the nuclear-submarine program.

Interview No. 7 with Admiral Alfred G. Ward, U.S. Navy (REtired)

Place: The Severn School, Severna Park, Maryland

Date: Thursday morning, 22 April 1971

Subject: Biography

By: John T. Mason, Jr.

Q: Admiral, today I think you wanted to continue your interesting story with your duty as commander of the amphibious forces in the Atlantic, beginning in August of 1961.

Adm. W.: That's right, Dr. Mason. I was very privileged to get this assignment, and here again I was one of the youngest of the vice admirals to be honored with three-star rank.

Q: Did you really find this a handicap?

Adm. W.: No, not at all. I had a ball. I had a wonderful time. My background is in operations and the brief time that I had as an amphibious squadron commander made it fairly easy for me to take over the reins of the Amphibious Forces, Atlantic Fleet. It was a pleasant and a busy time. It was pleasant becuase I was working with good people on interesting projects, and it was busy because the Soviets had come out into the Atlantic more frequently with their surface ships and their submarines. Their merchant marine was greatly expanded. We saw the traffic going into Cuba from the Soviet Union and realized that some kind of a battle for the supremacy of the Atlantic was under way, particularly in the merchant marine. The Soviet merchant marine had been greatly expanded and our merchant marine was shrinking.

Q: So what steps did we take in reaction to these observations?

Adm. W.: The steps we took were to do some contingency planning, and I was fortunate to have two different lieutenant generals in the Marine Corps with whom I worked directly. First, Joe Berger and later Bob Lucky, both of whom were terrific individuals, both of whom had clever, capable, smart staffs, and it was a privilege for me and my staff to work with these Marine staffs in planning contingency operations in the event we were called upon to go in and capture the island of Cuba or to take action in support of an insurrection in Cuba.

Q: That was the focal point, even at that point?

Adm. W.: Yes. We also worked with the Army planners and on many occasions the lieutenant general in command at Fort Bragg would come to our headquarters with his staff and we would plan on the locations that paratroopers would drop, we would plan on where the Marines would land, plan on what cruisers would be needed in order to provide the gunfire support that would be necessary to protect these landings. We made a regular invasion plan which would be available in the event of need.

It was inevitable, we felt, that something would happen in Cuba.

Q: How extensively were you using the facilities of Guantanamo then?

Adm. W.: Quite a bit. We did training with the Marines in landing in Guantanamo, we also did many shore bombardment exercises on the island of Vieques. It was a busy and interesting time in which to live.

Q: Did you use facilities along the coast also for practice?

Adm. W.: We did many practice landings on the coast of North Carolina. You can see a picture of one above you in which President Kennedy, together with the commandant of the Marine Corps and some of President Kennedy's guests, including the Shah of Iran and many prominent people from our government, are observing a landing of Marines at Camp Pendleton on the Atlantic coast.

Q: Did Admiral Anderson keep a close watch on this training process?

Adm. W.: Definitely, yes.

Q: You spoke about observing the fact that the Soviets were increasing their merchant marine and using the merchant marine as a part of their thrust into the Atlantic, were there any repercussions as far as our merchant marine was concerned? Did we anticipate building it up, improving it, and making it more competitive in the world?

Adm. W.: I'm afraid not. Our merchant marine was in a bad condition at that time and it has not much improved through the years. As you know, the Soviets have continued to expand their merchant marine and we are settling for a position that's much inferior to theirs.

Q: That's the forward arm of their march of empire, isn't it?

Adm. W.: Yes, and they're using it very effectively.

Q: Why don't we do something about ours? Why don't we emulate this move? We see how effective it is.

Adm. W.: We have several problems with regard to our merchant marine. The biggest one is the labor unions' control in which our people are unwilling to work for as long hours as the Norwegians or the Soviets are willing to work, and labor conditions are such in the merchant marine that we just can't be competitive, and our government is unwilling to spend the taxpayers' money in order to conduct a losing proposition, losing economic proposition, in trying to maintain their position of eminence on the world trade routes.

Q: You mean to subsidize it?

Adm. W.: We do subsidize it.

Q: The same problem exists elsewhere in our economy, doesn't it?

Adm. W.: Not to the great extent that it exists in the merchant marine.

Q: But it really puts us at a disadvantage in the world today, doesn't it, in a competitive sense?

Adm. W.: Let me go back to some of this planning, if I may.

Q: I wish you would.

Adm. W.: This planning stood us in good stead at the time of the Cuban confrontation later, in which President Kennedy decided to take firm action to stop this movement of equipment, of goods, and of supplies into Cuba. We were as ready as any nation has ever been to win a military victory in the period of October 1962. Fortunately, we didn't have to do this. President Kennedy's actions, which we will discuss later, were adequate. But our preparations which took place during the time I was in command of the amphibious force, preparations with the Marines, preparations with the Army, with the Air Force were very valuable in giving us confidence that we could do what the President asked, if and when he asked that it be done.

Q: This being so and it must have been known to the Russians, why did it not act as a deterrent before they went as far as they did?

Adm. W.: I think they were surprised at the boldness of the Kennedy action.

Q: They knew about the buildup, they knew about our exercises, our preparations.

Adm. W.: Certainly they did. They had many spy ships and electronic trawlers observing most of our actions. They knew that we were well prepared to conduct amphibious operations. We had reached a peak, I guess, in war experience and effectiveness in conducting amphibious operations, and this was known, I'm sure, to the Soviet Union.

Q: One of our naval strategists told me that a watershed event happened with Suez, and the fact that the United States did not implement with force a policy which they had said they would, and that this had a terrific effect on the Russians. Do you suppose there was a carryover in terms of their knowledge of our preparations in the Atlantic, and still thought that perhaps we wouldn't - when faced with the challenge - accept it?

Adm. W.: I'm sure this is right. I'm sure that the Soviets were surprised at the actions and the threat that the President had made, and I'm sure that had President Kennedy been less forceful they would have continued to go on in to Cuba.

Q: You speak about these electronic trawlers which the Russians have operating in various oceans of the world, what steps do we take, as a Navy, to counteract them? What can we do under international law?

Adm. W.: We can't do anything under international law- The seas are free and we want to maintain that freedom of the oceans. We would harm our own cause if we took offensive actions against trawlers that are not guilty of warlike actions just so long as they maintain their positions outside of our territorial waters. This is one of the problems which we face now around South America, particularly Chile, where they claim six hundred miles of territorial waters, which we refuse to sanction. This is one of the problems that we face out in the Far East with which we've had so much trouble.

Q: Do you have any incidents that you can cite during this period in your career in the Atlantic, of the Soviet trawlers being - snooping about and being somewhat obnoxious?

Adm. W.: They were always with us. They were not always obnoxious. They could accomplish their objectives by being present and by intercepting the messages and signals plus radio conversations, and we took no action to prevent this from happening.

Q: Do we use codes then to offset their ability to intercept?

Adm. W.: Oh, yes. Any of our classified messages were in code and we believed then and I believe now that these codes were secure and were not broken.

Q: Do they make any pretense of being what they would want to seem to be? Do they fish? Do they do anything of that sort?

Adm. W.: They no longer, and have not for many years, made much pretense of being anything other than what they are, and that is electronic intercept ships. They have radar antennas and radio communication antennas that clearly indicate their purpose and their mission. The positions that they take in areas in which fish are not plentiful are clear indications of their mission.

Q: Are they in civilian garb? The men who man these things?

Adm. W.: Oh, yes. There are not too many people on these trawlers and some women, which is foreign to what we do. We have our people in uniform and under military discipline and control.

Q: Is this not a rather unique effort on the part of a Navy, to employ these methods?

Adm. W.: Oh, no, not in the least. It's almost necessary to keep up with your possible opponent's capabilities, to find out how good he is, what we have to do in the event we do get into a shooting war to counter these actions.

Q: Did we at that time, then, employ similar vessels to spy on the Russian Navy in the Atlantic?

Adm. W.: I can't answer that.

To cover another aspect of this life of mine as commander, amphibious force, and that is the many trips that Joe Berger, and later Bob Lucky, and I made. We visited the Sixth Fleet, we saw amphibious operations there. We had the privilege of going and talking to the top Italians and top Greeks and to some Spanish people, too, about our amphibious operations in the Mediterranean. We were present when we had joint operations in the western part of the Mediterranean with units of the French fleet and units of the Italian fleet.

Q: This was a NATO operation?

Adm. W.: Under NATO auspices. We made many visits down to Vieques, St. Thomas, Guantanamo Bay. It was a busy time.

Q: What specifically would you learn from Mediterranean operations - amphibious operations?

Adm. W.: There were several things that we learned. One, the capabilities and limitations of the units of our allies. Another was the different climatic conditions, sound propagation in water in the Mediterranean being completely different, the differing effectiveness of submarine operations in those waters. As you probably know, we had some frogmen, and I'd like to talk about frogmen later, who were able to operate from submarines, coming out while the submarines were submerged, swimming underwater to determine underwater obstacles, make surveys of beaches at night, then coming back and getting back aboard the submarine. It was an interesting time.

Q: When you went to observe the operations in the Mediterranean, having performed some around Cuba and in the Caribbean, did you go with some preconceived ideas of effectiveness of certain things and then have to reverse your judgment?

Adm. W.: Dr. Mason, I'm afraid it wasn't that definitive. We would go over for a few days for operations, primarily to observe our unit in action under different commanders. That is, no longer under the commander of the Atlantic Fleet, but under the Sixth Fleet commander. But still men and ships which we had trained, actually units of the Atlantic Fleet, but under the control of another fleet commander. It was valuable to us and I'm sure it was valuable to our subordinates who knew that we were interested in what they were doing, and it made it possible for us to develop with our development force further improvements in the techniques we were using.

Q: In what areas had our techniques, amphibiouswise, made real strides since World War II, and what areas remain basically the same?

Adm. W.: Those that remain the same are the traditional way of a Marine landing over the beach - Marines going ashore in boats. The boats coming up to the beach and dumping the Marines and going off over the beach with the support of naval gunfire from offshore, with the support of naval supply ships and naval combatant ships providing them the necessary equipment to keep them on the land so that they can continue their operation. These were traditional over-the-beach landings.

Q: Similar to the island hopping in the Pacific?

Adm. W.: Similar to the island hopping in World War II. The innovations were the landings by helicopter behind the beach. This development took place during much of the time in which I was present. We were developing the techniques of doing both, landing by boat and sending in troops by helicopter landing behind the enemy lines and facing the beaches.

Q: That would automatically take the pressure off the beach landing?

Adm. W.: It would assist, yes, and make it possible to throw the enemy off balance because they were being faced from two directions instead of the one, which would be the one that they would expect.

We also used the helicopters for gunfire support. Many of them had machine guns and were able to assist the troops that were being landed behind the beach.

Other things were in the area of electronics, electronic intercepts, electronic jamming, all of the tricks of electronic warfare.

And, believe me, this development was an important one.

The underwater swimmers became more proficient - a mission that they would learn to get in and out of submarines while the submarines were submerged. This was a development which took place after World War II. We had special development forces Seal teams, sea, air, and land teams, in which troops were trained to get ashore by any of several different methods. Any one team always had people who could speak the language of the area possible opponents would speak. We had sailors who were expert in speaking Spanish, speaking French, speaking Japanese, and other languages.

Q: Did the abortive Bay of Pigs effort teach you anything in terms of amphibious operations?

Adm. W.: The only teaching was negative, and that is that you must have professionals in command and you must have professionals who have been in the training. You can't accomplish a complex operation without proper planning, and without training the people doing it.

I might add parenthetically that I had great fun working in the water with the underwater demolition teams. I think I was probably the first person above the rank of lieutenant who took very much interest in them. I would go down to St. Thomas and work out with them in some of their operations. I couldn't keep up with them, but I sure had fun trying.

Q: Had you had experience in diving?

Adm. W.: No, but I'd been a swimmer most of my life and had great fun using their equipment and going out and trying to work with them.

As a result of this interest, I believe that they had greater incentive to improve their techniques.

Q: This brings me to another question. With all the technical developments, the electronic equipment and so forth, you must have had to do a lot of homework in preparation to stay abreast of all these things?

Adm. W.: That's right, but I had staff people, too, who were expert in various fields.

Q: Yes, but this meant nevertheless that you had to be in command of it. How did you do this? What did you do?

Adm. W.: I made a point of going in to each of the different groups, electronics countermeasures people, the jamming people, the swimmers, the people who set off explosives ashore, and trying to learn what they were doing and how they were doing it, and make my interest known to them. I had a great time doing this.

Q: What were the security measures taken? Were you concerned that nothing should leak out to the potential enemy, or were you willing that something should?

Adm. W.: We kept most of the operations which I've just discussed very close in order to get into the area in which the electronics countermeasures people were making their experiments - had to go through several barbed-wire fences which were protected by Marines. Very close security. Not so with the underwater demolition teams. We worked out down there at St. Thomas, for example, in clear view of the tourists that were there. Our people became a tourist attraction for their usual operations of swimming near the beach and operations of being delivered near the beach by boat and then being picked up by boat close to the beaches.

Q: At Guantanamo are you not at a security disadvantage? I mean thinking in terms of a potential operation in Cuba itself and training on an edge of the Cuban island, were you not at a disadvantage?

Adm. W.: We actually didn't do too much underwater demolition in Guantanamo Bay. Our ships, the destroyers, would anchor in Guantanamo Bay, but we would leave Guantanamo Bay and do our gunfiring at targets off the shore and also firing at sleeves towed by aircraft. But any of the operations over which we would want to maintain security we conducted off Vieques or in the area between St. Thomas and San Juan.

Q: You mention Vieques so often and you have talked about it in the past, I don't know that you did it on tape, but is it not then a very great loss to us, to our Navy, to contemplate giving up the island?

Adm. W.: It would be a loss. I believe that we could stand the loss, but it would be a loss. It's an advantage to be able to have the ships offshore, shoot live ammunition against a target area in which a short distance away tanks are operating. This is real good training - about the best that people can get and closest to real action. I know of no other place where we can do this.

Q: There's no other uninhabited island in the area that would serve?

Adm. W.: Not to my knowledge.

Q: Would you talk about the disadvantages of Guantanamo as a base in a general sense, now that the rest of the island is under the control of a potential enemy, if not an outright enemy?

Adm. W.: Guantanamo was valuable as a training area since it can be used twelve months of the year. You can't operate out of Casco Bay, for example, twelve months of the year. The climate was good, the water conditions were good, the bay was close to open water. Within an hour of being at anchor a ship could be actually firing at a target being either towed by a ship or being towed by an aircraft. The facilities there for repairing ships, for making the targets, for handling ships that towed the targets were superb. Water conditions were good for underwater sound. It was a great training area. It was a place where, within a comparatively short time, a ship could leave its home port, divorce its interest from the families ashore, concentrate on the job to be done, and within a few weeks come back home and rejoin the existence which would be a normal for a sailor.

We had other advantages. We had good workmen down there. Most of these good workmen were Cubans who would work in the shops. They earned good pay, they liked the job, they liked the U. S. dollars. It was a very happy existence. We had some people who would come over from neighboring islands, Haiti and others, who would also help. Oddly enough, there was quite a Chinese colony there, of males only, who had come over twenty or thirty years ago and are still there. It was one of the best training areas that existed in the world, I would say. When Castro chose to close the gate, he put Cubans out of work and they had to go chop sugar cane and do other menial labor, and were no longer available for the skilled labor which they had been trained to do. It hurt the Cuban people, it destroyed much of the effectiveness of the base insofar as we were concerned. We still use it. It's a good base, but it is not as effective as it was before Castro.

Q: What about the labor force now? What did we substitute for the Cubans?

Adm. W.: We import Puerto Ricans and people from the other islands. We still have the Chinese. We don't have as many workmen there as we did when the Cubans were there. We have, for example, few, if any, dependents' schools and things of this type which we had in those days.

Q: So the whole operation is down-graded as a result of Castro?

Adm. W.: That's correct.

Q: What other aspects of the amphibious tour of duty did you have?

Adm. W.: Oddly enough, and it's one that you would not expect, I was on a speaking tour a great deal. I was called upon to tour many places, many cities, and speak about our operations, about the Navy.

Q: You mean in the continental United States?

Adm. W.: In the continental United States. Fourth of July speeches in Chicago and Birmingham and places of this type.

Q: What groups?

Adm. W.: Groups of any type, Kiwanis - the Fourth of July speech would be on radio for everybody in the area. This was a chore which any senior officer had. Because of my availability in the Norfolk area and, maybe, having some time which I could spend at this effort, I was put on tour.

Q: This was under the aegis of ChinFo?

Adm. W.: Yes.

Q: That must have been delightful. Tell me about one or two of those incidents.

Adm. W.: It was even more fun later when I was associated with NATO, because there I was not as busy as I had been in the amphibious force. I was "available Johnny," but my training while in the amphibious force in getting up before a large audience stood me in good stead when I later became a spokesman not only for the military but also for the State Department.

Q: Had you had experience doing this sort of thing prior to this period in your life, or was this entirely new?

Adm. W.: Not very much experience. I think every military officer has to do this occasionally on national holidays and things of this type. He is expected to participate in some way or another. I'd taken public speaking courses at George Washington University and places of this type in preparation for -

Q: But you'd taken those on your own? Your own initiative?

Adm. W.: That's correct.

Q: Would you make some statement at this point about the absolute necessity for the modern naval officer to have the ability to stand on his feet and express himself well?

Adm. W.: In my opinion this is an important part of the life and duty of every senior spokesman for the United States government, military and civilian. I'm sure that the people at the State Department would confirm the statement that they, too, have to represent our government in many forums. Certainly a military man is asked to do it because of particular relationships with the civilian populace. During this period, I would have to be present at the deaths of people in Chicago, say, and be expected to make proper remarks. It was not a traumatic experience for me. On the contrary, it was one which I welcomed.

Q: It exhilirated you!

Adm. W.: I felt I was doing a job.

Q: That's the effect it should have, because then you are uninhibited and speak for it. What percentage of your time was involved in this operation?

Adm. W.: Not too much during the amphibious force days. Immediately after the Cuban confrontation, I had to make many speeches. I think you have a copy of one of them that I made down in Miami -

Q: I do.

Adm. W.: And I made another one at Palm Beach. Immediately after the Cuban confrontation, I was asked to speak in many cities.

Q: You had an event that you could focus on, an event that had taken place. But, as amphibious commander, you were in the process of training for future events. Were you then able to say very much about that? Or did you?

Adm. W.: I think most of my material in the speeches that I made at this time dealt with the changing balance of power in the oceans and the position of the amphibious forces in exerting their influence to try and maintain some equality in power with the Soviets' thrust into the oceans.

In my home town, Mobile, for example, I was asked to make a talk before the Chamber of Commerce, which was also broadcast, about the military situation existing in the world as of that time and what influence the amphibious force had in the over-all picture.

Q: What reaction did you get from the general public to the discussion of the changing balance of power? Obviously, you were talking about the Russian buildup and the fact that we were threatened with becoming Number Two. What reaction did you get from the public?

Adm. W.: I got one of great interest and one of surprise. They had been thinking about the interest on their bank notes and about what new industries might be coming in to, say, for example, Mobile, about their local problems, and had not had a focus placed on the total world situation and where the United States fit into that situation, and where the people of Mobile fit into the over-all effort of the United States. And I believe that this was the most important message that I had to give them - to make them aware of their part in the world as it exists today and of the position of the UNited States in the power struggle that exists.

Q: We were somewhat lulled into a dangerous state of lethargy, were we not, in terms of international realities?

Adm. W.: The Cuban confrontation "unlulled," if that's a useful world. It suddenly awakened our people to the dangers that exist in confrontation with the Soviets.

Q: Admiral, how did this state of mind come to be? Was it in any way connected with the announced policy of national defense known as "massive retaliation"? Was there any connection with the lethargy and the sense of wellbeing which developed in the public mind?

Adm. W.: Oh, yes, I think so. I think the fact that the United States had maintained nuclear superiority for many years made our people - and made all of us - feel that we were secure in our position as the greatest military power in the world, and I believe this confrontation and the greatly increased strength of the Soviets both in nuclear power and in sea power, when these strengths became known it caused some uneasiness and some realization that we no longer had the umbrella of unilateral control over the world's destiny.

Q: Now, you're talking about the period in the early sixties when this realization came upon us as a people, your efforts and the efforts of many others to help bring this realization into being, and yet here we are in the early part of the seventies, and the situation has not really improved any. Why did not the public rise up and demand that something be done?

Adm. W.: I can't answer this one, Dr. Mason. I think you're more capable than I am on it. The situation has changed. The Soviets have continued to gain in relative strength in all areas. They've shown a much less combative attitude. This doesn't mean that they will always continue to do so, but they've been less pugnacious, less hard to get along with.

Q: But no lessening in their efforts to -

Adm. W.: No lessening in their efforts. On the contrary, they're continuing their efforts.

Q: What is necessary to bring us to the next stage? I mean, a realization, yes. You say we had arrived at that in large measure after the Cuban crisis in the early sixties. What is necessary to bring us beyond that to the implementation of that realization?

Adm. W.: I think continuing awareness of our people of the dangers involved if we get too far behind in this race and the fact that we will be under blackmail and subject to the will of the Kremlin rather than to our own thoughts.

Q: I think perhaps we've dealt with this period sufficiently well to go on now to the larger command which you assumed in October of 1962 as commander of the Second Fleet and of the Strike Fleet. It was a logical progression, was it not?

Adm. W.: It didn't seem very logical to me at the time. Let me tell you how this came about. I was sitting in my office, having had command of the amphibious force for about thirteen and a half months, just a little over a year, enjoying my duty and I had an odd phone call from a staff captain on the staff of Admiral Dennison, who was the commander-in-chief of the Atlantic Fleet -

Q: Had he been C-in-C during the time you were with the amphibious force - the whole time?

Adm. W.: Yes. This staff captain told me that I was to be relieved of my command the next day and I said, to whom am I talking, and he identified himself and I knew him. I said, well, what have I done wrong? And he said, "I don't know that." I said, "Who will relieve me?" and he said, "I don't know that." I said, "Well, I want to talk to Admiral Dennison." He said, "He's too busy, he can't talk to you."

I didn't know whether to believe the man or not, but I knew something was wrong. So I called Admiral Beakley, who was the deputy - you've heard these names before, I'd worked with Dennison and Beakley in the Pentagon, but they both were my superiors at this time. Ad. Beakley confirmed that I would be relieved tomorrow but told me that that was about all he could tell me.

Q: Did it seem ominous to you?

Adm. W.: It seemed very ominous. Later that afternoon, I had another phone call, this time from Admiral Beakley, explaining that I would not be relieved tomorrow, Thursday, but I would be relieved on Friday. Again I asked who would relieve me and he said again, "I don't know." Well, sure enough, the next day I was called and told that my friend Rivero would relieve me on Friday and that I was to prepare a change-of-command ceremony for that day, and that I would take command of the Second Fleet the next day, which was Saturday. Rivero showed up, having left Washington - the Pentagon - the day before and came down -

Q: This was in Norfolk?

Adm. W.: In Norfolk. And took command of the amphibious force, and the next morning, on schedule, I went over to the Second Fleet flagship, reported aboard, and had a change-of-command ceremony, and became the commander of the Second Fleet.

Q: What happened to Admiral Jack Taylor?

Adm. W.: Admiral Jack Taylor was sent out to duty in San Francisco. He was as much in the dark as I at this sudden effort. During the change-of-command ceremony, notes were being passed to me that said, in effect, "cut it short, you have work to do." So my speech lasted about two minutes when I took command, we had very few guests because there was no notice, no representative of the Atlantic Fleet staff was present at all. As soon as I could, I left the platform and went in and started reading some messages that ships were being ordered to sea that day, Saturday, other ships were being ordered to sea the next day on Sunday, direct from the Atlantic Fleet, not from the second Fleet commander. Well, I called up Admiral Beakley and I said, "Beke, what are you doing with my fleet? I want to see Admiral Dennison." He said, "The Admiral wants to see you, but he does not want to see you in his office. You can meet him in his airplane and go to Washington and be there within twenty minutes."

Q: At that moment.

Adm. W.: Yes. So I stopped by my house on the way to the airport, threw some underwear in a bag, and went to the airplane, and sure enough Admiral Dennison showed up shortly after I did, and we got in the plane and took off. During that forty minutes Admiral Dennison briefed me on the fact that we would blockade Cuba, that I would be the blockade commander, and that I would be in charge of all of the operations around the island of Cuba. He showed me some tentative plans that his staff had made on a blockade plan and together we modified those somewhat and decided what we would present to the Joint Chiefs of Staff on our arrival in Washington.

Immediately on arrival we went to see the Joint Chiefs.

Q: May I ask what was the advantage in keeping you in the dark until that very moment. When you were being consulted sometimes a chance for reflection has been advantageous?

Adm. W.: This was a result of the quickness with which the

situation developed in Washington. If you have read Eli Abel's book on the Cuban crisis, you will find that it was only a week before that consideration was given by anyone in government that action might be taken, and it was only two days before the change of command that the decision was actually being discussed, and the day before the time that I was called was about the time the decision was made that, yes, the U.S. government would take measures.

Q: And yet for a few weeks at least, we had had revelations on the floor of the Senate about this whole situation developing. SEnator Keating of New York was the mouthpiece for that.

Adm. W.: This is true and there had been many discussions by people in high places, most of which had never reached the public, about what action should be taken and how serious was this. And it was not until Senator Keating's call that we were made aware that the situation was becoming grave. Have you seen the movie "Topaz" or read the story Topaz?

Q: No.

Adm. W.: This is discussed and very accurately reflected in some of the movie scenes.

Q: CIA had information on this buildup for a certain amount of time. I got that story only yesterday.

Adm. W.: Yes, I'm sure it was known, but by only a few people, and the decision was actually made by President Kennedy in the White

House only a few days before the change of our fleet commanders and the fact that there would be a blockade. As you know, there was some question whether or not we would invade or launch an air strike, and President Kennedy made the decision, no, it would be a blockade.

Q: Would you, at this point in your narrative, outline the difference between a quarantine and a blockade?

Adm. W.: This is an interesting point. I'd like to divert just a minute before I hit it. During the meeting with the Joint Chiefs, we did show them the plans that we had, which seemed to be reasonable ones for a blockade, and the Chairman of the Joint Chiefs went to the White House war room -

Q: Was that Maxwell Taylor?

Adm. W.: Maxwell Taylor - and together with Admiral Dennison - I accompanied them but did not go in to the conferences with the high command, but stayed outside. I was given a copy of the speech that the President would make on Monday in which the word "blockade" was used, and as far as I knew, it would be a "blockade." On Monday, when I listened to the President make his speech - and incidentally on Monday I was well out at sea but listened to the radio -

Q: Monday night?

Adm. W.: Monday night. When he did make that speech Monday, the only word that was changed from the draft that I had in my hand was "blockade" was changed to "quarantine." There was no difference except one of semantics.

Q: Well, "quarantine" had been used by FDR in his famous Chicago speech, I remember, and perhaps that was the first time it had been used. But a blockade is always thought of as an act of war, is it not?

Adm. W.: Yes, a blockade is an act of war.

Q: And a quarantine?

Adm. W.: Your definition would be just as good as mine, but the word "blockade" was changed to "quarantine" in order to remove the stigma or the more serious impact had the word "blockade" been used, but there was no difference in practice. The United States government provided the Soviets with a list of forbidden materials which would be confiscated if an attempt was made to put them in to Cuba and, of course, high on this list were missiles of any type and the things that go to make a missile work, fuel, guidance equipment.

Now, to return to my story -

Q: I'm sorry!

Adm. W.: After I had gotten back to Norfolk after this briefing and after getting some instructions on what would be done, I did get additional tankers under way headed south with general orders to go to sea and head on a course 160° toward the coast of Florida and that they would be given some additional instructions later. We got destroyers under way in an almost similar position except that we put some restrictions on them - on the captains. They were to get under way on the weekend, but not to have a general recall on radio, recalling their people to the ships from their homes. They were permitted to call on the telephone and get such people as they could by those means. If they needed additional people, they were authorized to go to ships undergoing overhaul and borrow some of their men in order to get enough people so they could operate their ships. We had many ships get under way with very reduced numbers of crew members, some of whom were not their own, and this was for a very dangerous mission - a mission in which they may well have to shoot. None of us knew what would happen. We did not expect any numbers of Soviet warships, but we did not know the reactions that the Soviet ships might take.

By Monday, sufficient numbers of ships were at sea so that when the President made his speech on Monday night, we were on station around Cuba and off the east coast of the Bahamas to stop ships going through the Bahamas.

Q: What Soviet warships were in the area?

Adm. W.: None, to my knowledge, at that time.

Q: Submarines?

Adm. W.: Yes, there were none except submarines. There were submarines present. We did not know that. We discovered them. It was not known that Soviet submarines were present. One of our ships picked up a submerged contact, trailed it for about a day and a half, and the submarine was not nuclear-powered but a diesel engine submarine ~~that~~ so had to surface for air and surface close by the destroyer. Meanwhile we had gotten word to the White House and to Washington and were told to trail it but to take no offensive action.

Q: In the aggregate, how many were there actually?

Adm. W.: We detected four submarines. There may have been more, but we detected four and this was just by chance. The fact that we were on a war footing, we were conducting war operations that could well lead to war and we had all of our protection equipments operating on all ships.

Q: Where would those submarines have been based - their supply base?

Adm. W.: Probably Murmansk. When we trailed them halfway across the ocean, they were headed towards northern ports of the Soviet Union usually.

To add one more statement on this - when the submarine surfaced and the destroyer was escorting him, the first and only message that went out for some time was from the captain of the destroyer offering any possible assistance that the submarine might need.

Q: There happened to be a Russian-language officer on board the destroyer?

Adm. W.: Yes, there was, and this too was historic. In Washington, on Saturday, it was determined that we should have Russian-language officers on all of the ships on the quarantine line, so they punched a computer to find Russian linguists who were in or near the East Coast and these poor youngsters were given orders to be in Norfolk by noon Sunday, to be on board the ships.

Q: There was an adequate supply of them?

Adm. W.: Yes. Every ship on the line had a Russian-language linguist on board. It developed we really didn't need them. In the cruiser I was in, for example, we stopped a Russian ship and on the loudspeaker, known as a bull horn, in Russian we asked the ship to come up on a frequency in order that we could give him some instructions and talk to him and, invariably, the commanding officer of the Russian ship would reply in English, perfect English.

Q: They obviously had done something similar to what we did!

Adm. W.: I suspect that the skipper of a Soviet merchant ship is a fairly important individual and I suspect that most of them have been trained in the English language. They go to various ports throughout the world and English is now the universal language and I suspect it's desirable for them to be able to speak it.

Q: Actually, aren't they naval officers?

Adm. W.: I suspect. They're certainly well trained. One other aspect of this operation is that at the time of the speech we knew where most of the ships leaving the Black Sea were located. U. S. forces had taken pictures as they steamed through the Bosporus and take pictures again as they went through the strait at Gibraltar, so we knew what the ships looked like, we knew where they were as they continued to pass westward until about noon on Tuesday, when suddenly all of them stopped and stayed stopped for three days, then turned around and headed back towards the Soviet Union.

Q: How many vessels were involved in this?

Adm. W.: As I remember, there were about six which were capable of and which we believed were carrying missiles and missile-associated equipment, and the two that we were particularly interested in contacting did have missiles or missile cases on deck, and we were convinced that they did have missiles.

Q: Why did you select two in particular?

Adm. W.: Because of the photographs showing the missile cases along the deck. A missile is too large to get into the hold below decks and had to be put in bizarre-shaped tubes along the side of the deck and were quite easily identified.

Q: One of those two was flying the Lebanese flag, wasn't it?

Adm. W.: No. These were Soviet ships. The Lebanese ship Marucla was a supply ship. We stopped and searched her and found no implements of war on board, and as a result of a thorough search we were convinced she was carrying food supplies and other type supplies and equipment.

Q: Were these merchant vessels also transports bringing Russian personnel?

Adm. W.: Yes, we believed so. We saw some ships leaving Cuba,

Russian ships leaving Cuba and with undoubtedly Russian military personnel on board. We took some pictures from close aboard from helicopters, and they were fine-looking young men, clean healthy-looking.

Q: Your flagship was what?

Adm. W.: The Newport News.

Q: Did you come near to any one of these Soviet ships?

Adm. W.: Oh, yes, on several occasions.

Q: And photographed them from your cruiser?

Adm. W.: Yes, photographed from the cruiser and from helicopters just above the deck of the cruisers. Many interesting things transpired. We had a helicopter photographing from low altitutde. The pilot took his tie clasp off, which had a ship on it, and lowered it to the deck. The ship's skipper and the people on deck waved to him and asked him to return and put aline down and they tied a bottle of vodka on it and he raised it up to the helicopter. Don't ask me what happened to the bottle of vodka.

Q: Yes, on a naval vessel where it was prohibited! This indicates that there was not really a spirit of hostility on the part of the crews of the vessels.

Adm. W.: None whatsoever. We stopped one Russian ship and his first message by loudspeaker, which was very clearly heard on the deck of the cruiser, the flagship, he expressed in English condolences on the death of Mrs. Roosevelt which had been announced on the radio a short time before. When we released him we wished him God speed and good sailing and happy return home. This was the type of feeling that we had.

For the first few days we were afraid - well, not afraid because there was no reason to be afraid - but we were not sure what would happen. We had our ships darkened, we had our guns manned, but after the decision by the Soviets to turn their ships carrying war supplies around and head back, we lighted ships, took the people off the gun batteries, but maintained some alert, of course, for antisubmarine warfare.

Q: When did that Soviet decision seem to take place? Was it at noon on Tuesday?

Adm. W.: No, I think it was later than that. I have difficulty recalling, but I would think it was probably about Wednesday night, Wednesday evening.

Q: From the time the order came to have them stop in mid-ocean on Tuesday, there must have been deliberations to determine what they would do.

Adm. W.: That's right. It may have been Thursday before they turned around. I have it in my notes over here.

Q: Would you talk about the somewhat new technique, I think, is it not, that orders came directly from the White House to units of the fleet and so forth? I mean a very direct, close control of fleet operations? Was this not unique and new?

Adm. W.: Yes, this is new, and there is some justification for this in that we were accomplishing a political objective. We were not there to sink ships or shoot anyone. Our mission was to accomplish a political objective. President Kennedy in his wisdom accomplished his objective of stopping the movement of weapons into Cuba and, in my view, of removing the offensive missiles that had been landed in Cuba, getting them out of the country, in order to terminate the threat to the western hemisphere from these particular nuclear missiles. Everything we did had political impact. If we had sunk a Soviet ship, we would have started World War III. We could have. Everything that we did we reported directly by voice telephone, sometimes through a scrambler, to the Pentagon which was monitored also in the White House war room. For the first time we asked instructions on whether or not we should stop a Soviet ship known to be headed our way and the decision was made at the political level because it was a political decision rather than a military one.

We were there available to do the military job in the event war should start, but our actions had primarily political repercussions and were not military decisions.

Q: In actuality, wherein did the "quarantine" differ from the classical concept of a blockade which you obviously studied in the Naval Academy?

Adm. W.: This "quarantine" was a limited blockade. It was limited in that we permitted ships that we felt did not have missiles on board to go in to Cuba. For example, we did not stop any of the tankers carrying fuel oil into Cuba. We were told, as I think

I mentioned, what ships we were to stop and which ships we were not to stop. Had any of the ships with missiles continued westward, I am convinced that our instructions would have been to stop them and to prevent them from going in to Cuba, even if it had meant sinking them. It was a limited blockade, limited in that we were stopping specific military equipment from going in, though we were permitting supplies and equipment needed for harvesting sugar cane and for feeding the people or for operating machinery, these types of supplies and equipment were given the right -

Q: This was not an effort at starvation then?

Adm. W.: No.

Q: Incidentally, how ominous was the missile threat to the western world? I mean, how many missiles were involved, what was their potential as they had them deployed, that sort of thing?

Adm. W.: Those missiles had the capability of hitting as far as New York, Chicago, the midwest, Kansas City. They could not have, in our opinion, reached Seattle. They probably could not have reached San Francisco. They could have reached any of the Central American capitals, any of the capitals in the northern part of South America. They could have wreaked destruction on much of the United States. As I understand, and I'm not an expert on this, I believe that they had as many as twenty missiles that were operational and additional ones that would have become operational very shortly. We feel that none of these would have been effective had they been launched on the next Monday after the quarantine announcement was made. We feel that two or three days after that, they would have become effective, and this was one of the reasons for the urgency. The President wanted to take action before he was subjected to blackmail which Khrushchev could well have done, stating, you do this or New York will no longer be on the face of the map.

Q: Tell me, Admiral, how long did this operation take? When did the wind-down come? When did you lift the blockade, the quarantine?

Adm. W.: We were on station approximately thirty days. The wind-down came, started to wind down, after about six days, at the time when I indicated, we turned on the lights and permitted movies on deck and monitored the ships that were coming in to Cuba very closely. The only thing that happened of great interest in the reamining days was the action in detecting the submarines. We detected the first submarine about a week after the quarantine had become effective, and from then on we detected several others for a total of four.

Q: Could it have been that they were not actually in the area when the quarantine began and were given orders to get there?

Adm. W.: These submarines, as you know, go rather slowly, particularly if they want to stay submerged for any length of time, so that they had to be pretty close to the area at the time the quarantine became effective. We are convinced that they had left port long before there was any indication that the United States would take some action to stop the missiles from going in to Cuba.

Q: In your earlier command with the amphibious forces, were Soviet submarines observed in the Cuban area in that time?

Adm. W.: No. We had observed a submarine in the western part of the Atlantic prior to the Cuban operation. We had known that Soviet submarines were operating south of Iceland, but this was the first time we had found any as far south as Cuba.

The Soviets have continued to expand their submarine operations and are now operating throughout the Atlantic, including the South Atlantic.

Q: Unabashedly!

Adm. W.: Yes, and we don;t have too much capability for protecting the shipping in the South Atlantic, this is the reason that we put so much effort in trying to help train the South American navies in antisubmarine warfare.

Q: Are our hopes being realized in their abilities?

Adm. W.: They're improving. They have a limited capability, but they're improving.

Interview No. 8 with Admiral Alfred G. Ward, U.S. Navy (Retired)

Place: His office in the Severn School, Severna Park, Maryland

Date: Wednesday morning, 5 May 1971

Subject: Biography

By: John T. Mason, Jr.

Q: Admiral, last time you talked in most exciting fashion about the Cuban missile crisis. You were charged with enforcing the quarantine. Today, I wonder if, as an addendum to that story, you might make a summary of the points that were learned as a result of the episode, a summary of the results, perhaps as you summarized them in a speech you made shortly thereafter in Miami, Florida.

Adm. W.: I'd be very happy to, Dr. Mason. In that speech I said that I believed that history would acknowledge that the quarantine force was effective in accomplishing the tasks and missions that were assigned to that force by the President of the United States. As you know, our tasks were made easier by the Soviet decision to abide by the decision of the President in quarantining the island of Cuba for the introduction of additional missiles - offensive missiles - onto the island. No one could guess what the reactions of the Soviet government could be, so that we were prepared to go to general war if necessary in order to enforce the President's decision.

This was a powerful force we had in Task Force 135. We had the two great carriers, the nuclear-powered Enterprise and the Independence, both with their accompanying destroyers and a logistics resupply ship. The amphibious forces were loaded with Marines with the entire Fleet Marine Force of the Atlantic embarked in ships and remaining at sea during the critical phases of the operation.

Q: What, in terms of numbers, was this force? Do you know?

Adm. W.: There were approximately 25,000 Marines in the landing force, and in addition we had Marine aircraft that were available to support those Marines.

Admiral Whitey Taylor and the submarine warfare force put on a maximum effort. I mentioned that they detected some four Soviet submarines and trailed these submarines until they were clear of our operating theater. The Air Force had a bastion of strength in southern Florida that was unequalled within any specific geographical area within the United States at any other time. We had a great surveillance effort put on by both the Navy and Air Force aircraft. For the first time, the big bombers of the Air Force were used for surveillance, flying from islands in the middle Atlantic.

Q: Admiral, as a postscript to that remark, you told me last time that pictures were taken of the merchant vessels - Soviet vessels - as they left the Black Sea. Now, this was some time in advance of the crisis. How did it happen that we were so alert at that point?

Adm. W.: We had known for some time that the Soviets were having a military buildup in Cuba, that they had technicians and materials going in to Cuba. It was not until shortly before the crisis that we were able to identify some of these materials as being offensive missiles which were a threat to all North and Central America and part of South America. It was a big operation. My staff tells me that at one time we had some sixty-three ships in the quarantine force alone and that 183 ships were at sea in the Atlantic and the Caribbean during the operation.

We maintained a posture ready for either limited or general war. This posture was for real, for the first week of the quarantine and, as I indicated in the last session, we began to slack off at the end of that week, when we found that the Soviets were respecting the quarantine and had returned ships that were loaded with offensive missiles and those ships headed back to the Soviet Union.

We had an international aspect in this operation in that there was a Task Force 137 which was not under my control or command, but with which I coordinated efforts. These ships were from Central and South America, Rio Treaty Organization ships.

Q: Were they under SacLant, or what?

Adm. W.: They were coordinated by CinCLant. They had their own commander. We did have one U.S. ship in Task Force 137, and these operations were coordinated and controlled by the commander-in-chief, Atlantic, Admiral Dennison. The NATO aspect did not get into this operation at all, only one of interest and support.

What were the immediate results of the action? First, the United States' strength and firmness resulted in forcing the Soviet Union to back down in its program to arm Cuba. We eliminated, at least for the time being, the offensive threat, which was a real threat, to all the Americas. We acted calmly but forcefully. We left room for a solution short of war, and the Soviet Union demonstrated a respect for U.S. power.

Q: Admiral, again as a footnote, was the Monroe Doctrine a dead issue as far as this event was concerned?

Adm. W.: I would think so. Certainly the objectives of the Monroe Doctrine were in the forefront at this time but, as you know, we have permitted the Communists to take over some - to take over Chile, we have accepted some foreign powers in the Central American areas. I believe that the principles of the Monroe Doctrine are still objectives of the United States, but we have been a little less than perfect in our enforcement of the Doctrine.

Castro proved that he was not a free agent in this operation. Certainly he would have elected to have the missiles continue on into Cuba, and certainly he was unwilling to see the Soviet technicians leave, as they did towards the end of the quarantine. The shots were being called from the Kremlin and not from Havana. The offensive weapons were controlled by the Soviets in every respect. They were removed by the Soviets as a result of negotiations between the Soviets and the United States, and not as a result of Castro's influence.

United States statesmanship and power won out. By mounting a limited quarantine, we displayed traditional United States respect for human life and human values. Our objectives were limited to keeping out the offensive missiles and this limited objective was achieved. I think the strength of the Organization of American States was demonstrated by the formation of this international task force 137 and by the fact that this international task force did take part in enforcing the quarantine.

The employment of sea power in this case did not cause an escalation of the opposing power struggle between the two great giants. It left room for negotiations, and I believe that this is one of the unique advantages of using naval power, rather than ground and air which are much more liable to cause escalation.

Q: Why? Because of the necessary occupation of territory?

Adm. W.: Yes, occupation of territory and the fact that they are really not effective unless they do occupy territory or imperil the forces on territory.

Our principal NATO allies pledged their support to the actions taken by the United States government and demonstrated a hardening willingness for the U.S. to take the actions that were necessary to protect the western hemisphere.

Q: But there was no thought, or there was no time, I suppose for the employment of NATO naval units?

Adm. W.: There would have been time to get naval units there from NATO forces, but not in time for the initial action in the quarantine. As you probably know, the President talked to our NATO allies and our allies in Central and South America, or to their representatives, before the quarantine was announced and received some indication of support from those representatives. This was later confirmed by many other governments, our allies.

Our negotiations were carried out in the form and framework of the United Nations. The Secretary General, Mr. U Thant, was conducting negotiations at U.N. headquarters in New York and in Havana. It was noted that President Kennedy in his State of the Union message at the beginning of the next year, 1963, said that he did get support from the United Nations.

There was a new rule of law of the sea which became effective, and that is the quarantine. As we mentioned earlier, a blockade traditionally is an act of war. This quarantine was not considered an act of war and it did permit negotiations of the issues involved. It was respected by all states, including the Soviet Union, and I believe that henceforth it will become a part of the code of international law.

Q: Has it been employed any time since?

Adm. W.: Not to my knowledge, with the single exception of the enforcement of fishing rights by individual states, and this, as you know, Chile, has taken some rather severe actions in enforcing its fishing rights and used this precedent of a quarantine as an excuse for such action.

I mentioned that during this operations I was in direct communication with the Joint Chiefs of Staff and the White House by radio telephone, both by unclassified message traffic and by classified traffic, by voice as well as by teletype. What happened on the quarantine line had political implications that were of the greatest import, and it was necessary that I receive political advice and political guidance in many detailed aspects of the operation.

Q: Do you want to illustrate that?

Adm. W.: Yes. I may be repeating something, but we were told about the ship Marucla, informed the White House when the ship was stopped, the favorable reactions of the people on the ship in receiving our sailors and our officers who were making the inspection, their cooperation, so that this incident never got out of bounds. Had we not had such cooperation, it would have been necessary to get instructions from the White House as to what further actions should be taken. This, fortunately, did not transpire.

Q: There were no repercussions from Lebanon itself?

Adm. W.: None at all. This, too, I think, is indicative of the support for the quarantine by other governments and other nations.

If I could mention three principal results of the entire operation, the first would be that the Cuban problem is not over. Events to date indicate that there has been a disrupting influence on the solidarity of the Communist bloc. We believe that all of the missiles that were a threat to North, Central, and South America have been removed, but the problem of Soviet power in the western hemisphere is not solved.

Q: There's been another element of the Communist world interjected, has there not, with Mao Tse-tung's adherents?

Adm. W.: Oh, yes. The Chinese threat is a very real one, particularly as a result of their nuclear power. This problem is not resolved. President Kennedy in a speech later in the year in addressing the Cuban refugees in Miami said it was the strongest wish of the people of this country as well as the people of the hemisphere that Cuba should one day be free again. We have not yet accomplished this and it appears as though we won't be accomplishing it in the near future.

I think the second result is that the military forces of the United States demonstrated their immediate readiness to accomplish missions and objectives prescribed by the President and the government of the United States. If I may quote Admiral Anderson briefly, he said that "the entire operation has been a magnificent testimonial not only to the senior leaders of our government but also to those commanders and commanding officers at lower levels who were so quickly able to move their troops, large numbers of troops, and ships, many ships, and their aircraft on short notice to carry out the objectives of the United States."

Q: Was that a public statement?

Adm. W.: Yes, Sir, it was.

I think the third and final general conclusion pertains to sea power. The News and Courier of Charleston, South Carolina, expressed it in the best possible way by stating, and I quote: "Thinking people in the country should try to make their own assessment of the secret of national power. They pay for that power by means of taxes. Perhaps the key lesson of the Cuban crisis is that sea power remains the dominant force in the world's affairs."

Q: That, too, leads me to another question. The role of the press and the media as a whole in this crisis, what was the attitude of the Navy toward the publicity that was given?

Adm. W.: We had nothing but praise for the way the press handled the situation. There were some representatives of the press present at the demonstration at Vieques by the amphibious forces just prior to this operation. The press were asked not to reveal the presence of other ships being moved into the area, and they chose to comply with that request. They were terrific.

Q: Did you, by chance, have a representative of the press on the Newport News?

Adm. W.: No. I believe there were no representatives of the press at sea with the quarantine force, but we kept the press informed of our operations almost minute by minute.

Q: Did it mean that they didn't ask for that permission?

Adm. W.: It meant that the ships sailed before it was possible to get press people on board. We sailed on such short notice and under such secrecy that it was not feasible to get the press on board. After the operation had been under way for some time, the carriers did fly some press people out to land on board the carriers and be present in the carriers.

Q: Admiral, your command of the Second Fleet continued for a few months after the Cuban missile crisis. Would you account for your time during that time - during that period?

Adm. W.: The Second Fleet carried out the normal operations that the fleet in the Atlantic, the striking fleet of NATO, would carry out. We continued to operate with our NATO friends in the western part of the Atlantic. I had many cruisers and carriers as my flagship, actually going aboard and hoisting my flag in the attack carriers and had as my guests important individuals from both NATO nations and Central and South American nations.

Q: Did you observe any increase in enthusiasm on the part of NATO units as an aftermath of this Cuban crisis?

Adm. W.: Yes, I think that the Cuban crisis was a great incentive for our NATO friends to participate with American forces again and in more greatly detailed operations.

Q: The raison d'être -

Adm. W.: Right. They I'm sure were impressed with the effectiveness of our United States naval power and had a new impetus in cooperating with our naval forces. We had Dutch ships, we had British ships, and we had some French ships cooperating with us in both the western Atlantic and, of course, we continued to operate with the Sixth Fleet in the Mediterranean.

Q: Did the fleet entertain VIPs in any larger numbers as an aftermath?

Adm. W.: Yes, we did. There's no question about it.

Q: Congressmen and so forth?

Adm. W.: Yes, our own people as well as high officials of foreign governments. I've mentioned the fact that the Shah of Iran visited the fleet and observed operations.

Q: Yes. Did increased interest in the role of the Navy result in something tangible on Capitol Hill?

Adm. W.: I don't believe so, other than a general continuance, of course. At that time, as you know, we were still fighting for the budget dollar, but I believe the Cuban quarantine operation led the people of our country and therefore their elected represenatatives to understand more fully the necessity for maintaining military power, and I'm sure that it had some beneficial effects in maintaining the status not only of the Navy but also of the Air Force and the Army.

Q: In many quarters, the then Secretary of Defense was thought to disparage the role of military leaders. Was there any noticeable enhancement of the naval officer's role as a result of this action?

Adm. W.: With some trepidation I would go on record that the relationships between the people in naval operations and the Secretary of Defense did not improve during this time. The antagonisms were very real. As you remember, shortly after this operation, Admiral Anderson was relieved of his duties as chief of the Navy and the President appointed him ambassador to Portugal.

Q: Do you think there was any connection between the CNO's role in this crisis and that change in command?

Adm. W.: Yes, I believe there was. The Secretary of Defense, I believe, wished to control in even greater detail the operations of the military, and Admiral Anderson was trying to protect his commanders from what he considered to be interference.

Q: You say, Admiral, after the Cuban missile crisis was over, you spent some time in Washington giving various details of your command and one of your experiences was to have a personal interview with President Kennedy.

Adm.: That's correct. I was called to Washington on several occasions in connection with the planning that continued with both the Army and Air Force - of course, Marines were on my staff - and we continued to plan in detail. This entailed my going to the Joint Chiefs of Staff on several occasions and we discussed our contingency plans many times.

Q: This was in realization of the fact that the issue had not been completely resolved?

Adm. W.: Yes, and it applied not only to the Cuban crisis, which was quiescent at the time, but also to our relationships with the Soviets on a global basis. My area of command was all of the North Atlantic, but we certainly had interests in the South Atlantic and in the Norwegian Sea and would frequently go into those areas. It was a big responsibility and the Joint Chiefs were naturally interested in contingency plans being developed by the coordinated efforts of all of the military services. It is true that on one such visit I was called to the White House and discussed with the President some of the operations that were then in progress not only in the Atlantic, but the operations down at the South Pole.

Q: What was going on at the South Pole at that point?

Adm. W.: We were increasing out effort to continue the mapping of the continent at the pole and to coordinate our efforts with the nations of South America.

Q: Was the South Pole in the cognizance of the Second Fleet?

Adm. W.: No, it was not. We had only a supporting role.

Q: Whose cognizance was that?

Adm. W.: It was under the commander of the Atlantic - the Atlantic Command had control of the operations, but not the Second Fleet. As you are aware, I had direct relations with the commander of the Atlantic, Admiral Dennison, throughout this period and because I had worked for him in this general area before, we frequently discussed the problems associated with these expeditions.

Q: You said that your presence before the Joint Chiefs had to do with relations with the Soviets. Was there any change in Soviet relationships vis-à-vis the Navy as a result of the Cuban quarantine?

Adm. W.: I wouldn't say there was any radical change. I believe that the Soviets learned to respect America and American power more as a result of the Cuban quarantine operations, and that if anything their relations were improved.

Q: Was there an increase or a decrease in the visibility of Russian trawlers in the Atlantic?

Adm. W.: Yes, there was an increase, but I believe that this was a necessary - would have happened had there not been a Cuban operation.

Operations by Soviet intelligence-collecting trawlers, by submarines, and by surface ships were increasing.

Q: This suggests a general trend?

Adm. W.: Yes.

Q: Did this necessitate any change in the plans for the Second Fleet? Did it necessitate the augmenting of the SEcond Fleet with additional ships or anything of that sort?

Adm. W.: No. It increased our emphasis on electronic warfare, both offensive and defensive.

Q: Were these new developments that were coming en train, were they electronic devices that had been developed prior to this time and were only now being employed in the Second Fleet?

Adm. W.: Oh, this was a continuing development. The whole affair necessitated greater emphasis on the development, but this improvement in electronics, countermeasures and offensive electronics, capabilities had been going on continuously since World War II on both sides.

Q: This is the fruit of the R & D development in World War II?

Adm. W.: Yes.

Q: You have touched on this a little bit, but one of the results of the Cuban missile crisis and your role in it was to call upon you to speak publicly.

Adm. W.: Yes, I was on the platform frequently. As you can see from the stack of recorded speeches in front of you, there were many occasions to speak, not only on the East Coast but in several other areas within the United States.

Q: The Navy was most anxious to foster this action, were they?

Adm. W.: Yes. It was a time of interest to people throughout the United States and it was valuable for the Navy - of value to the Navy - that this story be told.

Q: Who was Chingo at that time?

Adm. W.: I think Hank Miller was.

Q: I think he was, and if he was, naturally, he wanted this story told to the advantage of the Navy!

Interview No. 9 with Admiral Alfred G. Ward, U.S. Navy (REtired)

Place: His office at the Severn School, Severna Park, Maryland

Date: Wednesday morning, 26 May 1971

Subject: Biography

By: John T. Mason, Jr.

Q: It's certainly good of you, Admiral, to give me some time this morning when you're winding up the affairs of your school for this semester, but you look very relaxed.! And so, we shall go on with Chapter No. 9. Last time you talked in some detail about the significant points of the Cuban missile crisis. You gave up command of the Second Fleet in 1963, I believe, and were succeeded by Vice Admiral Charles Martell. You got another interesting and important job in the office of the Chief of Naval Operations. You were named as deputy for plans and policy. This covers a lot of things. Do you want to take over, Sir?

Adm. W.: Yes. Thank you, Dr. Mason. Looking outside and seeing the boys walking from the last of their examinations preparing for commencement the day after tomorrow on this beautiful spring day is a most welcome experience.

I did leave the Second Fleet regretfully because I thoroughly enjoyed that tour to go to Washington to take over plans and operations. This was a very interesting time because the Eisenhower administration was out and a new direction was being given to the over-all policy for the Department of Defense by Mr. McNamara. It seemed to me that there were several principal concerns of Mr. McNamara. The first was the civilian control over every aspect of the military machine. The second was his great concern with the danger of an exchange of nuclear weapons which would have a devastating effect on civilization as we know it. And the third was the conservation of dollars. I believe that our president had a great deal to do with all three of these aspects of grand strategy and policy within the government. President Johnson was watching his dollars. He felt that he had a need to save the taxpayers' money during this period and I am convinced that he had close contact - daily contact - with Mr. McNamara in ensuring that the Department of Defense, as the greatest source of expenditure of dollars, conserve those dollars to the greatest degree possible.

Q: Would that statement also hold for President Kennedy, who was in office when you took over your job? He was assassinated in November of that year.

Adm. W.: No, I don't believe it extended to President Kennedy as much as it did to President Johnson. I believe that President Kennedy felt a more relaxed - had a more relaxed feeling of his control of government than did President Johnson after he took the reins. President Kennedy was a tremendous president during his time in office, in my opinion, and I think history will record him as one of our great presidents.

Q: He didn't have much time to accomplish a great deal.

Adm. W.: That's right. I think he gave a new direction, though, to our policies. I think he brought in people who were not mainline politicians but intelligentsia who were responsible for changing some of the directions of national policy at that time. And I believe this was for the good.

Q: Did you have any special contact with him in those last months of his administration?

Adm. W.: My personal contact was on a social basis. I did prepare many papers for consideration by higher levels of government, particularly in work with the Joint Chiefs of Staff.

Q: What were the nature of some of those papers?

Adm. W.: Many of them dealt with some of the issues which you have discussed, and that is the increased use of nuclear power in our ships, the greatly expanded nuclear arsenal of both the United States and the Soviet Union, the introduction of some of our new missile systems with their greatly increased destructive capability. I think these are probably the highlights of those few months.

Q: Would you talk a little about your point of view on some of those things?

Adm. W.: Yes. Speaking of nuclear power, I believe it was inevitable that our ships would be more and more powered by nuclear energy. I am mindful that early in this period Mr. McNamara made the decision on CVA-67, the new carrier. He prescribed that it be conventionally powered, again in order to save dollars. The difference in cost between conventional power and nuclear power is on the order of $100 million, and he felt that, at that time, our government could not afford the installation of nuclear-powered engines and nuclear reactors in this carrier. This decision is still subject to some discussion as to its validity. I believe never again will we build a ship - a major ship such as a carrier - without nuclear power.

Q: At that point in time, we stood alone, did we not, in terms of building major units of the fleet powered nuclearly?

Adm. W.: That's right. We had developed - and we alone - a sizeable sources of power using nuclear reactors. As you know, the Soviets at that time started to develop small nuclear engines and did have an icebreaker which had nuclear power, but, according to our intelligence sources, it was not a very sophisticated construction.

Q: As one reviews the events of that time, events that pertain to our Navy, there seems to have been a proliferation of small new type vessels of various kinds powered by atomic energy?

Adm. W.: Yes, I would agree with that. With the United States effort being principally in submarines and the Soviet effort being in other type units, such as icebreakers. They had in the next few years, at a slightly later time, much more emphasis on nuclear power in their submarines.

Q: What was the position of the Polaris in our defense system at that time?

Adm. W.: It was a very important part of our defense system. We had just introduced the first A-3 Polaris submarine, but we depended very heavily on Polaris as a principal component of our nuclear deterrent.

Q: Yes, I noted that the first underwater missile was fired from a Polaris submarine and there apparently was a great deal of publicity on that fact. That brings up an interesting question, at least interesting to me. Why would it be necessary to publicize various of these events which, in an earlier time, were held in high secrecy?

Adm. W.: I believe it was a difference in philosophy that the deterrent is a deterrent only if the world knows about the capability. That is, in a time of war when you're trying to fight an enemy and defeat his forces and sink his ships, you want to maintain secrecy as to your capabilities in order that you can accomplish your objectives more readily. This is not true in time of peace when you're trying to develop a war machine which you hope you will never have to use, and the only way you can ensure that you will never have to use it is to make it be known that it is one of the most powerful machines in the world and is capable of making destruction inevitable.

Q: Was this more or less a formal policy of the Defense Department?

Adm. W.: I think so.

Q: Promulgated by the Secretary?

Adm. W.: I believe so. I'm sure that Mr. McNamara was a master at this game of informing the world of what our strengths were, and I think he was successful. I think that our period of fairly stable peace is a result of that policy.

Q: Well, at that time, in 1963, 1964, the Russians hadn't achieved the kind of parity they now seem to have.

Adm. W.: I would agree with this.

Q: They were just beginning their great thrust, were they not?

Adm. W.: I would agree with this. They were behind us in both land-based and sea-based missiles, and they have caught up in these years.

Q: Was there any evidence of a sense of complacency on our part because of that knowledge?

Adm. W.: I don't believe that we were complacent at all. As a matter of fact, I think we were pushing ahead as fast as we could to try to maintain superiority, knowing full well that the Soviets were putting a great deal of their resources, a great deal of money, and effort into developing nuclear power - to increase their capabilities.

Q: Does this imply then that there was much emphasis at that time in R and D?

Adm. W.: Yes, it does.

Q: Were funds available to the researchers?

Adm. W.: Yes, I think funds were available to the researchers in order to develop techniques and new methods, which they actually did. They had them on the A-3, for example. The smaller sized weapons that greatly increased the destructive capability both of the Air Force and the Navy and, to a lesser extent, of the Army.

Q: There's a question I'd like to ask you about. In the campaign of 1960 there was so much said about a missile gap, that we had fallen behind, and all of that. Then after 1961 and 1962, there didn't seem to be such an apparent gap. What are your observations in that area?

Adm. W.: I believe that in the conventional equipment we may have had some gaps in missile technology, but in the nuclear field I believe that we did have superiority in the 1950s and maintained that superiority for a number of years. I believe that currently there is an essential parity, with both sides having the capability of destroying the other.

Q: What were some of the other papers you prepared for the Joint Chiefs?

Adm. W.: I suspect that some of the more important ones were in the political-military field throughout the world. One, I remember, is the basing agreement for our Polaris submarines in both Spain and in Scotland. These papers were prepared and submitted to the Joint Chiefs of Staff in their initial passage through governmental machinery. We had worked somewhat directly with the British authorities and with the Spanish authorities. They were fairly sensitive negotiations but were successful.

Q: What made them so sensitive? What were the basic problems involved? Take one at a time, the British with Holy Loch.

Adm. W.: We had problems not only with assuring the British of the safety - or comparative safety - of basing nuclear-powered ships in beautiful Holy Loch in Scotland, which is close to Glasgow...

Q: What kind of safety?

Adm. W.: As you probably know, these reactors need water in order to keep them cool and there was some question as to whether the affluent waste, the water that passes through the reactor, would be contaminated, and it was our job to work directly with British scientists and with British naval engineers to assure them of this safety, and/under our rules which were in existence at the time regarding the release of information on nuclear reactors was quite a difficult undertaking.

Q: Why was it such a problem with the British who were in possession of atomic power of various kinds, who might be thought to understand the ramifications of that?

Adm. W.: In my opinion, the United States' engineering in their nuclear reactors was the best in the world and we were not about to release details of this engineering feat to anyone, because of the doubt that had this information been released it would have been released to other people.

Q: We were barred by our Congress, were we not?

Adm. W.: Yes, and I believe that this was the cause for the congressional act.

Q: But still, the British being in possession of the ability to manufacture the atomic bomb and so forth must have had some widespread knowledge. Why, then, was it difficult to convince them of the safety of the Polaris being based at Holy Loch?

Adm. W.: Again, it's a question of the engineering techniques involved in the equipment itself as to what level of contamination will result from operations within a semi-enclosed body of water. The British had complete access to waters around our boats and because of this they were able to measure the very, very slight amount of radioactive waste that did come out. It was so slight as to be unimportant.

Q: Was there another question in their minds also of the fact that our Polaris submarines would be based there, did this make them feel in a sense that they'd be more vulnerable in case of an attack on the part of the Russians?

Adm. W.: I suspect that this is a debatable question. I believe that they were very happy to have United States power in the defense not only of the United States but also of the Free World. Very definitely, had a war or a threat of war existed, I'm sure that the British had as much reliance on our offensive weapon systems for the protection of Great Britain as they did to protect the United States. I think they welcomed them.

Q: This was a guarantee that they were also under the umbrella?

Adm. W.: They were under the umbrella and they didn't have to put out the pounds necessary to provide that umbrella.

Q: Did you have contact with any specific British officials in this matter? How was the arrangement worked out?

Adm. W.: Yes. We worked with the chief scientists of Great Britain and with the naval engineers and in developing the language of treaties and in getting permission to use the area there as a base. Not only was it a question of nuclear power and the spread of possible contamination, which I am sure they were convinced did not exist, but also it was a question of moving a lot of Americans into a small Scottish community and having to provide homes and living accommodations for them plus the families. As you know, our standard of living is a little bit higher than some of the people in Europe, and this was a concern to the administrators and to the politicians in the area.

Q: How many people were involved in this?

Adm. W.: We had a tender with about 700 men which would change back and forth and, from time to time, these nuclear submarines would come alongside of the tender for upkeep for a period of a month at a time. As of right now, we probably have two submarines alongside the tender. In the early days we had only one.

Q: I can see where this might be a matter of concern and, with hindsight, has it affected them in any way?

Adm. W.: No, it hasn't. The only way it's affected them has been to improve the cordial relations between the two peoples. I went over about three years ago and visited Holy Loch and found nothing but kind words and praise for the conduct of our people, the social relations between the Americans and the Scots. It's a very satisfactory arrangement.

Q: It didn't dislocate the economy, then?

Adm. W.: No, it assisted the economy somewhat. It did not dislocate it. And the same thing is true in Rota. Our base in Rota has been a great boon to southern Spain by bringing in people and money which has improved their standard of living.

Q: One other aspect of the British situation and also the Spanish: were there any repercussions from the Russians when this knowledge came out, that we were establishing missile-submarine bases in these areas?

Adm. W.: Not to my knowledge. As you know, there's a fairly continuous, low-key effort in the Soviet press and Soviet propaganda against the basing of U.S. nuclear power anywhere, any time, but it was not serious.

Q: The efforts at Holy Loch resulted in a formal treaty, did they?

Adm. W.: I don't believe it was a treaty. I believe it was an agreement, not quite the formality of a treaty. But we did negotiate an agreement with the British that made possible the basing of these warships. And we had also agreements for basing nuclear-capable aircraft - that is, aircraft capable of delivering nuclear weapons, Air Force aircraft - at British bases.

Q: Was that arrangement made simultaneously with the submarine base?

Adm. W.: Yes, almost simultaneously.

Q: Now would you talk a little about the Spanish base and the problems which were unique with that?

Adm. W.: The Spanish problem was more difficult in that Spain is not a member of NATO. With British bases the United States could state that these were forces earmarked or committed to NATO, but in Spain this had no meaning. But the Spanish are a practical type people and they, too, I am sure, were aware that in the event of a conflagration in Europe, American power would be available to help them as well as it would to help France or England or any other nation in Europe. The basing of submarines was not the only consideration. Again, the Air Force wanted to have aircraft with nuclear-delivery capabilities and did arrange to get these agreements made. We wanted an ammunition depot and we wanted a fuel depot and were successful in getting all of these.

Q: The Spanish bases were not new in a sense, were they? As I remember they were negotiated originally in the Eisenhower years.

Adm. W.: That's correct, particularly the bases in the islands off _____, and we did have some activity at Rota. But this introduction of nuclear-capable units and nuclear weapons into the area was sensitive.

Q: And you had the same problem of convincing the Spanish authorities of its safety?

Adm. W.: Yes, we did.

Q: And how did you deal with that?

Adm. W.: Again, it was a direct negotiation with individuals, as all agreements are, to persuade some key individuals in the military and in the government of Spain that these were not as dangerous as had been alleged and that it would not cause the fish to be killed or poisoned.

Q: Yes, for them that was a particular issue, wasn't it? WAs their understanding slower in forthcoming than that of the British?

Adm. W.: It took longer to negotiate the agreements with Spain than it did with the British and, as you probably know, we had to give some monetary compensation, too, to the Spanish.

Q: Yes. Was that longer period of time - do you ascribe it to the fact that they didn't have the basic knowledge of atomic energy that the British had?

Adm. W.: I think that, but I also think it was caused - we have worked very closely with the British for centuries and our military work together, our research people have exchanged information. We did not have this history of cooperation with the Spanish officials.

Q: Did you have any particular problems because the Spanish government is known as a dictatorship? This inevitably seems to have repercussions in the United States among liberals. Was there any problem involved?

Adm. W.: No. As a matter of fact, I suspect it was much easier for us to make negotiations because of the fact that it was a dictatorship. If you could convince a few individuals in the Spanish government, that was good enough. You didn't have to go out and sell the people who, in effect, had no vote in the decision.

Q: And would you say, then, the monetary considerations and the boost to the Spanish economy was a major element in inducing them to give consent?

Adm. W.: Yes, I would.

Q: You say that, three years ago, you visited Rota as well?

Adm. W.: Yes, I visited Rota periodically through the years and have seen the development of that base. I've met many of the Spanish people who live in the area and have observed the very friendly relations between those people and our people at Rota. It cultivated friendship. The people at Rota invite the Spanish in to go to churches, they invite Spanish pilots to fly in our aircraft. We make an effort to be friends.

Q: Is this an established policy?

Adm. W.: Yes, I'm sure it is.

Q: What is the particular advantage of the base at Rota?

Adm. W.: As you know, the Mediterranean is a key body of water and our Polaris submarines operate in the Mediterranean and just outside the Mediterranean, in the Atlantic, and they could reach targets which could not be reached from areas in the north or elsewhere. It's a part of our deterrent, the fact that we do have submarines on station ready to go on a moment's notice. It does provide a real deterrent.

Q: What is your prognosis for maintaining the Spanish bases, not only Rota, but the others?

Adm. W.: Well, I hesitate to guess. I would think that eventually we would probably not need to base the nuclear-capable units at Rota. I would think that the improved capability of our missiles and our submarines would negate the necessity for maintaining these type units in the Mediterranean, and that therefore Rota's usefulness would decrease as the capabilities of our systems improved.

Q: Would the same thing pertain to Holy Loch?

Adm. W.: Yes, the same thing would pertain to Holy Loch. As a matter of fact, there is some consideration now, I believe, that maybe we could bring our submarines back to the United States, which has some advantages because it would mean that their crews would be at home more often, and would not have to use Holy Loch. These considerations are not yet controlling, but could well become so.

Q: Is there no disadvantage in bringing them back and basing them here, in that in any massive attack upon us they would be destroyed along with others?

Adm. W.: But they would be destroyed at Rota also, and at Holy Loch

The disadvantage in bringing them back is the question of time on station, as submarines operating from Rota can be on station with weapons ready to hit targets in a much shorter time than if they were based in Norfolk or Charleston, South Carolina. From Charleston, South Carolina, it would take many days of transit to reach their launch positions. Not so from Holy Loch.

Q: Admiral, would you talk about the closing of the various military facilities throughout the country? Secretary McNamara, I believe, inaugurated this policy in October of 1963 when he announced that various bases were about to be closed.

Adm. W.: Yes. I suspect this was a natural development. After the end of the last war, our military had expanded considerably and some reduction was certainly indicated. Mr. McNamara has prided himself on his effectiveness and efficiency in getting the most for the government dollar, and I'm convinced that he and his staff felt that by reducing the numbers of bases, he would save money from closing those bases and that only a part of this money would be needed to increase the effectiveness of the remaining bases in order to maintain a comparable capability. And I believe he was right. I think at this time we needed some strong controls at the helm in order to make our military forces more efficient, and I think Mr. McNamara accomplished that. He also, I believe, was under political pressures to reduce the Defense Department budget, even though he doesn't admit this, and I think he was successful in doing this.

I think that there were several bad features in some of these actions, in that some of his analyses ~~were actions that he chose to take~~ were done by people who were not as experienced as people who had been in the game for a long time.

Q: The "Whizz Kids"?

Adm. W.: The Whizz Kids, definitely.

Q: Did you have - well, naturally, you did have contact with some of these people. What is your estimation of them as to their ability in those particular berths?

Adm. W.: I think many of them were very smart people. They deserved the title "Whizz Kids." I think that they did not have the experience or the background to make sound decisions in every aspect of their activities and, believe me, they didn't shy away from taking actions in areas in which they did not have experience. Many of them did have military advisers but frequently didn't listen to them. I think probably the political-military field was the hardest hit in that we had been talking with military people from other nations for years and now these discussions and these agreements were being made by civilians who had not ~~got~~ the background. In general, I think Mr. McNamara's administration was effective and efficient. I think that he served a useful purpose in his time.

Q: The attitudes and actions of his so-called Whizz Kids in ignoring the military might be said to reflect the attitudes of the Secretary himself - at least, there are many reports to that effect. Would you comment in that area?

Adm. W.: I certainly would. I'd like to. It would be very interesting to sit at the meeting of the Joint Chiefs of Staff in which the four chiefs of staff with their chairman and principal assistants would be present. Mr. McNamara would come in with possibly one aide or one assistant or maybe with his deputy, and Mr. McNamara was in control of the situation at all times. If a chief of staff of, say, the Air Force would make a statement - Curt LeMay would make many - McNamara would immediately take issue with him and would give a running discussion as to why this course of action should not be taken. And these were all impromptu sessions.

In the Joint Chiefs of Staff arena, there were no transcribed notes taken, as such. There was a recorder who recorded the sense of the discussion, usually an Air Force or Army colonel with no stenographic background, but the decisions would be recorded, and, believe me, Mr. McNamara was in control.

Q: Did he rely on the military attitudes at all for his opinions?

Adm. W.: Oh, I'm sure he did. I'm sure that Max Taylor was successful in some of his personal conversations in McNamara's office in getting some of his views across and generally Mr. McNamara would take Max Taylor with him to visit the President - not all the time, but frequently. Mr. McNamara had a great deal of knowledge - detailed knowledge - at his fingertips at all times. He studied his lessons and he studied them well. He was not an easy man to get along with. It was my view and, I believed, shared by others, that many of his decisions were made for him and that he had to develope the rationale that justified those decisions. I think many of them were dictated by financial considerations and political considerations.

Q: There have been various men who have said that in their opinion sessions were held on particular subjects but it was apparent to them that the Secretary had already made the decision before the session was held and before the discussions took place. Is this a fair estimate, in your opinion?

Adm. W.: Yes, it is a true estimate. I can cite one personal example - personal knowledge which would confirm this estimate, and that's to do with the withdrawal of dependents from Guantanamo Bay at the time of the confrontations with Castro. The Secretary of the Navy directed the CNO to withdraw dependents from Guantanamo and the CNO requested a rebuttal. I was present in the room with the Secretary of the Navy and the Secretary of Defense, with only three people being present -

Q: Secretary Anderson, was that?

Adm. W.: No, Nitze. Mr. McNamara, Mr. Nitze, and myself were together in Mr. McNamara's office, and Mr. Nitze gave a very reasoned discussion over a period of over an hour on why it would be inadvisable to pull the dependents out of Guantanamo Bay, with Mr. McNamara listening and making notes throughout his discussion. Occasionally, they would ask me some detailed question about the effectiveness of the various ratings that were there and what not, but the conversation was between Mr. McNamara and Mr. Nitze. And at the end of this period, it seemed to me that Mr.

finally stood up and said, "Mr. Secretary, you have your instructions to get the dependents out of Guantanamo Bay. Please carry out those instructions," which to me was an amazing statement as a result of these long discussions. I found out later from a friend in the White House - on the White House staff - that this decision had been made three days before and had only been given Mr. McNamara two days before, so that the discussion was a cover-up.

Q: Why that window dressing? Why was it necessary? It didn't do anything for Mr. Nitze.

Adm. W.: I believe it was desirable to try and prevent a schism between the political authorities in the Pentagon and the military authorities in the Pentagon, to make it known that a military authority and the secretary of a military service did have access and was able to make known his views to people who were making decisions.

Q: Admiral, so many of the military people even today react with great violence, almost, at the mention of the name of McNamara. What is this predicated on? You don't react that way. Is it predicated on his personality?

Adm. W.: I think it's partly his personality, but I thin, it's larger than that. I think it's the fact that Mr. McNamara was a good soldier and he carried out the dictates of the President of the United States and he made those dictates possible by accepting responsibility for them in his own person. He was smart, he was tough, he was ruthless, in my opinion, and I think he was probably good for the country. I say "probably," I'm not sure but I think he was probably good for the country. My friend George Anderson would not agree with this. There was certainly antipathy between those two individuals and for the reasons I've stated.

Q: McNamara served under both President Kennedy and President Johnson. Was there any noticeable difference in the policy which the Secretary of Defense pursued under Kennedy in contrast with Johnson?

Adm. W.: I think so, and I believe it's a fact that McNamara and Kennedy were more nearly alike than Johnson and McNamara. This is one reason, and the other reason is that I think President Johnson was trying his best to maintain a fairly stable and low-level increase in budget and he depended on Mr. McNamara to accomplish this for him. I think there was a great personal friendship and rapport between Kennedy and McNamara that did not exist between Johnson and McNamara. President Johnson was a pretty tough guy in demanding some of the things that he felt were good for the country.

Q: Since you served in both periods also, how did the respective services work under the Secretary of Defense in that time? Was amalgamation complete?

Adm. W.: Oh, the separate military services?

Q: Yes.

Adm. W.: No, there was no complete amalgamation. There was great jealousy and great disagreement between the services during the time I was associated with the Joint Chiefs of Staff. And, as you probably know, this reached its peak between Curt LeMay and Arleigh Burke. At a later time, under George Anderson, there was not quite the great antithesis. Curt LeMay was a very positive individual and very forceful - not "forceful", that's not the word, but he was a very positive man. He made his decisions, he announced them, and nothing would persuade him to change them. Frequently, decisions would go from the Joint Chiefs with split views and would be carried by MaxTaylor to the Secretary of Defense with these split views. I do not mean to imply that there was any lack of respect between Burke and Curt LeMay. In fact, there was great respect between the two of them, but they were very positive proponents of their individual services and of the views that they held.

Q: As I told you off tape, Carl Vinson in making his swan song at the Naval Academy is quoted as having said one sure way to unman the defense of this nation is the merger of the four services. This remark was made in 1964 at graduation and I wondered whether it reflected anything currently in the Department of Defense?

Adm. W.: I believe that there's no major move for the amalgamation of the services at the present time. There is a move to more closely coordinate the effectiveness of the services, and I think this is a good one. For example, I think in Vietnam that our coordinated effort is much better than it would have been had these same conditions existed under earlier leaders. I think the idea of a supreme commander is a very good one. I think that the fact that we have a CinCPac is necessary to the success of the operation, and I think the fact that we have an over-all commander on the ground in Vietnam is good, and I believe that no one would take issue - no one that's knowledgeable - would take serious issue with this type of coordinated control, but I believe also that complete amalgamation of the services would be the ruination of the effectiveness of our military machine.

Q: You witnessed, I believe, the establishment, at least the early functioning, of the CIA intelligence setup. Is this a good example of an effective amalgamation of effort?

Adm. W.: I'm not sure it's a good example because the DIA organization has been superimposed on other intelligence. Initially, I'm confident that it was the intention of Mr. McNamara to eliminate Navy intelligence, Army intelligence, and Air Force intelligence, and amalgamate them into one organization, DIA, but even he was not powerful enough to accomplish this, and I think that the decision to amalgamate was a very bad one. I think that some aspects of intelligence are peculiar to the Navy and should be in Navy hands. Our electronic warfare measures, for example, on board ship are getting more and more important to the success of operations and to have someone who is not Navy-oriented try and design, operate, and analyze the results of these equipments and the intake from these equipments would require someone specially trained.

Q: Did you have any dealings with General Carroll?

Adm. W.: Yes, I did. Being the Number Two man for the Navy in the Joint Chiefs of Staff arena, I had frequent contacts with General Carroll.

Q: Was he an ideal person to effect the establishment of this particular agency?

Adm. W.: Yes, I believe so. He was a very orderly and reasonable individual, and I think he did a very good job. I think the current DIA is good, too.

Q: Did you in that period when you were planning and establishing policy have anything to do with some of the White House staff? Was not Wisner the scientist there then?

Adm. W.: Yes, he was. I had very little contact with the White House staff in those days. I had very close contact with people in the State Department. Under my control of Op-61, which was the political-military division of the Navy who is charged with coordination and cooperation with State, I met many of the ambassadors, I knew the Under Secretaries, but I had very little direct contact with the White House.

Q: I noted that in May of 1964, we had the formation of the first nuclear-powered task group in the Sixth Fleet centering round the carrier Enterprise. This must have been a significant development in naval warfare.

Adm. W.: Yes, I think so. Nuclear power greatly increases the effectiveness of the fleet's ability - of warships. The Enterprise, as you know, is capable of traveling round the world many times without having to refuel and this, in itself, increases the capability.

Q: Indeed, this task group did go round the world, didn't it?

Adm. W.: Yes, it did.

Q: As kind of a flag-showing operation?

Adm. W.: Yes. This is no longer new because more and more of our ships are being provided with nuclear propulsion.

Q: Speaking of the <u>Enterprise</u> and her sisters, was there any controversy in the Navy Department at that time about the wisdom of putting so much money into nuclear carriers and one ship which then becomes quite vulnerable to a torpedo?

Adm. W.: There surely was. There were tremendous arguments by people of all services and by the civilian hierarchy in the Department. The Whizz Kids made many analyses as to the effectiveness - dollar effectiveness, nuclear power versus conventional power, and Curt LeMay would sound off at the drop of a hat at the millions of dollars required to provide a nuclear base for the airplanes and how much cheaper it would be to provide a base on land for these same aircraft. Burke and MacDonald would immediately reply, yes, but that land may not always be ours, but the deck of a ship can function anywhere on the globe and maintain its effectiveness and proficiency. These arguments would go on interminably.

Q: And inconclusively!

Adm. W.: They were inconclusive at that time, but I believe that the balance [handwritten correction above "volume"] of opinion now is running in favor of mobile air bases - and that means carriers. It will not be too long before we will be unwelcome in some of the bases we now have. It would be desirable for us to decrease our flow of dollars necessitated by having foreign bases. This same flow of dollars will not exist on the floating bases. I think that we'll find more and more dependence on carrier-based aviation.

Q: In the period when you were there, the idea was born, I believe, of putting missiles on the decks of merchant vessels and that sort of thing, and I believe the immediate reaction was one of pooh-poohing and ignoring this suggestion. Did you wrestle with it yourself?

Adm. W.: Yes, to some extent but not to the extent that George Miller did. It was one of his top projects. It has some merit, I'm sure. There are other devices that also have merit. The great advantage, of course, is to eliminate nuclear missiles on U.S. soil in order that these offensive weapons in our country will not draw the Soviet destructive capability to our land.

Interview No. 10 with Admiral Alfred G. Ward, U.S. Navy (Retired)

Place: His office in the Severn School, Severna Park, Maryland

Date: Wednesday morning, 29 September 1971

Subject: Biography

By: John T. Mason, Jr.

Q: Admiral, our last scheduled meeting had to be canceled abruptly because you had an unfortunate accident. I see no results from that accident, so I'm glad you recovered completely. Last time, you talked about your period of service as deputy CNO for plans and policy from August 1963 to July 1964, and immediately thereafter in July you assumed another job within the Department as deputy CNO for fleet operations and readiness. Will you talk about the scope of that assignment?

Adm. W.: Certainly, but I'd like to review for just a minute the background that caused me to become the deputy for fleet operations and readiness. As you will recall from previous discussions, I had been in command of the Second Fleet during the Cuban operation and had been pulled into the Pentagon at the end of the year as Commander, Second Fleet, to become the deputy for plans and policy. This was to be expected because I had been in the arena of the Joint Chiefs of Staff prior to this time, initially as Arleigh Burke's action officer for all matters involving the Joint Chiefs of Staff and, after making admiral, I again was associated with this arena. At the time of the death of Claude Ricketts, Dave

McDonald wanted to get a new deputy and he chose Admiral Rivero. This necessitated a change in the high command of the Navy, because Andy Jackson being the logical man to succeed me in that he had been my deputy in the plans and policy job, was highly capable and enjoyed the respect of Dave McDonald. Dave decided, in his wisdom, and I'm glad he did, that Andy would take over the Op-6 job and that I would move to Op-3.

The job in Op-3, that is in fleet operations and readiness, was a highly interesting job in that we had over-all management control of the fleet operations and also the readiness of the fleet. This involved getting involved in new construction, in the details of new construction, what type of a fleet we needed, how many ships and what kinds were needed, and it involved going before the Congress and justifying the Navy's budget for ship-building. It involved working directly with the fleet commanders and their staffs in developing a pattern of operations, such mundane things as percentages of time that ships should be at sea under the budget restrictions we had and yet be able to accomplish the missions of maintaining a presence in the various oceans of the world. It was a busy time. There were no great decisions made, but I think we made steady progress during this time. As you are aware, we had improvement in our ships, particularly in the amphibious forces. The submarine program was going well and continued to go well in this period. On frequent occasions I had to go up and justify before the Congress the needs of the Navy and, there again, I would stress to an the Congress interest in the amphibious part of the fleet. I had a good staff, I had good people working for me and I thoroughly enjoyed the assignment.

Q: Admiral, there was one question which arose and it has as much to do with this era of your activity as to the previous one I believe. Back in 1963, a selection program began for nuclear-power training because a shortage of volunteers seemed to be developing. Would you comment on that?

Adm. W.: During those days Admiral Rickover maintained pretty strict control over everything to do with nuclear power, its development, its use, the way the ships were built, and the people who operated those ships. It was rather a difficult time for the people in Personnel because of this across-the-board control that Admiral Hyman Rickover had. It was resented somewhat, but even more than that, it caused a rift in the structure of personnel training, personnel selection, and personnel assignment. Rickover no longer has this direct control over people -

Q: Did he give it up voluntarily?

Adm. W.: No, he gave it up under great protest through numbers of years.

Q: It was an autocratic control, wasn't it?

Adm. W.: Yes, it was. He still has some say in the selection of the captains of nuclear-powered ships. Unless a young man has Rickover's approval he doesn't get assigned to command a nuclear-powered ship, and I believe the same is true for the nuclear engineers in the carriers and in the cruisers. I don't find that this is too bad as long as he shows a little better feeling for the person, which seems to have eased slightly, very slightly.

Q: What was your relationship with Admiral Rickover when you were in plans and policy?

Adm. W.: By my own choice I had as few relations as possible with Admiral Rickover. I rarely saw him. I had to attend a few meetings with him with the CNO. I avoided him and I think he made it a point not to get under my feet in what I was trying to do.

Q: One of the ranking naval officers in the Department told me that in the days of Admiral Anderson, for a portion of the time at least, when there were conferences that pertained to atomic energy and such matters, Rickover wasn't even invited.

Adm. W.: I suspect that's true. I think Admiral Anderson had the same feeling towards Hyman Rickover that I had. Let me say two good things about him. He had the Congress on his side and, fortunately, his side was the Navy side as far as nuclear power goes and we did many things, got much support from the Congress because of Admiral Rickover. Had Admiral Rickover not been there we would not have had the success with the Congress in getting money appropriated for nuclear-powered ships. The second thing he did in which I have great praise for him, was that he got the taxpayers' dollar value for every dollar spent in nuclear power. He was as rough with the General Electric Company, Westinghouse Corporation, and other suppliers of parts that went into the development of nuclear power - he did more than any other person could possibly have done. He was mean, he was rough, he was ruthless, but he served the taxpayers' part in getting the most for their money.

Q: What was back of his great success and genius with the Congress? Was it the fact that it was nuclear power he was dealing with and promoting a popular issue with the Congress or was it his own public relations job, or what?

Adm. W.: I think it was a combination of several things. One is, as you know, he's Jewish and therefore a minority race and therefore he is representative of a minority, and the Congress was very careful not to alienate minorities. But more importantly, he treated the Congress in a way in which no other person I know has ever treated them. He would go into a hearing and be very subservient to various members of the Congress and make sure that any time any member made a statement he, Rickover, would agree with that statement, would amplify it, so that any application would change it sufficiently so it would accomplish both the purposes of the congressman and of Rickover, and he was a master at it. I've seen him testify and just looked in amazement at his success in the way he handled a congressional hearing.

Q: But, curiously, this was not his way of relating to fellow naval officers?

Adm. W.: That sure is correct! He was absolutely ruthless in his dealings with people in the Navy. He hated the uniform, rarely wore it. I don't remember seeing him wear it since he was promoted to rear admiral.

Q: How did he relate to the Secretary of Defense?

Adm. W.: From the knowledge I have, he was no more successful with the Secretary of Defense than he was with the Secretary of the Navy and the Chief of Naval Operations.

Q: Did you take any part of his book in your relations with Congress in your testimony?

Adm. W.: I don't believe I can say yes to that question. My testimonies were more of a routine matter in which I would present a program and would try to justify that program. I had some help in the form of the Chief of the Bureau of Ships, for example, who would be present and who would also testify as to the need for these particular vessels and why the designs of the ships were as they were. I was never questioned critically by the Congress, nor was the Chief of the Bureau of Ships during the testimony for new construction. The Congress always treated me with dignity and never was I subjected to some of the pressures and some of the adverse treatment that other people received.

Q: What sort of preparation did you engage in for these appearances before the congressional committees?

Adm. W.: We trained at great length. We would make an initial presentation before our own staffs and then later with the Secretary of the Navy and the Chief of Naval Operations as to what we would intend to say, and would actually make a presentation.

Q: With someone acting as the devil's advocate?

Adm. W.: Yes, and it was helpful.

Q: Did the JAG office help you in the preparation?

Adm. W.: Frequently, and invariably when the Secretary was involved.

Q: Who were your acknowledged friends in the Congress? What committees did you testify before?

Adm. W.: I guess the best friend I had in any naval outfit was Mendel Rivers. Senator Stennis was also very helpful in the Senate.

Q: What about Rivers' successor as chairman of that committee? Wasn't he active at that time?

Adm. W.: Yes. Mr. Hebert was helpful. He yielded to Mendel Rivers and always had a second-place play during the time that Mr. Rivers had the chairmanship. I think Mr. Hebert is a good chairman.

Q: Are there any incidents that come to your mind now in connection with these hearings that might be worthy of recording?

Adm. W.: I guess one of the best ones was involved with a new type of fast boat to be used for landing Marines over the beaches, and this particular subcommittee took a great interest in this development. The program was approved by the Congress and the contract was actually signed with Boeing and it paid off. It was a good program. On another occasion, Jerauld Wright came up to support one part of a program and he was certainly helpful.

Q: Did you have an opportunity to correct your testimony afterwards?

Adm. W.: Yes, we all did. I had one particular problem which I cite as being a fairly general one, in that we had been directed by the Secretary of Defense on a detail of one program and the Congress asked for these details and we'd give it to them honestly and it became quite critical because, in order to answer questions, we had to violate instructions issued by the office of the Secretary of Defense. At that time I asked to give this information as a matter of record later, and Mr. Rivers ruled that I could do so. But even then it was very touchy because we had been directed not to give this information to Congress. The Chief of the Bureau of Ships had a good friend on the committee, I had a good friend in the form of the administrative assistant to the committee who actually ran the committee business for Mr. Rivers, and together with doing some spadework, we were able to avoid confrontation. I believe that this is not unusual.

Q: This creates an awkward situation, then, doesn't it, when the Congress asks for specific information and the Department or what-have-you refuses to give it? It shatters rapport, doesn't it?

Adm. W.: Yes, it does, and if it does come up to a confrontation in which you say that the Department of Defense prohibits you from saying it, the probability is that you would not be on duty in the Pentagon very much longer.

Q: What about the press? I mean they're always so eager to ferret out things during committee hearings. Did you have any

Ward #10 - 252

experiences with them?

Adm. W.: No, because most of the hearings that I attended were in closed session. Most of them were pretty highly classified.

Q: So then the record of the testimony wasn't made public?

Adm. W.: No, that's right. Ususally a sanitized version of it would be made public, that is, the committee staff would delete those parts that they felt were classified and release the rest of it, and frequently they would send over drafts of their proposed releases to the person who provided the testimony and get their views as to whether or not anything that was highly classified remained in what they proposed to release. We worked well together.

Q: It must have been something of a harrowing experience, however, to testify and know just when to cease.

Adm. W.: Some people are better than others on the stand and Hyman Rickover is the best as far as his relations with the Congress are concerned. Dave McDonald did very well with the Congress. I think all of the CNOs have done well, but they work hard at doing a good job. And of course the details of the programs in which the Congress is most interested are given by deputies rather than by the chiefs themselves.

Q: Admiral, you mentioned just a few moments ago another area in which you operated. That is, your contacts with the various fleet commanders and your concern that they should operate their fleets at sea but, at the same time, within budgetary limitations. With the advent of nuclear power, was this quite as much a problem? The Enterprise, for instance, could operate indefinitely.

Adm. W.: I don't believe the problem is one of ability to remain at sea. It's one of personnel and the CNO has agreed with the statement I just made. During the time that I was in Op-3, because of the global commitments of the Navy, our ships were forced to remain at sea for long periods of time. We had carriers, for example, that would be out in the Western Pacific for more than a year at a time, and you cannot maintain personnel strength and personnel morale if a young man or young married officer has to be away from home for more than a year, maybe home for a few months, then go again for another year. And even during the few months between his deployments, he's probably at work on training at sea, so that it was pretty much impossible, particularly for the carrier forces to permit their people to have a reasonable life other than on board ship, and our re-enlistment rates were deplorable. Admiral Zumwalt is trying to correct this now by relaxing schedules at sea somewhat. It's still a rough problem.

Q: Why has this problem grown in importance in our time? In earlier days it didn't seem to be so paramount as an issue with officers or men.

Adm. W.: That's true. When I was a young officer, the ships that were deployed to the Western Pacific or on the Asiatic Station and China Station could take their families with them. The families would go on transports and set up homes in Shanghai and the Philippines or somewhere else and the ships would operate from those places, so there was no break-up of family life. It was a very pleasant experience for them - that is, some of the people took their families out. The bachelors, of course, had themselves a ball in the Orient without being subjected to pressures of families.

Since World War II our commitments have required that we maintain carriers in the Mediterranean and the Western Pacific, and the carriers require destroyers and cruisers for their support, so that much of our fleet is operating at great distances from their home ports much of the time. With these parameters it's just not possible to have men live a normal life as you would expect in peacetime.

Q:: In conversations with wives of senior officers, they seem to express the opinion that their attitude in their younger days was somewhat different from the attitude of the young Navy wife today.

Adm. W.: Conditions are so different. For example, when I was a young officer, we'd stay in the San Diego or Long Beach area most of the year. Occasionally we'd take a trip up to Seattle. When we went to Seattle my wife would get in the car and go to Seattle to be with me up there. There were very few times when we had long separations. We'd go out to sea on Monday and be back in port on Thursday night or Friday - maybe two weeks out of four. No longer true. The separations now are long and they have a tremendously adverse effect on the re-enlistment rate. Again, the present CNO is making Herculean efforts to ameliorate some of the problems that the young people now face.

Q: And meeting with some success, isn't he?

Adm. W.: Yes, he is meeting with some success. He's trying to reduce the operating schedule so that they can get home at more frequent intervals, but this is difficult with our global commitments at the present time.

Q: During the time that you were in Fleet Readiness, you must, of necessity, have worked very closely with the Bureau of Personnel?

Adm. W.: No, I really didn't. I had frequent meetings with the Bureau of Personnel on training, but my work was primarily with the fleet commanders and the fleet commanders worked with the personnel people.

Q: Did your interest extend to educational programs and so forth within the different fleets?

Adm. W.: Not directly, no. I was more interested in shipbuilding and in operating schedules and in commitments.

Q: Did this involve you, then, with the long-range planning people?

Adm. W.: Yes, it did, particularly with regard to designs of ships and the operation of ships.

Q: It has been said, and just recently, that the Russian attitude toward her navy and the direction of the navy changed somewhat after the Cuban missile crisis. Was this reflected in the time when you were in fleet operations?

Adm. W.: Oh, yes, definitely. Prior to the Cuban operation, the Soviet Navy did not venture far at sea. Most of their surface ships would remain north of Iceland or in their land-locked water areas or, out in the Western Pacific, they would normally not come down below Japan. But this gradually changed and now they have worldwide operations, and this, of course, necessitated additional surveillance on our part and further increased our own commitments. The Soviets, as I mentioned, had some submarines off Cuba during those operations and this was the first time that we had seen them this far away from their homeland. Now it's not unusual for Soviet submarines to be in the Indian Ocean, the South Pacific and in waters throughout the world.

Q: Then, during your period, it was a kind of a watershed period, wasn't it, being cognizant of this new development and new attitude? What plans were you making for U.S. presence - naval presence - in the Indian Ocean?

Adm. W.: As you know we have a small force in the Persian Gulf that operates in the Indian Ocean -

Q: Rather miniscule, isn't it?

Adm. W.: It's very small - a plane tender, a flagship, and a couple of destroyers. But they do operate in the Indian Ocean - go down to the Seychelles and in to the various islands south of India, and occasionally some of our units that are operating off Vietnam will go over into the Indonesia area and into the Indian

Ocean. But our presence is small, and there is a limit to the coverage that our Navy can provide of the waters of the world because of the fact that I mentioned our heavy commitments to maintain our presence elsewhere and in strength off Southeast Asia and in the Mediterranean.

Q: But still, the gradual - maybe more than gradual - withdrawal of the Royal Navy ~~of some of these carriers~~ made it imperative for us to do something to fill the vacuum, didn't it?

Adm. W.: Particularly in places like Singapore, Trincomalee, there is a vacuum there.

Q: With this knowledge, did it mean that you made attempts to really step up the building program?

Adm. W.: Oh, no. We made steps but the fact that ships are becoming more expensive and the fact that war, except in the Western Pacific, is not foremost in the minds of the people of the United States, ~~and~~ our Navy is getting much smaller, rather than any larger. We are losing ships and losing our control of the oceans.

Q: The period of your service coincided with the beginnings of our involvement in the Vietnam situation, did it not? I believe that the first conference that Secretary McNamara had at CinCPac was in July of 1964. What can you say about that area? I mean how did it reflect on your own operations? What was our philosophy at that point?

Adm. W.: I may have claimed a little more control over the fleet than I had intended to do, in that the fleet commanders under the area commanders, that is the commander-in-chief of the Pacific, had direct control of the operations of the Pacific Fleet, and then the Pacific Fleet commander having detailed control through his commanders of the ships at sea. My part in this whole thing was to try and ensure that the requirements of fleet commanders were met, so far as we could. I was involved in ensuring that the manufacture of munitions would be adequate, but depended on the fleet commanders to provide information on what they needed. I had, again, to justify new ships before the Congress, but this was not the direct control that you implied. We did not have this direct control from Washington.

Q: Well, at that stage of the game, what was our philosophy vis-à-vis the conflict in Southeast Asia? Surely that was reflected in your budgeting?

Adm. W.: Oh, yes, that's right, and I think our people like George Anderson, Dave McDonald, and Tom Moorer are better qualified than I on this one. I've attended many meetings of the Joint Chiefs of Staff in which policies toward Southeast Asia were discussed and the Chairman of the Joint Chiefs would make known the views to Mr. McNamara who, in turn, would make those views known to the President.

Q: Did it go always in that direction, or did it come in the opposite direction at times, from the President on down?

Adm. W.: I'm sure it must have, and Mr. McNamara would make known the views of the commander-in-chief, Jack McCain, or would make known the views of the Joint Chiefs of Staff and usually McCain would go to the Joint Chiefs of Staff, but not always. These views and requirements and requests for support, requests for increased numbers of people would go through Mr. McNamara and he would go to the President.

Q: I seem to see reflected in those early actions some indication of the current policy, Vietnamization policy, the handing of the weapons to the friendly power and telling them to get on with it. Would you say that that was so?

Adm. W.: Yes, I agree.

Q: Sometime back you mentioned the death of Admiral Claude Ricketts who was serving as deputy CNO. Would you say something about him? He had such a fine reputation.

Adm. W.: Claude Ricketts was a terrific man - I've never known a man with higher ideals, higher standards, for himself and for those around him. He was a brilliant naval officer, he gave of himself, he was very effective in handling men and his control of the events around which he was involved. He was a successful naval officer in every respect. He was a natural to come in as vice CNO. He worked as hard as any person I've ever known. His staff were effective. He gave them guidance and leadership which was terrific. He demanded excellence in those around him and his personality and his ideals were such that the people around him were willing to exert themselves to justify his faith in them. He worked so hard that I'm sure he prejudiced his own length of life by stretching himself to the fullest.

Q: Did you have any particular problems with the submarine boys in keeping the program in balance during the time that you were appearing before the Congress and dealing with construction?

Adm. W.: No, I don't believe so. The program had been set up several years before. As you know, it was an ongoing program and each year you'd decide what should be your five-year plan, so that nothing is changed in any short time frame. I had great support from the submarine officers working in the Pentagon and in the various fleets. I made many trips on board submarines, both the nuclear-powered attack submarines and the Polaris submarines that were operating out of the Firth of Forth. I had good rapport with submarine commanders. I had no problems.

Q: Secretary McNamara is noted for the development of what is known as systems analysis in terms of financing naval ships and whole programs. Would you talk about that?

Adm. W.: Yes. I was heavily involved in justifying the shipbuilding program and before we could get a shipbuilding program through the Department of Defense for presentation to the Congress, we had to justify it on the basis of systems analysis. That is, we had to figure out what the planning for the ship would cost, what the building of the ship would cost, what the fuel costs would be over its lifetime, and provide alternatives, that is, rather than putting on a particular weapons system, what would happen if we changed that weapon system to another similar one that would do the job at possibly lower cost? We had to go through the systems analysis process in determining whether or not a ship should be powered by nuclear energy or by fuel oil.

These analyses were in great depth, cost some money, but were necessary before we could get approval from the Secretary of Defense for a new weapons system. Of interest, the man with whom I worked the most on this was Dr. Albert Hall, who was in the office of the Secretary of Defense at the time as a deputy assistant secretary, and he is the same Albert Hall who taught me at MIT when I was a graduate student and who is my current boss as the Chairman of the Board of Trustees of the Severn School.

Q: Did he have these ideas when he was at MIT?

Adm. W.: No, I'm sure he didn't. He was a technician, an electrical engineer of the finest order. He worked under Dr. Alain Enthoven, who was the instigator of the systems analysis and was one of his valued supporters.

Q: Did the system really work?

Adm. W.: Dr. Mason, you'll get many answers to that question from many people. An awful lot of people felt that the primary result of this analysis was to delay programs and to permit the government to save money by these delays and not to exceed the amount of money that the President said we could spend for the military program. In my opinion, the systems analysis program is superb if it's done by honest people looking for honest answers. It's awfully easy for a small input that appears to be harmless made by a man who wants to reach an objective, say, of reducing the cost of the weapon system can accomplish. That is, an analyst can change what looks like a simple input and by so doing negate the value of the whole system, but, at the same time, reduce the cost quite considerably.

Q: Is it in operation still?

Adm. W.: Yes, it's in operation, but not to the extent that it was under the McNamara era. I'm sure that Dr. Enthoven was honest. I'm equally sure that many of the people who worked for Dr. Enthoven got the answers that they wanted rather than those that would have resulted from honest appraisals not using the system.

Q: What happens when the system, in terms of a given ship under construction or proposed, went awry? What happens then?

Adm. W.: We usually had some recourse to getting reconsideration. Let me tell you a personal experience. I was in the room one time when Secretary Nitze asked his aide, who was at that time Zumwalt, if he could prove the value of a result that was being discussed - and I think it was the cost of a weapon system - by systems analysis. Zumwalt turned to him and said, "Mr. Secretary, I can prove anything you tell me to prove by using systems analysis."

Q: A weighty remark! I would see many built-in problems with a system like that. Would it not mean, when you are thinking of building a naval vessel, that it would predetermine the shipyard where it was to be built?

Adm. W.: No, I don't believe so.

Q: Well, aren't there different prevailing wages in different localities in the country?

Adm. W.: Yes, there are, but actually the value of the systems analysis is to try and determine whether nuclear power or steam is desirable, or whether or not you want to go to a new system of turboprop engines. I guess I have to fall back on the Bud Zumwalt answer that you can prove anything by varying inputs.

Q: What repercussions did this have with congressional committees? It's so different from the old systems where they had to go back year after year for a supplementary appropriation. Has this enabled the Congress to maintain an active control? Were there any repercussions as a result of this?

Adm. W.: I think the complexity of weapons systems is such that the Congress could not, with their own staff, develop a cost-analysis which would be valid. They had to depend upon the experts in the Department of Defense to tell them that if they wanted these kinds of performances by this kind of a weapon system, it would cost so much. I believe that the Congress staffs were not qualified to check these computations.

This had one other effect, and that is that major decisions were made by people pretty far down the line. As you undoubtedly know, the Secretary of Defense has a deputy and many assistant secretaries of Defense, and each of the assistant secretaries of

Defense has a deputy assistant secretary of Defense, and under Mr. McNamara they were a large number. Frequently these would be young engineers or young people who had not much experience in building ships or in managing large programs, but they had tremendous power, and they had the power by virtue of the systems analysis process in many cases. They would use these techniques in order to prove a point and frequently would have more influence with the Secretary than would, say, the chief of the Navy or the Joint Chiefs of Staff.

Q: This really wasn't a very healthy development, then?

Adm. W.: It sure wasn't and it was one of the reasons why I believe that Mr. McNamara - it was one of the causes of Mr. McNamara's downfall.

Q: Did these young officials seek expert advice from Navy people where Navy matters were concerned?

Adm. W.: No, most of them seemed to resent the more senior people in the military services. They were in the driver's seat and they didn't ask for advice - that is, many of them. Some of them did.

Ward #11 - 265

Interview No. 11 with Admiral Alfred G. Ward, U.S. Navy (Retired)
Place: His office in the Severn School, Severna Park, Maryland
Date: Wednesday morning, 8 December 1971
Subject: Biography
By: John T. Mason, Jr.

Q: It's wonderful to see you this morning, Admiral. This should be a most interesting chapter. You served from April 1965 to 1968 - July, I believe - as the U.S. representative on the NATO Military Committee, and there were some exciting things taking place during that time. I hope you'll tell me about them. In the first place, will you tell me how you got this assignment?

Adm. W.: I suspect it was rather natural that with the background I had I was assigned to this position. As you know, I had been in plans in the Navy, working with the Joint Chiefs of Staff matters for several years, first in Op-602 which was a division of the plans division under Dennison, then moved up as a three-star admiral working as the action officer for Arleigh Burke and later Dave McDonald. So that I had been in the Joint Chiefs of Staff arena for half of my life as an admiral.

Prior to becoming the NATO Military Committee representative I had had Op-06 and then had shifted to Op-03 in operations which we covered in the last interview. One morning after the death of Admiral Ricketts, Dave McDonald called me in and told me that he was going to make some changes in organization and he designated Rivero as being vice chief and he upgraded me to a four-star job on the NATO Military Committee, and Andy Jackson took over the job that I had previously held.

Q: Tell me about the NATO Committee itself. Why was it located in Washington, and what was the scope of the Military Committee's activities?

Adm. W.: The Military Committee was founded soon after NATO was established as one of the early bodies and influential bodies in the NATO organization. We had some rather influential people who held the job from all the services, but primarily Army. This was felt to be necessary in order to give some direction to the Supreme Allied Commanders in Europe and in the Atlantic and also to act as advisers to the council of NATO. The political body of the council, of course, was composed of ambassador-level representatives from each of the nations, and the Military Committee, the military body, of NATO was composed of very senior officers, usually four-star people from the major nations, who dealt with political-military problems and who gave advice and guidance to the Supreme Commander. This was performed in Washington because the United States had all the power and any decisions that were made had to have U.S. concurrence, or they didn't get made, because most of the troops and by far the preponderance of the power were in the U.S.

Q: Even before France withdrew actively from NATO, this must have been a rather unpalatable thing for her, wasn't it?

Adm. W.: I don't believe so. The French Government at the time of the founding of NATO was not as strong as it was at a later date under de Gaulle, and actually it was to the benefit of France, in my opinion, to have representatives in the seat of the military power in the world, which was the United States at that time. And they had very capable people who were sent over to Washington so that they could feel the pulse and make their influence felt in the decisions that were being made. Originally, there was a center group within the Military Committee called the Standing Group, and the Standing Group was composed of only three people, representatives from the United States, the United Kingdom, and France, and before any problem was brought to the NATO Military Committee - any major problem - the Standing Group considered this problem and invariably would get the opinions or the views or the decisions of their home governments before making a vote - the vote had to be unanimous between these three nations, or it didn't get made.

Q: In other words, each one of these three nations exercised a kind of a veto over what the Military Committee was to consider?

Adm. W.: That's right.

Q: And they were comparable, then, to the Security Council?

Adm. W.: Yes.

Q: Your appointment as a four-star naval officer, did this underscore the importance which was placed upon the role of the Navy in the NATO force?

Adm. W.: I believe that to a certain degree. ~~That is~~, I believe that this was not the reason for putting a Navy man in. It was because they felt that the Navy had not been represented for some time - incidentally, I was not the first one. Admiral Freddie Boone had this job that I had at an earlier date.

Q: But it was rotated between -

Adm. W.: It was rotated between the services.

Q: When you took office, almost immediately thereafter, there was a matter although, I suppose, not of immediate concern to NATO, but it certainly shook the foundations, and that was our intervention in the Dominican Republic, which happened towards the end of April that year. Did it have its repercussions in your committee?

Adm. W.: It was discussed in our committee, but really was not a NATO matter in that it had no direct effect on NATO as a body. It really had very little effect.

Q: Do you recall the reactions of the other NATO representatives to this action?

Adm. W.: There was no formal recognition by the other representatives. There was some interest and I was asked to explain as much as I could of the situation as it existed, but the other representatives took no action towards making their governments' views known through the NATO Military Committee.

Q: Had you been briefed in terms of background to the whole incident, so that you could deal with it?

Adm. W.: Oh, yes. I kept very close contact with my previous office as support for the CNO and the JCS arena and there were no secrets that were not made known to me at that time.

Let me discuss a little bit more the Standing Group. Other nations resented to a great degree this veto authority of the three great powers —

Q: At that time, there were what, fifteen nations?

Adm. W.: Fifteen nations, yes, and it was felt that they were second-class citizens and there should not be a group that had such veto authority, and our government concurred in this point of view. So the United States took the lead in trying to get the Standing Group abolished and was successful in so doing. De Gaulle held out, oh, I think half a year after we made this proposal before he finally agreed. But at that time he was becoming anti-NATO and I'm sure that the decision he made was based on the fact that even at that time he planned to withdraw from NATO's Military Committee. Shortly after his consent to the disestablishment of the Standing Group he, in fact, did withdraw.

Q: Would you say, then, it hastened the French withdrawal?

Adm. W.: No, I don't believe so. I think it was the other way around. I think his plan to withdraw had been considered for some time and that he vetoed the disestablishment of the NATO Standing Group until he had made up his mind that this was in the wind and he would do so.

Q: Did the British cherish this additional authority which they exercised?

Adm. W.: I'm not sure that I would use the word "cherish." They thought it was important in the early days but I believe that they together with the United States recognized that the other nations were becoming restive and the only sensible thing to do was to disestablish the Standing Group.

Q: Did it act during its existence, do you think, as a kind of deterrent to the full cooperation, militarily speaking, with the other allies in NATO?

Adm. W.: I believe instead of acting as a block in the road to progre[ss] I believe the other nations rather welcomed it initially, in that the United States again, with all its power, and the United Kingdom becoming a nuclear power of sorts, and with France being the main power on the continent in the early days, that this was a rather logical arrangement, but that the increase in strength of Germany, tremendous increase in strength of Germany, and the resurgence of military power in Italy and in Greece resulted in the former arrangement being no longer suitable.

Q: During the first few months of your service as the U.S. representative, there was a great increase of communist activity on the Vietnamese front. Did this have repercussions in your committee?

Adm. W.: No, not really. Our interest was Europe and our charter was only in Europe. The NATO areas of interest were Europe and the Atlantic.

Q: Nevertheless, in many of your speeches the subject of international communism was an important topic which you did discuss.

Adm. W.: Yes, this is correct, and there was keen interest in the situation and many briefings. For example, I would get some of the people who had been in Vietnam or who were interested and influential in the course of events in other parts of the world, particularly Vietnam, and we'd have these representatives come down and brief the NATO Military Committee, just as a matter of information, not for any decisions by the Military Committee.

Q: I suppose when you look at world communism, you can't break it into fragments. I mean, it's a monolithic movement, isn't it?

Adm. W.: I would take exception to the "monolithic" term because communism in China is not the same communism that exists in the Soviet Union.

Q: Well, do you want to discuss the whole subject of communism as you saw it as a representative on the committee a little further?

Adm. W.: Yes, I would like to discuss it further, and there is substance to the statement that you made that international communism is a worldwide organization, and ~~certainly~~ this is true that the communist efforts in France, for example, and in Italy are certainly tied to the communists in the Soviet Union and are getting support from that worldwide movement. I think we are fortunate in the United States that while we have some communists, we seem to be *far better* than most other of our NATO nations in this regard.

Q: Is this predicated on the fact that some of the members of the fifteen might be classed as emerging nations?

Adm. W.: Oh, yes, that I believe is so and much closer to the threat of communism than we. For example, Denmark and Norway have to be very ~~fearful~~ careful in the actions they take in NATO and in their own governments in order not to cause too much of a breach between themselves and the power of the Soviet Union.

Q: Just the mere proximity!

Adm. W.: A typical example is we would want to conduct some exercises up in northern Norway during the time when I was fairly new in the Military Committee, and Norway would invariably, at that time, veto such an exercises for fear that it would cause some retaliation from across the border. Later, they felt confident enough so that they would have token exercises up there, and I actually attended some of these small-scale operations at the North Cape.

Q: In a sense, the vetoing of a NATO exercise which was designed to be protective of member nations was a denial of the purpose of NATO, wasn't it?

Adm. W.: Yes, but you had to be pragmatic. Even we, the United States, would not overrule the desire of Norway, for example, to keep a balance in their relationships with their neighbors and to try to maintain the situation such as it would not become out of hand. We had no problems within our government. If Norway didn't want to have an exercise, we were not about to insist on it.

Q: Then the decisions in the Military Committee were highly flavored by political considerations as well. You couldn't segregate the two?

Adm. W.: That's correct, and actually the votes and the decisions made by the committee were a result of both military and political guidance and consideration by the several governments.

Q: So your voice was influenced somewhat by the attitude of our State Department. How closely did you work with the State Department?

Adm. W.: Very close to the State Department. Most of the decision-making process would follow this chain: a point would be raised in the Military Committee and ask for views of governments. I would go to the Joint Chiefs of Staff and ask them for guidance on this problem as to whether we should do it or not do it, or what position we should take on the problem. The JCS would ask the Secretary of Defense who, in turn, would get some views of the State Department and, if necessary, of the President, and as a result of getting these views, the Joint Chiefs would give me guidance on what position to take, and I think most governments carried out this type of an arrangement. Certainly the French did, the Germans did, the British did.

Q: This being a rather involved process, or it sounds so to me, it meant that decisions for actions taken by the Military Committee were not very immediate?

Adm. W.: That's correct, and particularly in the days of the Standing Group because, again, the Standing Group had a veto over any one nation of the Standing Group could veto any action by the Military Committee. It really wasn't too bad, though, because most things got done, but they were slow. We were not asked to make decisions on immediate actions. For example, if the autobahn into Berlin were closed, the Military Committee was informed of this but the actions were actually taken by the governments themselves.

Q: So that you couldn't cite an example, then, where this slow process really interfered with the effectiveness of your decision?

Adm. W.: It was so slow that it did have some drawbacks and it did interfere and for this reason the U.S. was successful in eliminating the Standing Group.

Q: Can you cite an example which provoked this decision on our part?

Adm. W.: No, I'm afraid not.

Q: I take it, then, that by going to the Joint Chiefs of Staff, the U.S. representatives and more particularly a Navy man was able to get the thinking of the military and the Air Force as well?

Adm. W.: Yes, all major decisions were made by the U.S. government, with the Joint Chiefs of Staff taking an initial position and getting the concurrence of the State Department and the President on major issues.

Q: Since we're in this area of combined decision-making, tell me how closely you worked with Ambassador Harlan Cleveland, whom you mentioned quite often in your speeches.

Adm. W.: I worked very closely with him, both before I moved to Europe and, of course, very closely afterwards. His office was in the NATO building in Paris initially, and I too had an office in the NATO building in Paris and I had a deputy who was an Army major general who was permanently in Paris maintaining my office for me. I would go to Paris almost once a month for a period of several days, maybe a week.

Q: But your main headquarters were in -

Adm. W.: In Washington.

Q: Through the whole period of your assignment?

Adm. W.: No, just for the first year and a half. For the first year and a half of my assignment my offices were in Washington, but I did maintain this office and a staff in Paris. My staff in Paris would work very closely with Ambassador Cleveland's political staff in NATO, and we would phone each other or send messages back and forth daily, so that we had direct contact not only at top level but all the way down between the two staffs. Then, the last year and a half I was in Brussels with offices just across the corridor from Ambassador Cleveland. One of my titles was Military Adviser to Ambassador Cleveland. This brings up an interesting point. Ambassador Cleveland, when I was still in my assignment to the Military Committee as representative of the United States, asked that I report to him and this was a cause celebre in that the Joint Chiefs of Staff wanted and directed that I report to the Joint Chiefs of Staff and not to Ambassador Cleveland. Secretary McNamara got into this controversy and discussed it with the Secretary of State and it was decided that I would be responsible to the Joint Chiefs of Staff directly.

Q: Why this opinion on the part of Cleveland?

Adm. W.: He felt that the U.S. government should speak with one voice and that he, as the ambassador, should be that voice. Incidentally, we had no problems at all because we were both reasonable, I'm sure, and the ambassador and I got along fine and never had a problem. We didn't permit problems to exist between our staffs either.

Q: I suppose his attitude reflected the traditional one of the diplomat, did it not?

Adm. W.: Yes, it did.

Q: The head of mission was always the mouthpiece?

Adm. W.: Yes, and he was the head of mission within the political body of NATO, but the Military Committee did not have authority, without getting governmental approval, to take any actions at all, or almost no authority. There were exceptions to that, though. Frequently a question would arise that demanded an answer and I didn't hesitate to give an answer when I felt there was not time to go back to the government. Of course, I wouldn't have given an answer that would impinge on a political situation, but insofar as guidance to military commanders -

Q: In a truly military sense. How effective was Ambassador Cleveland as head of the mission?

Adm. W.: He was the most influential member in the NATO Council, with the possible exception of Manlio Brosio, who was the chairman of the Council. But Mr. Brosio would take no action on any major issue without first discussing it with Ambassador Cleveland, and he usually would discuss it with no other ambassador unless some other nation was vitally concerned. Ambassador Cleveland was the most influential member of the council, by virtue of two reasons. One is the power of the United States, and the other one is his own great personal presence and influence and the fact that he's a brilliant man.

Q: Was he a U.S. career diplomat?

Adm. W.: Yes, I would say - of course, he was an educator. He taught in college first and then he did join the State Department and was considered to be one of their most valuable ambassadors. President Johnson used him a great deal in things not to do with NATO. If President Johnson wanted to get a bill through Congress he would send for Ambassador Cleveland and tell him to go and spend two weeks talking to congressmen on an issue. Ambassador Cleveland was most effective. As you probably know, he's currently the president of the University of Hawaii.

Q: Is he a descendant of the Grover Cleveland family?

Adm. W.: I don;t know. I don't believe so.

Q: Turning to another subject, during the fifties we had a policy which was termed a defense policy, which was termed "massive retaliation" and this was changed during your term as U.S. representative on the Military Committee of NATO to another policy of "flexible response." Do you want to contrast the two and talk about the merits of both, if they had any?

Adm. W.: Yes. I think the growing nuclear power of the Soviet Union necessitated some change in the policies of the United States and of NATO. Initially, of course, with the U.S. having the preponderance of nuclear arsenals and nuclear power, the U.S. could have a policy of massive nuclear retaliation and could threaten the Soviet Union or any other power with destruction without any fear of retaliation in the event that they tried to conquer the world by conventional means.

Q: It was the big stick!

Adm. W.: It was the big stick, but this is no longer true. We now have a balance of power so that we can have mutual destruction by both great super powers, if one or the other decides to use nuclear power.

Q: Would you talk about the formulation of this new "flexible response" idea? How did it come into being? Whose idea was it?

Adm. W.: I think it was a natural result of thinking within all governments and certainly within our own government. I know that the Joint Chiefs of Staff struggled over this for many many sessions and I'm sure that the thinking within our own State Department and within our military authorities were seeing this as the only thing that you could do - try and stop any small-scale actions by small-scale response.

Q: Is the response on different levels?

Adm. W.: Yes, it is.

Q: Can you give me a good definition for "flexible response"?

Adm. W.: Yes. Should the Soviets take action against Berlin in a small measure, even to the smallest idea of closing the access to Berlin, the U.S. would take a small-scale response to try and persuade them that this is not the right thing to do and would make the response in the same general order of magnitude as the Soviet response and try by all means to hold down the escalation of such a responsive action.

Q: Treat it as a kind of a brush fire?

Adm. W.: Yes.

Q: The idea of massive retaliation, that policy, the question has been raised from time to time as to our intent in expressing such a policy. Do you think from your own intimate knowledge of the situation when you left that we really intended to go through with such a policy if we had been forced to do so?

Adm. W.: I think not. I believe that had the Soviets launched a major thrust into Germany, I believe that we may have responded to it with all the power that we had - conventional power - and that had our conventional power not been adequate I think the pressure would have been such that we probably would have used collective nuclear weapons. I believe that we would not use them now, but in the early days I think we probably would.

Q: Did that policy and its existence over a period of perhaps a decade, or more, have some influence on the attitude of the American people in general towards world responsibility?

Adm. W.: Yes, I believe so. I know that in the early days in the planning of the Joint Chiefs of Staff most of this planning was based on collective nuclear weapons, even in the Vietnam situation. It was expected that if we ever did put U. S. forces into Vietnam - if the decision was made to do so - these forces would have to use nuclear weapons. Of course, the course of events changed that policy and we didn't use them, and I think it's an excellent thing that we changed our policy. I believe it would have been terrible if we'd ever used nuclear weapons.

Q: You traveled considerably throughout the U. S. and were an astute observer. Did you sense the kind of false security which perhaps a policy like that would engender among people at large?

Adm. W.: Well, at that time, had the Soviets decided to make a major assault I believe that the U. S. decision would have been to use nuclear weapons. I believe that very few people in the world and I was one of them who did not foresee the ground actions that did take place in Southeast Asia. I think I've talked to you on this subject before, but I did have long conversations with President Diem and he certainly did not predict the actions that have since transpired.

Q: In April of 1967 a nuclear planning group of NATO met in Washington. You were a part of that, I assume. Would you talk about it, and did this in any sense violate the spirit of the

Atomic Energy Act which limited our sharing of any knowledge of atomic energy with foreign powers?

Adm. W.: In answer to your second question, I believe there was no violation of the act in itself. This is my judgment. Other people may take a different view of it. The reason I say this is that we did not disclose in our nuclear planning group the details of the manufacture of fissionable material, and I believe that the purpose of the act itself was to maintain our knowledge of the processes of making fissionable materials. The formation of this nuclear planning group, I believe, was a natural result and one that has been extremely valuable and proved to be the correct decision of the United States. The Secretary of Defense, I'm sure, took the lead in this action, Mr. McNamara, and he did it because he felt that it was necessary to get the support and cooperation - more support and more cooperation - from the nations in Europe in the confrontations against the Soviets, and I believe he succeeded in accomplishing this objective. The planning group actually went into details on the effectiveness of nuclear weapons and on the ways in which they could be used, and much of the information had been and still is highly classified, but the United States government chose to make known to selected individuals of other nations enough data so that they could plan effectively in the employment of weapons and in their own defense, too, because, as you know, we do have weapons which would be used in the event of a major war in Germany and we did have them in southern Europe but they have since been moved.

Q: Did the formation of this group do much to dispel the feeling on the part of the twelve members of NATO, other than the three principal powers, that they were not second-class citizens?

Adm. W.: Yes, I believe there's no doubt about it. I think the elimination of the Standing Group and the fact that the U.S. government did make available these planning factors and planning data were successful in making them feel that they were part of a team and a unified effort to maintain the defense of Europe.

Q: You talked about a certain selective process in talking with various nations. This touches on the policy of security then, doesn't it? How was this effective when you were dealing with such a group of nations with such varied backgrounds?

Adm. W.: Some of the nations dealt themselves out of this policy - consideration - and were not members of the nuclear planning group.

Q: Why?

Adm. W.: Because of the sensitivities of other nations. For example, Denmark is not a member of the nuclear planning group. Denmark feels that they are too close to the Soviet Union and they prefer not to be part of this group and they have not participated in the planning.

Q: The fact that they're not a part, does this signify that they disapprove of the existence of the group?

Adm. W.: No, not at all. I think that they're very happy that the group does exist and I think that they're very pleased that the United States made the decision to pull other nations into this plan.

I think they feel that their security has been enhanced by such action, but they themselves do not want to cause any further disruption in relationships with their close neighbors.

Q: What other nations ruled themselves out?

Adm. W.: I believe Norway is not a member of the nuclear planning group. I'm not sure about Turkey. I don't remember whether Turkey is a member or not.

Q: To go on to the larger subject of dealing with security in fifteen nations as a group, were there any specific problems that one had to face?

Adm. W.: Security problems?

Q: Yes.

Adm. W.: Yes, there were problems. We were not permitted, for example, to release detailed information on our own U. S. war plans. We were authorized to provide general information on the support we would have. Of course, as you know, most of the planning for the defense of Europe is done by the Allied commanders, SHAPE, and all of the SHAPE plans are sent to the Military Committee for review. We didn't actually approve or disapprove them, but we reviewed them, and if any nation had any comment to make, we would make it to the Supreme Allied Commander. And on the staff of the Supreme Allied Commander there were representatives of all the NATO nations.

Q: Did you feel any handicaps because of the difficulty in dealing with your fellows as the U.S. representative?

Adm. W.: No. I did not. As a matter of fact, because of actions such as Mr. McNamara's in releasing some of the information to selected individuals, I think the UNited States position was greatly enhanced. My relations with the other representatives on the Military Committee were excellent, and all of them felt that they could come into my office and get information that was immediately available. If I decided I had to get authority to release something, I would always ask for it, but it was never necessary for me to make this position known to a caller. Sometimes the answers were pretty general, but they respected it.

Q: Did you have personal conversations at any time with Secretary McNamara as to the scope of your job?

Adm. W.: Oh, yes, Sir, both when I took the job and at routine intervals thereafter. I would frequently travel with him in his aircraft to Europe for NATO meetings or conferences, and after we moved to Brussels we'd attend conferences with him and with Ambassador Cleveland, and with his successors.

Q: Can you recall - can you cite anything of particular interest in your relationships with him in terms of this NATO group?

Adm. W.: Well, I think the best one is the one we just discussed, and that is the formation of the nuclear planning group in NATO. That did take a great deal of discussion back and forth between Ambassador Cleveland's staff and my staff.

Q: Did you also have personal conversations with Dean Rusk in this area and with President Johnson?

Adm. W.: With Dean Rusk, yes. With President Johnson, no. I was present with President Johnson on several occasions, but I never had personal discussions with him. I did with Dean Rusk. As a matter of fact, my relationships with Dean Rusk were really good. I have great admiration for that man. He was terrific. At a NATO meeting of the Council when Mr. Rusk started to speak that room was absolutely quiet and never was it quiet except when Mr. Rusk was speaking. Every word he used was appropriate. He's a brilliant man. He says more in a few words than any man I've ever known.

Q: It's appropriate then that he's now in a classroom!

Adm. W.: Yes.

Q: Tell me, in your dealing with European problems and because of your own particular background of experience which you've related to me, did you not often feel that there was some small gap in the total picture in Spain's absence from the NATO group?

Adm. W.: Spain is an odd problem. I can understand why General Franco did not want necessarily to be part of NATO and the antipathy in many of the European NATO nations against Spain is almost unbelievable. I'm sure that this is because of the democratic views of the northern European nations, particularly Norway and Denmark, against the dictatorship of Franco and the evident hatred for the Spanish government and everything pertaining to Spain. It's a very fortunate thing that Spain is not a member of the NATO organization.

Q: Did this have its roots in the Spanish civil war?

Adm. W.: Undoubtedly, and we must recognize that there's very little freedom within either Spain or Portugal, insofar as political views are concerned.

Q: But Portugal's a member of NATO and a contributing member. Why was she accepted and Spain not?

Adm. W.: There's no freedom of action in Portugal and there isn't in Spain and I believe it's partly to do with the benevolent dictatorship in Portugal and the rather strict dictatorship in Spain. Portugal has seen, maybe, some rough times in regard to their colonies, the cruel government of their colonies. Of course, there's also some opposition to Turkey and to Greece.

Q: When I asked that question originally I had in mind your role in establishing the bases in Spain and your knowledge of their contribution to our own defense set-up. Did you not feel something of a gap when you were discussing NATO defense in the lack of this representation?

Adm. W.: Rather than answer that directly - or commenting directly - let me express a view that I think that the defense of Europe is enhanced by the fact that Spain is not a member of NATO. I believe that if Spain were to become a member of NATO, the differing views and different philosophies from the northern European countries and Spain would cause tremendous difficulties. Now we do have the use of bases in Spain by U.S. forces and, therefore, those forces would be available to support the defense of Europe and therefore NATO.

And I think this is recognized by the other nations.

Q: In other words, you, as U.S. representative on this Military Committee, were the mouthpiece for the Spanish bases as well?

Adm. W.: In a way. I certainly didn't speak for Spain, but I did speak for the U.S. forces in Spain, and many of those forces were available to NATO, both air and naval. Our base at Rota, for example, is supporting our Polaris submarine effort which is there for the defense of Europe.

Q: Do you want to discuss the whole question of the French withdrawal from NATO and its impact on the total set-up and any specific incidents that you can recall?

Adm. W.: Well, typical of my reaction to the French withdrawal is explained by an incident that happened in my own home. I had a visitor who was the senior officer in the French Navy and therefore quite an influential person in NATO because he was the head of the French Navy.

Q: What's his name?

Adm. W.: Cabanier. Admiral Cabanier came to make a visit to Norfolk and take a look at the U.S. fleet and was a guest in our home. He was a polished gentleman. Spoke beautiful English and we conversed in English while he was in my house. I returned his call in Paris and Admiral Cabanier spoke not one word of English and through an interpreter and I, in my poor French, tried to speak to him and he pulled me off to the side away from the other people who were listening, and he said, "Admiral, if you don't speak good French, don't speak at all." From then on, we spoke through an interpreter.

Q: Even though he was perfectly capable of -

Adm. W.: Oh, he spoke beautiful English. And I've visited in his home and in his home we always spoke through interpreters.

Q: This was a social convention or national pride or what?

Adm. W.: National pride. De Gaulle did the same thing. He would only speak in French. The people who worked for him followed that tradition, and it was a proud tradition. French being the language of diplomats and the language to be used in polite society, they spoke only in French and they still do.

This happened in the NATO Military Committee with General Houssay, a four-star French Army general. He would speak only in French in any formal gathering. Personally in my home he would speak English.

Q: Well, you gave that as an illustration in response to my request about the impact of the French withdrawal.

Adm. W.: I believe that the French withdrew because they felt that they were - that their national integrity or their national policy-making decisions were circumvented in some small way by NATO, and De Gaulle wanted absolute freedom to control his forces and to control French destinies. He did not want any political undertaking to which he had to be subordinated. Therefore, he withdrew.

Q: Was the French representative on the Military Committee withdrawn?

Adm. W.: Yes.

Q: Was he distressed at this?

Adm. W.: No, I don't believe so. General Houssay was a very fine person and one of my very good friends. We got on very well together. We sometimes would get orders from our respective governments that were conflicting and we understood this. This was our job and we took the position our government told us to take. But as an individual he was a wonderful person and we visited in each other's homes since leaving the Military Committee. He was withdrawn and I'm sure he felt this was the proper decision.

Q: You didn't have an opportunity to hear him express himself?

Adm. W.: No. He would never make such a statement.

Q: What impact did the withdrawal have on the other members? Here, France was at the very core of the NATO staff physically and in some other ways. What did this do to the morale of some of the lesser countries?

Adm. W.: It certainly didn't hurt the United States morale because we still believe that in time of war France will fight to preserve the integrity of France primarily, but of the rest of Europe incidentally. Their welfare and wellbeing is tied intimately into the rest of Europe, and the French military leaders do plan with SHAPE what they would do in the event of an attack into Germany. This planning continues on a bilateral basis between the U. S. and France or between SHAPE and France.

Q: So there's a partial cooperation still?

Adm. W.: Yes.

Q: Was there any problem while France was active, in terms of freedom of expression and discussion with her? I recall that before World War II broke out in Europe, there was some hesitancy in disclosing everything and speaking very franklin to the French.

Adm. W.: I suspect that there was some withholding from complete cooperation. By virtue of De Gaulle's own nature, France was France. General Houssay, I'm sure felt that sometimes he would ask for instructions and it would take an interminable time before such instructions were forthcoming and sometimes they would not be what he hoped they would. Therefore, the ability of the Standing Group to function effectively was curtailed. On one issue I think it took six months to get an answer out of the French government.

Q: And this held up the whole thing?

Adm. W.: We had veto authority and if we didn't want to use it we just didn't.

Q: So you said - and this was in the background of your remark that it didn't affect the morale of the U. S. when they withdrew.

Adm. W. No, it certainly did not. I think we're much better off with our headquarters in Brussels than we ever would have been in Paris.

Q: Did General De Gaulle not feel - at least it was reported in the press - that his sudden demand that NATO move out was something of an insult to some of the other powers involved?

Adm. W.: Yes, I guess so, but I really don't know. I know many of them felt that it was an insult. I don't think the U.S. felt so very much. I think we're very much better off in Brussels.

Q: You said that the last year and a half of your assignment was spent in Brussels, that you moved your headquarters from Washington to Brussels. Was this the result of the French effort - when NATO moved to Brussels, is that when you moved there?

Adm. W.: Yes.

Q: What happened to the Military Committee in Washington then?

Adm. W.: It moved to Brussels, and this made great sense because it was an awkward and inefficient system, having the political body on one side of the Atlantic and the military body on the other side of the Atlantic, and by virtue of having offices in the same building, the U.S. delegation being in one building - area - and other delegations in other areas, it was very easy to coordinate efforts within the staff and take positions which were helpful, and I'm sure that Ambassador Cleveland would agree with this. I'm sure that he was benefited by having me and my staff immediately adjacent to him physically and therefore able to go with him on a trip through other NATO nations, act as his military adviser and work together.

Q: And this did not work any hardship on you? I mean, the physical removal from Washington to Brussels.

Adm. W.: No. Again, we had a liaison outfit back in the Pentagon and we were on the telephone with him almost daily and if I needed instructions on some position to take on an issue it was so very easy to get it.

Q: That was made possible because of the ease of modern communications and travel?

Adm. W.: Yes.

Q: How often did you have to come back to Washington?

Adm. W.: I came back about every six weeks, and General Wheeler was frequently in Brussels. He was Chairman of the Joint Chiefs of Staff. He would go over and would generally accompany the Secretary of Defense, sometimes in a different airplane but always would be present when the Secretary of Defense was in Brussels.

Q: Tell me about your personal arrangements in Brussels.

Adm. W.: They were very nice. I sent an aide over a little early to try and find a home for us and he found a beautiful home right on Avenue FRanklin Roosevelt, which is comparable to Massachusetts Avenue in Washington, D.C., the home of the embassies. We had a beautiful home. Ambassador Cleveland had an even more elaborate home just a few blocks away. The physical arrangements were good. I had a chauffeur, a soldier who spoke perfect French. He was born in Canada so this helped in getting round the city. He had been there earlier. The offices were not quite completed when we got there, but they too are very nice.

Our relationships with the other delegations were actually enhanced because of the proximity to the Secretary General and to other delegations, both military and political, made our work very easy.

Of interest, I was with Secretary General Manlio Brosio frequently. He was Italian, of course, and a tremendously successful Secretary General. He listened keenly to what the U.S. Secretary of Defense stated and, as I mentioned earlier, his No. 1 confidant and adviser was Ambassador Cleveland. We had very good relations.

Q: Did the fact that you were resident in Brussels augment your social life and social responsibilities?

Adm. W.: Well, it was pretty strenuous on both sides of the ocean. In Washington, by virtue of being in the host country we had considerable social obligations, both socially and militarily, in that on the military side I felt obligated to take the Military Committee around to various U.S. military bases, including to California to see a shot by a Minuteman and other missile shoots. I took them down to Cape Kennedy. Took them out to sea on a carrier, and these kind of things.

Q: There was a grand tour, then?

Adm. W.: Well, continuing. A program of touring and seeing the military power of the United States. It was effective, too. They recognized that the power of NATO is the United States.

On the other side of the ocean, we were able to visit foreign countries and representatives in their home nations frequently, and we did go and visit many of the NATO exercises. I mentioned one at North Cape in Norway. We flew down to an exercise in Greece. It was a very rewarding and interesting period.

Q: And this was much more than you were able to accomplish when you were in Washington, the visits to the European capitals?

Adm. W.: Yes. Ambassador Cleveland did not travel in Europe as I was doing since he was in Washington more frequently. I had access to an airplane, so if the Ambassador wanted to make a trip in Europe he would call up and invite me to go with him. "You get the airplane and we'll go visit SHAPE or Italy or Norway," so it worked very well.

Q: What about the dinner and cocktail circuit responsibilities?

Adm. W.: They were strenuous, I guess that's the right word. We were entertained by Belgian officials, including the prime minister.

The Foreign Minister and the Prime Minister both entertained us, and we had many formal dinners, and a formal dinner in Belgium is really formal, with many, many courses and much, much food.

Q: And many hours!

Adm. W.: Yes, and many wines.

Q: Were you provided with an adequate allowance for your own share of entertaining?

Adm. W.: Yes, I was, and we entertained frequently but much more simply than the officials in Europe. My successor, General Bert Spivey, did even more than I. He had movie equipment installed in his basement in the house in which I had previously lived, and he would invite people in for a buffet dinner and then take them downstairs to the movie.

Q: A very successful way of handling guests! Are there any incidents in connection with this social activity that you might like to recall and record?

Adm. W.: Yes, it was a very pleasant experience. One of my best friends was the chairman of the Military Committee, a Belgian general. We had dealt previously with him as chief of staff of the Belgian Army, and he and I were very good friends, General Baron de Cumont. They entertained frequently and they were in our home frequently. We did such projects as wine-bottling parties. He would get two or three kegs of FRench or Belgian wine and we'd go to my basement and bottle it and have buffet supper and sample the wine while we were doing it with the various other guests, mostly members of the Military Committee and their wives - rather informal clothing. It was a very happy atmosphere.

Q: Did your French improve and does Mrs. Ward speak French fluently?

Adm. W.: No, Mrs. Ward speaks very little French but enough to shop, and I speak enough to order a meal and make my wishes known, but it's not good French. Our little daughter was probably the best of the three.

Q: What kind of a staff did you have?

Adm. W.: We had just like any other -

Q: Filipino stewards?

Adm. W.: Yes, and they got on very well in Brussels.

Q: I'd like to open up a different subject which flows from some of your speeches. I'd like to ask this question: in view of the lessons we learned from our cooperation with the NATO powers and the very great importance of the naval units as a part of the total defense picture, why did we, then, with that knowledge and our own growing role in the world, why did we allow our Navy to grow old?

Adm. W.: I'm not the right man to answer that question. I think maybe you should go to the Congressmen for this one. Certainly the Navy has grown old and has gradually lost its preeminent position as the most powerful Navy in the world. I think the United States is making a mistake in not putting more of its resources and its wealth and its interest in building our Navy.

Q: In terms of what you've just said, how does it stack up with what you said in March 1967 in Oklahoma City when you said, "no nation which has given up control of the sea has ever again regained it"?

Adm. W.: I don't believe that we have actually given up control of the sea, though we certainly are on the verge of so doing. Soviet power and Soviet strength in its merchant marine, for example, is tremendous, and our merchant marine is almost nonexistent. Our naval power itself, our warships, I believe that we still have the greatest strength in certain areas. For instance, I believe our carriers and aviation are still the most effective in the world. I think our Polaris submarines are still the best ships in the world of that type, and I believe that we have sufficient numbers of Polaris submarines to in fact have a retaliatory capability of sufficient magnitude to deter aggression. I think our surface fleet is growing old and therefore is losing its superiority in naval power, and this is particularly true in our destroyers and ships that are carrying guns and missiles. I think it behooves our nation to put more effort into our surface Navy.

Q: Is there any possible relationship between the difficulty, the experience, with the Congress in getting more support for modern naval vessels, is there any connection between that acknowledged situation and that earlier doctrine of massive retaliation?

Adm. W.: Yes, I'm sure there is. In the doctrine of massive retaliation, it's really not vital that we have the preponderant strength at sea or conventional armies, but that theory, I think, has fallen and is no longer a valid one. I think no one believes that massive retaliation is a proper response to military action. Massive retaliation could only result in the destruction of the world as we know it, and therefore it is not an available option. If this is true, the conventional job becomes more important.

Q: But then why the failure at the next step, to think it terms of building up our conventional forces more, especially the Navy?

Adm. W.: I agree with what you are implying, that our government is making a mistake in not paying more attention to conventional naval power.

Q: Admiral, there was a specific question I wanted to ask you but it opens up a larger area. During your time as the military representative, I think it was when we began that experiment with the Claude V. Ricketts, the destroyer, using a kind of a cosmopolitan crew of NATO members. Was this a successful thing, and in the larger sense is it successful to combine elements from military forces from various NATO countries and work together as a single unit?

Adm. W.: Well, this was an experiment and I think as an experiment it was successful insofar as the ship was effective, the people got along very well together, there were no major problems after the initial ones of satisfying some of the peculiar food desires of some of our friends. Personally, I believe that it would be more effective to have mixed task forces, that is, British destroyers and U.S. destroyers working together, rather than mixing the crews up because I believe Americans get along with Americans more effectively than Americans get along with the Portuguese, for example. But I think as an experiment this was highly successful, and I think it was a good thing because it let some of the other nations' people see how we live in our ships and we could see how they behaved. And I think as far as the relationships between people and nations are concerned, this was good, but it's really not the most effective way of operating the NATO forces.

Q: Was it expanded? Or was it discontinued?

Adm. W.: No. When you say "discontinued" I think this was definitely experimental and I suspect that it will happen again. We exchange crews occasionally. As you probably know we have a French midshipman come over here during the summer and during the winter, too. We exchange midshipmen between the two nations and with other nations, and I think this type of thing will go on, but on a very small scale.

Q: As you sat with your peers in the military sphere on this defense committee, how did they feel about an experiment of this sort? Were they more optimistic than we?

Adm. W.: I don't believe that they considered it a very important experiment. I think they thought it was good, but I believe most of them had the same view that I have, that it was good for a one-time effort or maybe infrequent effort, but it's not the most

Ward #11 - 300

effective way of doing it.

Q: Who proposed this specific experiment? Did Admiral Ricketts himself?

Adm. W.: I think so. No, it would not have been Admiral Ricketts because, you see, the ship was not named Ricketts until after Admiral Rickett's death.

Q: Then it was something else.

Adm. W.: Yes, he did propose it, as a matter of fact. He did think this was a good thing.

Q: Tell me about the NATO Defense College.

Adm. W.: The NATO Defense College is -

Q: There's no date on this, but your remarks are in this collection You were present at a briefing of the staff and the students of the NATO Defense College.

Adm. W.: The NATO Defense College is in Italy - in Rome. It has officers from all NATO nations. It has a commandant whose nationality varies. The first one, of course, was Italian. It's a beautiful site. People go to the college for a period of about six months and they study the NATO war plans, the plans that SHAPE has, and the plans that the Supreme Commander, Atlantic, has. They are given briefings by the staff officers at both the Supreme Allied Commanders and by various members of the NATO Military Committee. The Military Committee visits the college about once during each of the sessions of the college. It's considered to be a desirable thing to get particularly European nations knowledgeable on the available force levels for the defense of Europe, to have them see in the field some of the military units of the various nations. Usually the NATO Defense College visits the United States once during each year or oftener during each course, and I think it's a good thing.

Q: This implies that it's rather small, then, in numbers.

Adm. W.: Yes, it is. I believe there are about 40 to 60 officers at one time.

Q: Are they junior officers, promising junior officers?

Adm. W.: Major level - lieutenant commander, major - about that level.

Q: How do we make our selections?

Adm. W.: They're made by service chiefs. They will nominate officers for the Defense College - that is, Chief of Staff of the Army, Chief of Staff of the Navy - and the members are rotated between the services, and officers from all services go. The instructors are on a full-time basis for a period of about three years.

Q: It's an acknowledged fact, I think, that the media in the United States, and especially television these days, have a tremendous impact on the attitudes and thinking of our people, and certainly in terms of military matters. This was not necessarily true in some of the European nations. Was there any problem that resulted because of this situation?

Adm. W.: No, I don't believe so. You are right that our media do influence our own thinking a great deal. I don't believe that the Europeans are as sophisticated as we are in this regard, and I believe that the media do not have the control or tremendous influence that exists here in this country.

Q: Did this create a problem for you as the U.S. representative on this committee then? The media in this country influencing people and situations, whereas you were dealing with men who were not so influenced and restrained?

Adm. W.: It didn't affect me personally, I'm sure, but I've cited the example of President Johnson's use of Ambassador Cleveland on the Congress, and frequently the President's position would not be that that the majority of the media chose to support, and I think that this is the reason for the President asking Ambassador Cleveland to spend a month in the halls of Congress, to try and present the other side of a picture. I was not influenced by this problem.

Q: This may not have any direct relationship to your job as the military representative on this committee, but you did in one of your speeches in Seattle, Washington, in 1967 - you made a very intriguing statement and I wonder if you can support it and substantiate it. "In my view," you said, "patriotism in America today is greater than ever."

Adm. W.: That was true in those days, but I believe that the

Vietnam situation has changed that opinion. This was prior to the big war in Vietnam when that statement was made. I believe that situation has changed.

Let me make one statement and see if we can terminate this, and that is that I was privileged to visit prime ministers, ambassadors, kings, queens, during my period in NATO and invariably I found a great wealth of affection for America and things American, and I believe that this was a real affection. I was entertained by the King of the Belgians and he certainly is very sympathetic to the problems that we had and was most hospitable.

Q: I'd like to comment myself that even though you walked with kings, it doesn't seem to have turned your head! And so this is the conclusion of your service on this NATO committee -

Adm. W.: I retired.

Q: Came your retirement from the Navy - and that was when?

Adm. W.: Three and a half years ago.

Q: You retired in July of 1967?

Adm. W.: 1968.

Q: Well, I thank you very much, Sir.

INDEX

to interviews with

ALFRED G. WARD

Admiral, U. S. Navy (Retired)

Aircraft Carriers, views on, 108-110

ALABAMA, BB, 42

Amphibious Force 8, commander of, 93; arctic mission, 94; oceanography, 95, 98; exercises in Atlantic, 96

Amphibious Forces, 167 ff, 174-178, 184

Amphibious Operations, 46-47

Anderson, Adm. George, 210 (quotation on Cuban missile crisis); 213, 239, 246 (on Adm. Rickover), 258

AS training, 120-121

Atlantic Fleet Command, 101-102; committee appearances, 106; aspects of electronic warfare, 107

Baguio, 144

Bao Dai, Emperor, 132-133, 140

Bau Dai, Buddhist sect, 138-140

Bay of Pigs, 157, 160-165, 177

Beakley, VAdm. Wallace M., 80, 92, 157-159

Bell Labs, 22

Berger, Lt. Gen. Joe, 168, 174

Boone, Adm. Walter Frederick, 268

Bramble, Professor, 16

Brosio, The Hon. Manlio, Secretary General of NATO, 276-277, 293

Brown, Admiral Charles R. (Cat), 77

Brown, Dr. Gordon, 20-21, 23

Brussels, 275, 291-293

Burke, Adm. Arleigh, 49, 81-82, 86, 88, 91, 157, 159-160, 163-164, 239, 244

Busick, Capt. William, 70

Cabanier, Adm. 287

Camp Pendleton, 169

Carroll, Gen. Joseph F., 240-241

Casco Bay, 51-52

Castro, Fidel, 181, 206, 236

Central Intelligence Agency, 240

Chesapeake Bay, training, 35

Churchill, Sir Winston, 139

Cleveland, The Hon. Harlan, U. S. Ambassador to NATO, 274-276; desire to have U. S. Representative on Military Committee report through him, 275-276; 277, 291, 293, 294, 302

Com Dev For, 52

Communism, discussion of, 270-272

Congressional Committee Hearings: appearances before, 249; preparation for hearings, 249-251; press reporting of hearings, 251-25

Conolly, Adm. Richard, 154

Coral Sea, 43

CruDiv 1: Showing the flag in Japan, 124-128; 147-150

Cuba, invasion plans, 168-169, 171-172

Cuban Missile Crisis: See entries under 2nd Fleet Command

Dahlgren Proving Ground, 27

de Cumont, Gen. Baron, 295

Deep Freeze, Operation, 117-119

Denmark, 282

Dennison, Adm. Robert, 80, 82, 92, 187, 189, 191, 215

Destroyer Force, Commander, on staff of, 69

Diem, President of South Vietnam: character sketch, 132-135, 137, 139, 140-142, 280

Dominican Republic, U. S. Intervention, 268

Draper, Dr. Stark, 20; gyro-sight developed, 20; 23, 25, 26

Dufek, RAdm. George, 118

Dulles, The Hon. John Foster, 81-82

Durbrow, The Hon. Elbridge, U. S. Ambassador to South Vietnam, 133-134

Eisenhower, President Dwight D., 82-83, 121-122, 130, 135, 160

ENTERPRISE, CV, 37, 241-242, 253

Enthoven, Dr. Alain C., 261-262

Espiritu Santo, Battle of, 36, 43

Fahrion, Adm. Frank G. (Spike), 69-70, 72, 77-78

Fleet Operations, Ward's duties as Assistant CNO, 155-158, 244-245

France: her partial withdrawal from NATO, 287-291

Frogmen, 175

Gates, The Hon. Thomas, 92

Ghormley, VAdm. Robert Lee, 45, 48

Guadalcanal, 34-35, 43, 45

Guantanamo, 169, 180-181, 236

Gun Factory, Washington Navy Yard, 27

Hagen, Dr. Harold, 21

Hall, Dr. Albert, 23-24, 261

Halsey, Ft. Adm. William, 45-46

Hart, Admiral T. C., 9-10; philosophy of education for the Naval Academy, 10; predictions for the future of the Navy, 11

Heavisides, Operational Calculus, 16

Hebert, The Hon. F. Edward, 250

Helicopters, 176

Hill, Adm. Harry, 46

Hiroshima, 125

Hokkaido, 66, 131

HOLLISTER, DD, 56-60

Holy Loch, discussions of Polaris base in Scotland, 225-228, 232

Hong Kong, 131

Hooper, VAdm. Edwin, 12, 20, 32

HORNET, CV, 33-35; lost in Slot, 38

Hoshina, Admiral, Japanese Navy, 67

Houssey, General, 288-290

Hussey, VAdm. George, 50

Icebreakers, 99

Indian Ocean Naval Policy, 256-257

International Business Machines, IBM, 22

International Control Commission, 136-137

Jackson, VAdm. Andrew McBurney, 245, 266

Japanese People, comments on, 129-130

Johnson, President Lyndon, 219, 238, 277

Kachibama Wan, 58-60

Keating, Senator Kenneth, 190

Kennedy, President John F., 10, 169, 190-191, 197, 209-210, 214, 219-220, 238

Kivette, VAdm. F. N., (Knappy), 147

Korea, 63-65

Kwajalein, 44

La Place Transformations, 17, 22

Lee, VAdm. Fitzhue, 75

Lee, Adm. Willis, 42-43, 47, 51

LeMay, General Curtis, 92, 239, 241

LEXINGTON, CV, 36

Lucky, Lt. Gen. Robert, 168, 174

MacArthur, Gen. Douglas, 61, 129

MacArthur, Douglas II, Ambassador to Japan, 125, 127, 129, 131

Mao-Tse-tung, 209

MARCULA, Lebanese Supply Ship, 196, 209

Martell, VAdm. Charles, 218

Martin-Marietta, 23

M.I.T. (Massachusetts Institute of Technology): P.G. work, 19-27; Computer technology, 20, 22-23; servo-mechanisms, 20-21; 24; post-course tour, 26

Massive Retaliation Doctrine, contrasted with doctrine of flexible response, 277-279; definition of doctrine of flexible response, 279-280

McCain, Adm. John R., 259

McDonald, Adm. David, 245, 252, 258, 265

McNamara, The Hon. Robert, Secretary of defense, 213; new directions in defense, 218-220, 223; closing of military bases in U. S., 233-234; estimate of McNamara, 234-238; illustration of

McNamara decisions, 236-237; McNamara with Presidents Kennedy and Johnson, 238; attitude towards C.I.A., 240; attitude toward RAdm. Rickover, 249; Vietnam Conference, 257-259; systems analysis, 260-261; 264; 275

Midway, Battle of, 33, 35

Miller, RAdm. George, missiles on merchant ships, 243

Miller, Rip, 70

Mobile, Alabama, 1-2, 184-185

Monroe Doctrine, 206

Moorer, Adm. Thomas, 258

Morale problems with Fleet, 111-114

Mustin, VAdm. Lloyd, 12, 20, 26, 32, 51, 120

Nagasaki, 61-63, 126, 129

NATO Command, 103-105; exercises, 105

NATO Defense College, 300-301

NATO, Military Committee Representative, 265-267; NATO Standing Group 267-270, 273; interest in international communism, 270-271; political considerations in decision making, 272-274; committee procedures, 273; relocation in Brussels, 275, 291-296; discussion of security matters in Military Committee, 283; Ward's personal accommodations in Brussels, 293-296

NATO, Nuclear Planning Group, 280-283

NATO: support in Cuban crisis, 207, 212; cooperation in supplying crew for DD CLAUDE V. RICKETS, 298-300

Naval Gun Factory: 27, 49-50, 53-56, 2nd tour, 72-73

Navy Preparatory Schools, 4, 6

Naval War College, 79; 91, 151-152-153-154-155

Navy, Strategic Plans, 80, 83-84; cooperation with O.N.I., 84; work for C.N.O. as member of Joint Chiefs, 85, 87; Quemoy, 87

Nautilus, SS, 117

NEWPORT NEWS, 197, 211 (flagship)

New York Navy Yard, 27, post graduate assignment

Nimitz, Fleet Admiral C. W., 40-41

Nitze, Secretary Paul, 236-237, 262

Nomura, Admiral in Japanese Navy, 67

NORTHAMPTON, Cruiser, first tour of duty with, 12-15

North Cape, 272, 294

NORTH CAROLINA, BB, 27, 30; new type of equipment, 27; cryptology devices, 30; security measures, 30-31; comments on personnel, 31-32, 38, 33-35, 37; her presence in South Pacific a morale builder, 37; torpedo hit, 38; augmented A/A guns, 39-40; combat information center, 41-42; method of communicating to other ships, 42; use in bombardments, 44-45; 26

Northwest Passage, 98

Norway, 272; vetoes NATO exercises in northern waters, 272; 283, 285

Nu, Madame, 132, 136

Nuclear Planning Group in NATO, 281, 284, 292

Nuclear Power, 220; discussion of navy policy, 220-225; 241; personnel requirements for nuclear-powered ships, 246; as pertains to Russian navy, 277-278

Ohara, Admiral (Japanese), 126

Patrick, RAdm. G. S., 124

USS PERRY, 13-14

Personnel Problems and Budget, 252-255

Pirie, VAdm. Robert Burns, 101

POLARIS, 221-222; bases in Scotland and Spain, 224-226, 228; 231; estimate of value, 297

Political-Military papers, 224

P. G. School, 15-16; first half at Naval Academy, 16-18; M.I.T., 19-27

Quemoy and Matsu, 87

Radar Development, 24, 28-29, 36-37; fade charts, development of, 44

Ricketts, VAdm. Claude V., 244, 259-260; 265

CLAUDE V. RICKETTS, DD, 298-300

Rickover, RAdm. Hyman George, 246-248, 252

Rivero, Adm. Horacio, Jr., 12, 20, 26, 32, 188, 244, 266

Rivers, The Hon. Mandel, 250-251

Roosevelt, Mrs. Eleanor, 198

Roosevelt, President F. D., 18, 139

Rota, discussion of Polaris base in Spain, 228-232, 287

Royal Navy, 105

Rusk, The Hon. Dean, Secretary of State, 283

Russian Fleet Deployment, 116

Russian Merchant Marine, 167, 169

Russian Navy, 148

Russian Trawlers, 172-174, 215-216

Saigon, 131-132

St. Thomas, Virgini Islands, 177-178

SARATOGA, CV, 36, 48

SEATO, 142, fleet exercises, 143

Sea Power: comment on in NEWS and COURIER, newspaper of Charleston, S.C., 210

Second Fleet, Adm. Ward's command of: circumstances of this command assignment, 187; change of command ceremony, 188; plane ride to Washington, 189; blockade vs quarantine, 191-192, 199-200; details of quarantine story, 192-196; presence of Russian subs, 193-195, 201-202; Russian language officers, 194-195; missile carrying ships, 196; White House control of situation, 198-199; estimate of missile threat, 200-201; length of operation, 201-202; summary of events, 203-208; SacLant role, 205; NATO support, 207; role of Press and media, 211; Russian reactions to the crisis, 255-256; post missile crisis concerns, 214; U. S. reactions, 185-186

Sendai, Japan, 130

Severn School, 4; Mr. Teel, founder, 4; 24, 261

Seychelles, 256

Shah of Iran, 110

SHAPE, 283, 290, 294, 300

Sigma XI, honorary fraternity, 25

Singapore, 257

South Pole, 214

Spain, comments on her absence from NATO, 285-287

Speech making, 181-184; post-Cuban crisis engagements, 216

Sperry Corp., 20, 26

Spivey, Gen. Delmar Taft (Bert), 295

Spring, RAdm. Arthur, 143

Stennis, Senator John C. 250

Submarine Building Program, U. S. Navy, 260

Submarine Force, expansion efforts, 165-166

Systems analysis, 260-264

Tachen Islands, 80-81

Taipei, 144

Taiwan, 144-145; comments on post war recovery, navy, etc., 145

Takai, 126

Tarawa, 45

Taylor, Adm. Jack, 188

Taylor, General Maxwell, 191, 235

Thompson, Capt. Raymond W., 47

USS TOLEDO, 128, 143

Topaz, 190 (Cuban Missile Crisis)

Trincomalee, 257

Tsou, Admiral (Nationalist Chinese), 146; his son, Peter, 146-147

Turkey, 283

Underwater demolition, 177-179 (Caribbean exercises)

Vieques, 96; value to navy, 96-97, 169, 179, 211

Viet Nam, picture of conditions in time of President Diem, 139--142; 257-258; use of nuclear weapons, 280

Vietnamization, 259

Vinson, The Hon. Carl, 239

VIP's with Fleet, 110

Ward, Adm. A. G., early data, 1-3; education, 2-3; naval academy appointment, 3-5; academy days, 5-7; summer cruises, 7; Lucky Bag editor, 7-8; course description, 8; MS from MIT, 25; Rear Admiral, 88-91; retirement, 303

WASHINGTON, BB, 32, 34, 42

Wellborn, VAdm. Charles, 13

Werntz, Bobby, prep school, 4

Wheeler, Gen. Earle G., 292

White House staff, 241

Whiting, VAdm. F. E. M. (Red), 32

Whitmire, Don, 70

Whiz Kids, 234-242

Williams, General Samuel T. (Hanging Sam), 135, 141-142

Wright, Admiral Jerauld, 96, 101-102; his performance in NATO command, Atlantic, 103-105, 250

Zumwalt, Adm. Elmo, 253-254, 262-263

Tokyo, September 1, 1959.

Dear Admiral Ward:

    I was delighted to read your fascinating letter of August 21 and to see the pictures and the other mementos of the visit of Cruiser Division One of CINCPAC Fleet to various ports in Japan. I had already heard a good deal of the wonderful work you and your men have done in promoting friendly relations between the peoples of Japan and the United States during your visit here. I have read of your calls in the newspapers and I have also heard glowing reports from distinguished Japanese in the areas you have visited. The Commander and all of the officers and men of Cruiser Division One deserve thanks and a hearty well done. I shall keep your letter and its attachments as an example of what can be done to promote closer relations between Japan and the United States and to advance our interests here through close and friendly personal contacts.

    I have also put copies of your letter commending Mr. Takai, Mr. Medd, Mr. Knowles and Mr. Peattie in their personnel files.

    With every good wish.

                                    Sincerely,

                                      Douglas MacArthur II
                                    Ambassador to Japan

A. G. Ward, Rear Admiral, USN,
   Commander Cruiser Division ONE,
      c/o Fleet Post Office,
         San Francisco, California.

ROUTINE　　　　　　　　　　　　　　　　　　　　　　　　　　UNCLASSIFIED

080754Z

FROM: COMSEVENTHFLT
TO: USS TOLEDO
INFO: COMCRUDESPAC / COMDESFLOT ONE / CINCPACFLT

PERSONAL FOR RADM WARD AND CAPT LOUGHLIN FROM VADM KIVETTE X I AM SURE THAT NO SHIP IN RECENT YEARS HAS LEFT BEHIND MORE ASIAN FRIENDS UPON HER REDEPLOYMENT X TOGETHER YOU HAVE GIVEN OUTSTANDING SUPPORT TO OUR PEACEFUL OBJECTIVES IN WESTPAC WHILE MAINTAINING YOUR FIGHTING TRIM X IT TAKES ALL KINDS OF WORK TO WIN THIS PEACE AND YOU HAVE DONE YOUR WORK WELL X GOOD LUCK AND A HAPPY HOMECOMING

THE SECRETARY OF THE NAVY
WASHINGTON

The President of the United States takes pleasure in presenting the DISTINGUISHED SERVICE MEDAL to

ADMIRAL ALFRED G. WARD
UNITED STATES NAVY

for service as set forth in the following

CITATION:

For exceptionally meritorious service to the Government of the United States in duties of great responsibility as Deputy Chief of Naval Operations (Plans and Policy) from August 1963 to July 1964 and as Deputy Chief of Naval Operations (Fleet Operations and Readiness) from July 1964 to March 1965. Serving with distinction in these two particularly demanding assignments, Admiral Ward participated directly in the formation of strategic concepts and plans for the defense of the United States, and in the establishment of security policy designed to strengthen and preserve peace throughout the world. He displayed an unusually perceptive understanding of complex politico-military considerations in the negotiation of basing agreements for Polaris submarines at Holy Loch, Scotland, and Rota, Spain, making a major contribution to the preparation for these significant negotiations which were successfully concluded in February and July 1964, respectively. During this period of tensions, crises and active hostilities in Southeast Asia, Admiral Ward exhibited foresight and a thorough understanding, both of possible measures available to our Naval forces, and of the likely response to be expected of our adversaries. By his brilliant leadership and outstanding professional competence, he contributed greatly to the security of the United States and to the preservation of world peace. His distinguished accomplishments reflect the highest credit upon himself and the United States Naval Service.

For the President,

Paul H. Nitze
Secretary of the Navy

THE SECRETARY OF THE NAVY
WASHINGTON

The President of the United States takes pleasure in presenting Gold Star in lieu of the SECOND DISTINGUISHED SERVICE MEDAL to

ADMIRAL ALFRED G. WARD
UNITED STATES NAVY

for service as set forth in the following

CITATION:

For exceptionally meritorious service to the Government of the United States in a position of great responsibility as the United States Representative to the NATO Military Committee in Permanent Session in Washington, D. C., and upon its relocation in Brussels, Belgium, from March 1965 to June 1968. Exercising outstanding professional competence and skillful diplomacy, Admiral Ward provided invaluable contributions to United States objectives in NATO military matters and to the fruitful work of the Military Committee and the Major NATO Commanders. He was instrumental in developing and adopting the new NATO Flexible Response strategy and was highly successful in negotiating U. S. positions with respect to force postures. In addition, Admiral Ward was largely responsible for establishing a definitive role for the Military Committee in NATO nuclear planning; contributed greatly to development and approval of the NATO Standing Naval Force Atlantic; and contributed in large measure to the Military Committee development and approval of a new concept for reinforcing the flanks of the Alliance. This concept and the Standing Naval Force contributed directly toward implementing the New Strategy and furthering security interests of the United States. Admiral Ward's distinguished performance of duty reflects great credit upon himself and the United States Naval Service.

For the President,

Paul R. Ignatius

Secretary of the Navy

COMMITTEE OF ONE HUNDRED OF MIAMI BEACH

ADDRESS

BY

VICE ADMIRAL ALFRED G. WARD, USN
COMMANDER SECOND FLEET

AT

THE SURF CLUB

FEBRUARY 16, 1963

FOREWORD

Due principally to the inclement weather that prevailed during the Navy Gala Dinner Dance at The Surf Club on the evening of February 16, 1963, it was possible to hear only an abbreviated version of Vice Admiral Ward's address to the Committee. Through Admiral Ward's courtesy, and with his kind consent, the complete text is provided herewith to all members of the Committee of One Hundred. Our members will find much to ponder within these pages. We are grateful to Admiral Ward for the complete candor of his remarks and he did us great honor in presenting this address to us.

James Gerity, Jr.
President

"SEA POWER IN THE CUBAN CRISIS"

When I was informed by Admiral Anderson's office that the Committee of One Hundred would welcome a visit by a major ship of the Second Fleet about this time of the year, I was an enthusiastic volunteer to bring in the flagship. I had learned of Admiral Anderson's warm reception here last year and his high regard for members of the Committee of One Hundred, both collectively and individually. Neither my wife nor I have been in this area before, and this provided us an opportunity to find out why so many smart people in these United States come to the Miami/Miami Beach/Fort Lauderdale area in the wintertime. In the short time we have been here, we have found that answer. You may be assured that this will not be our last visit to this area. We hope that we may contribute in some small measure to the objectives of the Committee of One Hundred of bringing together, under the banner of friendliness and good will, men who have broad interest in human progress, believe in real fellowship, and desire the betterment of this area.

We are well aware of the problems and the challenges facing the people of Southern Florida with the Cuban situation and in the many aspects of that situation. We know of the adjustments that have to be made by the displaced citizens of that country who are having to make new lives for themselves in order to remain free. We know, too, of the problems generated here by an influx of people who have not had the same language or the same heritage that belong to us.

I am interested in the Cuban situation because of my previous association with the crisis that started on October 22nd, and because of the fact that I command a fleet which would undoubtedly be a part of any United States effort should the military become involved in carrying out our national objectives in this area. Of interest to you is that today and every day there are units of the Second Fleet in this area; there are units in the Puerto Rican area; we continue to maintain a sizeable number of ships in training at Guantanamo; and we are privileged to send our ships into this great area for rest, relaxation and surcease from our work at sea. The Miami/Fort Lauderdale area ranks at the top in the choice of our men as a port of call. Your climate, your friendliness, your understanding and your hospitality make the lives of our officers and our men more enjoyable and rewarding.

The Cuban crisis was the most significant event on the military scene in 1962 and, in my opinion, was the single most important episode in the history of the world during that year. This evening I would like to talk to you about the Cuban crisis in three phases:

The first, a description of the role played by military forces in the crisis, including some personal observations of actions at the scene of Quarantine Force operations;

Second, the immediate results of the crisis; and

Third, a study of a few of the lessons learned or, to state this in other words, some analyses of the effects of the crisis.

The Navy's role in the Cuban crisis was described in an editorial in the Norfolk-Virginian Pilot on October 30. I would like to quote some extracts from that editorial:

"President Kennedy's choice of a naval quarantine as the backbone of United States resistance to the Soviet Union's missile bases in Cuba will fascinate the historians of sea power. The measure was selected as an alternative, or as preliminary, to an attack on the offending weapons. Events have indicated how awkward was the position in which it placed the Kremlin.

"The history of the blockade, including the so-called pacific blockade, has been reviewed in these columns. The point has been made that in this nuclear age, military and diplomatic precedents are all but valueless and the classic definitions lose their meaning. Mr. Kennedy simply seized upon the most effective measure, short of violence, that he judged to be available to him.

"The significance of what the President did lies not in the past but in the present. That is according to the demands of the times. He seized from Mr. Khrushchev the initiative and strapped upon him a choice far more bitter than the one he had resolved by ordering a blockading force into the Caribbean rather than by shooting.

"Mr. Khrushchev's . . . apparent willingness to pull in his horns with as much grace as he can muster is, therefore, another tribute to the U. S. Navy's strength and readiness. The Navy's performance has been none the less dramatic for its being carried out so near to home bases and command centers. Our fleets have demonstrated many times in the Cold War -- off Lebanon and in the Formosa Straits, to take two outstanding examples -- a capacity to deal effectively with crisis.

"Navy Day went almost unnoticed Saturday while Task Force 136 guarded the sea approaches to Cuba. But the nation's gratitude to its sea arm, and its satisfaction in its control of the seas, makes every day of this continuing crisis a Navy Day."

Let me repeat a part of the story of the Quarantine Force.

I relieved Admiral Jack Taylor as Commander Second Fleet on Saturday, October 20. I spent the rest of that weekend with Admiral Dennison at his headquarters and in the Pentagon.

On Monday morning at 0830 I held a conference of commanding officers and unit commanders of cruisers, destroyers and escort ships based in Norfolk. Admiral Allen held a similar conference in Charleston with commanders of his destroyers there. These captains were informed for the first time that the President would make an address to the nation that evening, that their ships were being assigned to the Quarantine Force and that they were to sail that day for an indefinite period. Some of these ships had recently returned from the Sixth Fleet in the Mediterranean and had many men on vacation. Not one Captain expressed any opposition to being directed to sail on short notice. They all went about their business of recalling men on leave in the local Tidewater area, of loading urgently needed supplies and equipment and of getting ready. Some ships who had large numbers of men on leave borrowed men from ships undergoing major overhaul in the shipyard. The general consensus was to the effect that they were privileged to serve their country in a time of crisis and to be able to contribute to the attainment of our national objectives. You could have been proud of them; I was.

The President did make his speech on that memorable Monday evening, the ships did sail on schedule on that same evening, the President's quarantine proclamation was signed the next day, Tuesday, to be effective on Wednesday morning; and after a 27-knot speed of advance, ships were on station, on time, on the quarantine line ready to carry out their orders.

During the next month the Quarantine Force intercepted Soviet and Communist Bloc ships and ships under charter to the Soviet Government headed for Cuba, and intercepted and photographed Soviet ships leaving Cuba.

In general the ships that were stopped were cooperative. There were no unpleasant incidents that adversely affected the accomplishment of our mission. This, I believe, reflects favorably on the caliber of the Masters of the merchantmen flying the flags of many countries, including the Soviet Union, and also is a tribute to the awareness of our officers and men of the U. S. Navy of the sensitive nature of their mission. Let me relate a few examples —

The decision was made by the U. S. government that a boarding party should inspect the Lebanese freighter MARUCLA. The destroyer JOHN R. PIERCE made the intercept just after dark. Since boarding under any conditions would be tricky, and inspection during darkness only partially effective at best, it was decided to postpone boarding until daylight. A nearby destroyer, JOSEPH P. KENNEDY, JR., with a division commander embarked, was ordered to join PIERCE. The boarding party included the Executive Officers of both destroyers. The men were dressed in their Dress Whites, were unarmed, and presented a smart military appearance. The inspection was conducted smartly and effectively. No prohibited cargoes were found and the ship was cleared to proceed. There was no hostility or personal antipathy in evidence. There were smiles, greetings, and some handshakes.

In order to take good photographs, intercepting ships necessarily had to approach quite close to the Merchantmen; sometimes possibly alarmingly so. The destroyer BIDDLE came close to the Soviet ship KOMSOVOL carrying missiles out of Cuba, with the Soviet ship sounding the danger signal by several short blasts on his whistle. The destroyer maintained his close position until the pictures were taken. They were good. Initially the KOMSOVOL Master spoke over voice radio in poor but understandable English. A U. S. Naval officer in BIDDLE replied in Russian. The Master's next message was in Russian with the BIDDLE replying in English. This change of language repeated itself several times, apparently enjoyed by both. Captain Roth of the BIDDLE invited the Soviet Master to come aboard for lunch. After a long silence the Master replied that he had a previous commitment.

When NEWPORT NEWS intercepted the Soviet tanker POLZONOV, good morning messages, using signal flags and the International Code, were exchanged. Voice communications were established with English language being spoken. The Soviet Master expressed sympathy in the death of Eleanor Roosevelt. When asked to uncover the missiles on deck, he stated that he had been intercepted by a U. S. warship on the previous day and had been cleared, but without delay he proceeded to remove part of the tarpaulins, exposing missile cases to view. When the NEWPORT NEWS helicopter passed close over the ship with passengers in the helo hanging out of the doors taking pictures, many of the more than 50 young men on deck waved greetings. Most of these men looked to be of college age and were dressed either in sport shirts and slacks or in shorts with no shirts. They were nice looking with good physiques, looking not unlike our own sailormen. In departing NEWPORT NEWS sent: "WISH YOU GOOD SAILING ON YOUR TRIP HOME. GOODBYE AND GOOD LUCK." The POLZONOV replied, "THANKS TO YOU. GOODBYE."

The WASP intercepted the Soviet ship ALAPAYEVSK. Communications were good. The U. S. officer in the helicopter over the ship spoke in Russian, with the Soviets replying in good English. There were about 200 young men on deck, many not wearing shirts. They appeared friendly and almost jubilant. Perhaps they were missile crews happy to be going home. The helo hovered over the ship twice. There was much waving of hands in greeting. Captain Middleton, the Chief of Staff to Admiral Bulo, was in the helicopter, took off his tie clasp and lowered it on a line to the deck as a gesture of good will. A short time later the helo was motioned over the ship by the men on deck and, when a line was lowered, a gift of a bottle of vodka was attached. I'm reluctant to tell this story, since if I'm asked what happened to the vodka on board a dry ship of the Quarantine Force I must admit I don't know.

I believe history will acknowledge that the Quarantine Force was effective in accomplishing the tasks assigned.

As you know, our tasks were made easier by the decision of the Soviet government to respect the quarantine and to turn back many of their ships headed for Cuba.

No one could guess what the reaction of the Soviet government would be, so the United States forces had to be prepared for general war, for possible Soviet reprisal actions in Berlin or South Vietnam, or for any combination of offensive communist moves. While Task Force 136, the Quarantine Force under my command, was doing its assigned job, there were other powerful military forces in position of immediate readiness.

U. S. Navy forces included Task Force 135, consisting of two powerful attack carrier groups centered around the nuclear-powered ENTERPRISE and the USS INDEPENDENCE, both groups with their own destroyer screens and logistic resupply ships. These groups operated to the South of Cuba.

The Amphibious Force loaded the U. S. Marines of the Fleet Marine Force of the Atlantic Fleet and remained at sea. This landing force was augmented by a powerful brigade from the Fleet Marine Force based in Southern California.

As you know, wives and children were evacuated from our base at Guantanamo Bay, but the total base population was swelled by strong U. S. Marine defensive units.

U. S. Marine aircraft were positioned within striking distance.

Admiral Whitey Taylor's Anti-Submarine Warfare force put up on a maximum effort both to conduct ASW and also to locate and track Soviet merchantmen. These forces detected Soviet submarines and maintained contact until submarine exhaustion, forcing the subs to surface to recharge batteries. The Navy patrol aircraft, assisted by SAC aircraft, maintained surveillance over the broad ocean areas between Europe and Cuba and reported locations and movements of Bloc shipping, thereby making my job easier.

The U. S. Air Force increased the alert measures for the strategic retaliatory force and positioned tactical aircraft at bases in Florida within striking distance.

As you also know, we increased our surveillance effort, using U. S. Air Force and U. S. Navy aircraft. The President awarded medals to many of these pilots. Some U. S. Army forces were moved to staging areas and much Army equipment was prepositioned.

As I have indicated, this was a big operation, involving large forces. My staff tells me that 63 ships at one time or another participated in the Quarantine Force alone, and that 183 ships were at sea in the Atlantic and the Caribbean during the operation. Over 33,000 marines and large numbers of army and air force personnel were displaced from home bases.

The Navy maintained a posture of readiness for "limited and general war" objectives." Admiral Dennison as the Commander in Chief of the Atlantic Command could schedule his component Army, Navy and Air Force forces to fulfill any commitments required. It would seem improbable that these readiness measures went unnoticed in the Kremlin.

An international aspect was provided by Task Force 137, a force charged with establishment of a quarantine line between Puerto Rico and the northern coast of South America. As you remember, there was convened in Washington on October 23, the day after the President's report to the Nation, an urgent meeting of the Council of the Organization of American States and the free nations of the Western Hemisphere, acting collectively under the Rio Treaty, and they were unanimous in strong action to meet the Soviet threat. The Council of the OAS, in its resolution of October 23, called for the immediate dismantling and withdrawal from Cuba of all missiles and other weapons with offensive capability and recommended that the member states take all measures to ensure that the Government of Cuba cannot continue to receive from the Sino-Soviet powers military material and related supplies which may threaten the peace and security of the Continent and to prevent the missiles in Cuba with offensive capability from ever becoming an active threat to the peace and security of the Continent. The OAS stand was another key factor in inducing the Soviet Union to withdraw its weapons from Cuba. The Rio Treaty and all other collective arrangements of the Inter-American system remain in full force.

As a result of this action, the majority of the free states of the Western Hemisphere agreed to make contributions toward the attainment of these goals. Argentina immediately dispatched at maximum speed two destroyers. Venezuela provided two ships, as did the Dominican Republic. These six destroyer types plus the U.S. destroyer MULLINNIX formed Task Force 137 under the command of Admiral Tyree.

Now, what were the immediate Results of these actions? First, U. S. strength and firmness resulted in the USSR backing down on its program of arming Cuba. The Soviet Union, with the complicity and acquiescence of the Cuban Communist regime, had posed a threat to the peace and security of the Western Hemisphere and had attempted to upset the balance of power by secretly placing offensive weapons systems in Cuba with capacity to wreak nuclear havoc on large areas of North, Central and South America. The U. S. acted calmly and forcefully but left room for a solution short of war, and the Soviet Union demonstrated its respect for U. S. power.

Second, Castro proved that he is not a free agent, but a puppet of the USSR. The Cuban people, who had already lost their freedom, now saw that their government had lost its independence. Cuba is a communist outpost in the hemisphere.

The offensive weapons were installed to serve Soviet purposes; they were controlled by the Soviets; they were removed by the Soviets as a result of negotiations between the U.S. and the USSR. At one time Castro claimed the IL-28 bombers were Cuban property, he had to reverse himself completely on this point.

Third, U. S. statesmanship and power won out. By mounting a limited quarantine the U.S. displayed its traditional respect for human life and values. The quarantine was intended to keep out offensive weapons only, and this limited objective was attained.

Fourth, The OAS found the Cuban communist regime to be "incompatible with the principles and objectives of the Inter-American system". The OAS was greatly strengthened and given new meaning by actions taken as a result of the Cuban crisis.

Fifth, Employment of sea power in this case did not cause escalation of the opposing power struggle into a shooting war and yet it did provide the elements required for success in attaining national objectives.

Sixth, Our principal NATO allies pledged support to the actions taken by the U.S. government and were heartened by the demonstrated willingness of the U.S. to fight if necessary to gain objectives considered to be vital. This crisis tended to strengthen the North Atlantic Treaty Organization.

Seventh, Negotiations were largely carried out within the form and framework of the United Nations. The Secretary General, Mr. U Thant, conducted negotiations in UN headquarters in New York and in Havana. It is noteworthy that President Kennedy in his State of the Union message at the outset of 1963 stated that one of the four platforms for progress in international affairs is full and continued support of the United Nations. He stated, "Today the United Nations is primarily the protector of the small and the weak, and a safety valve for the strong. Tomorrow it can form the framework for a world of law".

Eighth, A new rule of the international law of the sea has come into being and has been accepted by all principal states. Traditionally and in accordance with international law a BLOCKADE is an act of war, designed to force an enemy state to comply with the will of a blockading country. In contrast, a QUARANTINE is a selective effort to deal with a specific threat to peace. The Cuban Quarantine was imposed in accordance with the resolution of the Council of the OAS and the terms of the Rio Treaty. The Quarantine was respected by all states, including the USSR and will henceforth be a part of the code we call international law.

Another immediate result is the increased level of command and control of military operations from Washington. There was a time when military affairs were the primary if not the sole concern of generals and admirals. This period ended with the beginning of World War I, which ushered in what has been described as the totalitarianization of war. The necessity for coordinating the whole resources of a nation toward a specific objective has become too vast to be handled effectively by one class of leaders. It has become the responsibility of the whole people and the government. As Clemenceau put it in the First World War "war is much too serious a matter to be entrusted to Generals."

During the recent Cuban crisis, I, as Commander of the Quarantine Force, was in direct communication by telephone (High Command Net) with Admiral Dennison in Norfolk and with the office of the Chief of Naval Operations in Washington. What happened on the quarantine line influenced reactions in Moscow, in the United Nations, and in the Organization of American States.

Admiral Anderson has this to say:

"During recent weeks I have been privileged to be associated with the events which have occupied the minds, the attention, and the prayers of Americans and many others in other countries of the world. Never before have I been so impressed with the intimate relationship between the application of military power and the political power and policy of our country. Twice each day, as a member of the Joint Chiefs of Staff, I met with my colleagues; we've met daily with the Secretary of Defense and on occasion with higher officials of our Government and with the President of the United States. I can attest to you the great devotion of every single one of those officials and officers, their dedication to your welfare, to the preservation of the honor and the security of the United States, the things which we hold dear."

In attempting to analyze long range effects of the Cuban crisis, I would like to limit my thoughts to three principal subjects and mention each only briefly:

FIRST -- The Cuban problem is not over but events to date seem to have had a disrupting influence to the solidarity of the Communist Bloc. Withdrawal of offensive weapons from Cuba has not solved the problem of the presence in Cuba of a Communist dictatorship or the use of Cuba as a base for Communist subversion and aggression. The continued presence in Cuba of about 17,000

Soviet military personnel casts a continuing intervention of foreign military power in this hemisphere. In his December 29 speech at Miami to Cuban refugees, the President said:

> "It is the strongest wish of the people of this country as well as the people in this hemisphere that Cuba shall one day be free again."

While the alliances within the free world, and particularly the NATO and OAS alliances, have been strengthened, there seems to be growing evidences of rifts between Communist China and the Kremlin and some increased disaffection between communist parties in undeveloped nations and their masters in the USSR. South and Central American nations in particular are seeming to take increased measures to control communist minorities in their countries. Mr. Khrushchev seems to be a little more amenable toward attempting to reach some solutions, albeit possibly temporary ones, with the West. This does not mean that the Cold War is over. We must continue to maintain our guard and our strength.

SECOND -- The military forces of the United States demonstrated their immediate readiness to accomplish missions and objectives prescribed by the President and to meet the commitments necessary to maintain our free way of life. Again I quote Admiral Anderson:

> "The entire operation has been a magnificent testimonial not only to the senior leaders of our Government, but also to those commanders and commanding officers at lower levels who were so quickly able to move their troops -- large number of troops -- their ships -- many ships -- and their aircraft of many types in position to carry out lengthy, tedious, and often very sensitive operations with a high degree of leadership, professional competence, courage, and diplomatic skill."

I would like to add that the men in the ships were superb. During the period in which we were short-handed as a result of sailing with reduced numbers of men on board, individuals had to double-up on watches and be on duty many long hours every day. I have never known morale in the services to be higher. As indicated earlier, there was an underlying feeling of pride in serving their country and of contributing to the attainment of national objectives by each and every one on board the ships of the Quarantine Force. I am told by my Army and Air Force compatriots that this high morale and dedication of purpose was also in evidence in their forces.

The THIRD and final general conclusion pertains to sea power. An editorial in the Charleston, South Carolina newspaper, "The News and Courier" of December 18th states, and I quote:

> "Thinking people in the country should try to make their own assessment of the secret of national power. They pay for that power by means of taxes.
>
> "Perhaps the key lesson of the Cuban crisis is that sea power remains the dominant force in world affairs.

"A powerful case can be presented to show that control of the oceans is the deciding factor in the Cold War. This truth should not be overlooked by citizens whose security is being protected at sea."

By a judicious combination of its multi-purpose units, sea power is able to apply measured force which can cope with provocative situations as circumstances dictate. No greater force need be employed than is necessary to achieve the objective. As proven in the Cuban crisis employment of sea power is less likely to cause escalation of limited or cold war. I agree with the statement made by Admiral Anderson that "the versatility, the flexibility, the mobility and, above all, the readiness and spirit of our Navy are indeed assets of which I believe our country can be justly proud."

And, in conclusion, one final thought: U.S. strength and firmness in the Cuban crisis won out. We should never forget the advice given us by President Theodore Roosevelt when he said:

"If we stand idly by ... if we shrink from hard contests where men must win at hazard of their lives and at risk of all they hold dear, then the bolder and stronger people will pass us by and will win for themselves the domination of the world."

ADDRESS TO BE GIVEN AT A RESERVE OFFICERS' ASSOCIATION DINNER, OKLAHOMA CITY, OKLAHOMA, BY ADMIRAL ALFRED G. WARD, U. S. NAVY, U. S. REPRESENTATIVE TO THE MILITARY COMMITTEE, NORTH ATLANTIC TREATY ORGANIZATION ON SATURDAY, 18 MARCH 1967

Members of the Reserve Officers' Association, Members of the Navy League, and Honored Guests:

I have been most pleased with my visit here in your fine city for the past two days. It has given me another splendid opportunity to renew my acquaintances in this part of our country and yesterday I had the privilege of talking with the members of the Chamber of Commerce about the United States Navy. When I received the invitation to address you tonight, I happened to be reading a current News magazine which featured an article on the overwhelming might of America. I was both surprised by and proud of the statistics which were outlined. The power which this country possesses, I believe, is worth reviewing because, the military power I will discuss is but a small portion of the greatness of America.

The United States has only 7 percent of the earth's surface and less than 6 percent of the world's population, yet against this small percentage, we have one-third of the total output of production of all goods and services; we have one out of every three college students in the world; we have an income per person which is 40 percent higher than our nearest competitor Sweden; and the average Russian earns 60 percent less than the average American. In terms of military might the article concluded, we have more men under arms than any other nation; the best equipped Air Force on earth; four times the long-range missile force as that of Russia; and as my friends in your Chamber of Commerce heard yesterday, we have the world's greatest Navy and the only major fleet of aircraft carriers.

Statistically then, the power of America is awesome. We have the productive capacity, natural resources, and technology to remain great. Our vast machinery runs on oil from this fine state, it is constructed of metals refined in our eastern states, it is cared for by the bright students from universities throughout the country, and it is transported by the world's leading civil aviation, railroad, and trucking corporations. Yet for all of these statistics and for all of this power; this is not my theme tonight. Rather it is my intention to speak to you of the strength of this country in the terms of her greatest asset. I shall be talking to you of the men and women of America, and specifically of the men and women of our Armed Forces. I hope to convey in some measure the dedication which I have noted throughout my career, and I hope to reassure you that our young men and women today measure up in every respect with the men and women who pioneered, industrialized, and fought for our nation in the past. For it is the men and women from Oklahoma City, from other cities and villages in Oklahoma, from other States in these United States and from all of the free world who are the most important assets with whom we join in the battle against those who would destroy our democracy.

But I will speak first of a subtle change in the minds of Americans regarding our concept of war. For although those of us here today recognize the importance of our serviceman, our Reserve Force, and our veteran, I find that in these days of a continuing need for strong Armed Forces--too often our military must be composed of "unsung" heroes who have gone to war unaccompanied by national acclaim. Your sons in the Service from the Berlin Wall to the

Vietnamese rice paddies don't know the burst of patriotic fever that the Revolutionary knew when he heard "Yankee Doodle" - nor the comfort of the Civil War Anthem - "The Battle Hymn of the Republic". Most of us can remember with a surge of pride George M. Cohan's World War One hit: "Over There". Even the mechanized scope of World War Two could inspire a song or two which filled the needs of a man in the Pacific or on the Beach of Normandy - remember - "Praise the Lord and Pass the Ammunition", or sentimentally - "The White Cliffs of Dover"?

No song came from the War in Korea. There was no tune appropriate to arouse the nation during the Cuban Missile

Crisis. It seems incongruous to associate Massive Nuclear Weapons with a musical theme. Even though the United States now has over three hundred thousan military ashore in Vietnam and some sixty thousand more in the fleet just off the coast, supporting Vietnam operations, there is no widely recognized song identified with this conflict.

Songs are a small point I know - but they tell a significant story - the nature of conflict today is unlike the romantic conflicts of centuries past. So, too, is our display of patriotic emotion. The challenges to democracy now are world-wide, aggravating, frustrating and continual. And although the surge of public emotion is not as apparent as it has been before, in my view, patriotism in America today is greater than ever. It has to be, because we are facing a challenge which requires the largest peacetime Armed Forces in our history. These forces require our continuing support year after year. Thus our patriotism has changed from a periodic demonstrative patriotism to quiet, patient patriotism, shared the world over by a greater number of Americans than ever before. Today's serviceman quietly serves all year long in hardship, danger, and loneliness. Within this background, then, let me speak of our military capabilities.

The United States today possesses the mightiest military power in the whole of human history. Statistics alone are not good to tell you the story of our military capabilities; but some statistics are meaningful. Right this minute more than three million three hundred thousand Americans are on active military duty. Seven out of every eight of these are volunteers. Behind this active duty force stands another four million Reserves all of whom are volunteers. Concerning this Reserve force, I believe if we are successful in bringing the Vietnam crisis to a conclusion without a general call-up of Reserves, the uninformed may seize upon this as a reason to reduce the support for the Reserves. You and I know that when regular forces are heavily committed, the need for strong and ready reserves becomes even more important. It may be overlooked that Reserves *were* ready if additional contingencies arose. Alert and articulate people of knowledge must make the general public aware of these fundamental points.

You might reasonably ask is there a sensible plan or an objective in the building of U.S. military force. I believe there are two principles which guide us. The first is to develop that force structure necessary to support U.S. foreign policy, and the second, is to procure and operate this force at the lowest possible cost. We have been attentive in recent years to these two basic principles, and our strides forward are well worth mentioning. From 1960 to 1965 the United States achieved a 45 percent increase in combat ready Army Divisions; a 100 percent increase in airlift capability; a 51 percent increase in Air Force Fighter Squadrons; a 100 percent increase in Naval ship construction to modernize our fleet; a 1000 percent increase in the Special Forces trained to combat world-wide counter insurgency. These increases you will notice were in our conventional forces. At the same time we have not neglected our nuclear capability. In fact, we have achieved a 200 percent increase in the number of nuclear warheads and the total megatonnage of our strategic alert forces. And we have achieved a 100 percent increase in the number of tactical nuclear weapons in Western Europe since 1961.

What I think we all know, is that since World War Two we in this country have taken upon our shoulders the most serious task of guarding the precious concepts of liberty and freedom throughout the world. We are a strong nation. As a strong nation it is our responsibility to lead. We must lead willingly and without compromise in order that the threats posed by Communism to smaller and less affluent nations will not be so great as to force these nations to give up their fight.

Our willingness to deter Communism has been demonstrated in Berlin, the middle east, Latin America and Southeast Asia, where each crisis required a different level of force. Therefore, each attests in a different way to the wisdom of the system which we have adopted for the management of our Armed Forces. I have used the word management advisedly since as I am sure the business leaders here tonight know the management of the United States Armed Forces require efficiency, skill and economy. It is important that we have the communications and transportation to permit us to employ the strength which we possess at the right time, at the right place - and with a minimum of warning. I think that an analysis of our military and quasi military engagements in the past two decades shows clearly that we can say that we are prepared. A closer examination will also show that the flexibility in our response is indicative of techniques (some of which are old and others which are new) are appropriate to the situation and are sensitive to the changing requirements of the politico military situation in the world.

The strength of U.S. military forces of course contributes in a large measure to the real strength of world-wide treaty organizations. In Europe a strong NATO is and has been the deterrent. Between World War Two and 1949 ten nations and six hundred million people fell under

Communist domination. With the establishment of NATO in 1949 not one foot of European soil has been lost to the Free World. NATO today, in spite of recent French actions, remains united in its determination to resist Communist domination. In the Far East the commitment of Armed Forces to the struggle in Vietnam includes forces from our Pacific Allies. I know that you, as I, have been gratified by recent renewed pledges of our Asian Allies that in Asia, as elsewhere in the world, the American fighting man will stand shoulder to shoulder with men of those countries which border the Communists.

But I am speaking tonight in the terms of primary sources of the power of the United States -- the youth of our country and the dedication of our citizens. Our future lies in a continuation of the philosophies which have produced our current capabilities. We are, in the military, constantly aware of the great technological change which has engulfed our country. But we are equally aware that the most complex piece of equipment requires a trained technician who is both knowledgeable and interested. Many of today's technicians are barely out of their teens. They come to us from your homes endowed with the knowledge and interest which you have in keeping the current position of the United States as the mightiest military power in history. Thus in a large sense the future goals of our country remain in the hands of young men and young women whom you have reared, educated and taught the value and pride in being an American.

I am sure that many of us, at one time, questioned the toughness of our young people. We wondered if the long hair, the tight breeches, the Beatle craze reflected a change in the fibre of young Americans. We wondered, too, if the trouble raisers, the recalcitrants against any discipline and even against accepted rules of conduct, if these malconformists represented a completely new breed of men. We no longer have to be concerned with young America. Our young men have been tested against the appalling terrain in Vietnam, against a way of living completely foreign to them, against obstacles and against enemies who fight savagely and without restraint. Our young men have proven their physical and moral stamina! Without hurrah they have stood the test!

I have been speaking of the tremendous capability present in our Armed Forces and I have tried to speak of this capability in the terms of the human being. We have found our military manpower in the two decades since World War Two to be adequate, and to be well enough organized to achieve our goals. Traditionally, most of the members of our Armed Forces have been private citizens - called to arms. This has changed somewhat, but nevertheless to the professional military as well as to the citizen soldier, primary considerations remain home, family, church, business, friends and essential to all of these, freedom. No-one wants to make war; but no American will permit the loss of those personal freedoms so vital to the strength of his country. If I can ask that you remember but one thing from my visit, it is to remember that I have found in all of my years of service and I find today that the young men and young women who comprise our military force are aware of their responsibilities They are dedicated to achieving victory for the United States and for the Free World. This is the same dedication that has inspired victory since 1776. I should like to close by quoting from the first American to escape from Viet Cong imprisonment. This was a young Navy flier who, after being shot down, survived, unarmed through days of terrifying experiences in the jungles of Vietnam - constantly pursued. I think that this young man, when interviewed, was not consciously aware of Patrick Henry's famous declaration of "Give me liberty or give me death"; yet, he spoke in the spirit of youth and citizen dedication which I have been describing when he said:

"You really don't know what freedom is until you have had to escape from

Communist captivity. I had rather die free in the bushes than die in the Communist's hands."

- The End -

Mayor Braman,
MEMBERS OF THE CHAMBER OF COMMERCE,
~~MEDAL OF HONOR WINNERS~~, HONORED
GUESTS:

IT IS ALWAYS GOOD TO BE BACK WITH MY MANY FRIENDS HERE IN SEATTLE. THROUGH THE YEARS I HAVE WATCHED THIS FINE PORT CITY GROW AND PROSPER AND I HAVE SAILED IN AND OUT OF YOUR FINE HARBOR MANY TIMES; SO, I KNOW THAT YOUR CITY HAS SERVED OUR NATION WELL IN WAR AND IN PEACE. AND I KNOW THE IMPORTANCE OF THE SEATTLE AREA TO OUR CURRENT EFFORTS IN VIETNAM.
BECAUSE OF YOUR CONTINUED INTEREST IN THE STRENGTH OF OUR UNITED STATES I THINK THAT THIS AUDIENCE MIGHT BE

INTERESTED AS I WAS IN A RECENT NEWS MAGAZINE ARTICLE WHICH DISCUSSED THE OVERWHELMING MIGHT OF AMERICA. THE OVER-ALL POWER WHICH THIS COUNTRY POSSESSES IS WORTH REVIEWING BECAUSE I PLAN TO TALK ABOUT MILITARY POWER BUT AS THIS ARTICLE CLEARLY POINTS OUT MILITARY POWER IS BUT A SMALL PORTION OF THE OVER-ALL GREATNESS OF AMERICA.

THE UNITED STATES HAS ONLY SEVEN PER CENT OF THE EARTH'S SURFACE AND

AND LESS THAN SIX PER CENT OF THE WORLD'S POPULATION, YET AGAINST THIS SMALL PERCENTAGE, WE HAVE ONE-THIRD OF THE TOTAL OUTPUT OF PRODUCTION OF ALL GOODS AND SERVICES; WE HAVE ONE OUT OF EVERY THREE COLLEGE STUDENTS IN THE WORLD; WE HAVE AN INCOME PER PERSON WHICH IS FORTY PER CENT HIGHER THAN OUR NEAREST COMPETITOR SWEDEN; AND THE AVERAGE RUSSIAN EARNS SIXTY PER CENT LESS THAN THE AVERAGE AMERICAN. IN TERMS OF MILITARY MIGHT, THE ARTICLE CONCLUDED, WE HAVE MORE MEN UNDER ARMS THAN ANY OTHER NATION; THE BEST EQUIPPED AIR FORCE ON EARTH; FOUR TIMES THE LONG-RANGE MISSILE FORCE AS THAT OF RUSSIA; AND I AM PLEASED TO REPORT WE HAVE THE WORLD'S GREATEST NAVY

AND THE ONLY MAJOR FLEET OF AIRCRAFT CARRIERS.

STATISTICALLY THEN, THE POWER OF AMERICA IS AWESOME. WE HAVE THE PRODUCTIVE CAPACITY, NATURAL RESOURCES, AND TECHNOLOGY TO REMAIN GREAT. OUR VAST MACHINERY IS DEVELOPED HERE IN THIS FINE STATE FROM METALS REFINED IN OUR EASTERN STATES; IT IS CARED FOR BY THE BRIGHT STUDENTS FROM UNIVERSITIES THROUGHOUT OUR COUNTRY, AND IT IS TRANSPORTED BY THE WORLD'S LEADING CIVIL AVIATION, RAILROAD, AND TRUCKING CORPORATIONS. YET FOR ALL OF THESE STATISTICS AND FOR ALL OF THIS POWER; THIS IS NOT MY THEME TODAY. RATHER IT IS MY INTENTION TO SPEAK TO YOU OF THE

STRENGTH OF THIS COUNTRY IN THE TERMS OF HER GREATEST ASSET. I SHALL BE TALKING TO YOU OF THE MEN AND WOMEN OF AMERICA, AND SPECIFICALLY OF THE MEN AND WOMEN OF OUR ARMED FORCES WHOM YOU HONOR THIS WEEK. I HOPE TO CONVEY IN SOME MEASURE THE DEDICATION WHICH I HAVE NOTED THROUGHOUT MY CAREER, AND I HOPE TO REASSURE YOU THAT OUR YOUNG MEN AND WOMEN TODAY MEASURE UP IN EVERY RESPECT WITH THE MEN AND WOMEN WHO PIONEERED, INDUSTRIALIZED, AND FOUGHT FOR OUR NATION IN THE PAST.

BUT I WILL SPEAK FIRST OF A SUBTLE CHANGE IN THE MINDS OF AMERICANS REGARDING OUR CONCEPT OF WAR. FOR ALTHOUGH YOUR ARMED FORCES WEEK ENTHUSIASM ~~MEMORIAL TO MEDAL OF HONOR WINNERS~~

CONFIRMS SEATTLE's UNUSUALLY FINE RECOGNITION OF OUR SERVICEMAN AND OUR VETERAN, I FIND THAT IN THESE DAYS OF A CONTINUING NEED FOR STRONG ARMED FORCES — TOO OFTEN OUR MILITARY MUST BE COMPOSED OF "UNSUNG" HEROES WHO HAVE GONE TO WAR UNACCOMPANIED BY NATIONAL ACCLAIM. OUR YOUNGSTERS IN THE SERVICE FROM THE BERLIN WALL TO THE VIETNAMESE RICE PADDIES DON'T REALLY KNOW THE BURST OF PATRIOTIC FEVER THAT THE REVOLUTIONARY KNEW WHEN HE HEARD "YANKEE DOODLE" — NOR THE COMFORT OF THE CIVIL WAR ANTHEM — "THE BATTLE HYMN OF THE REPUBLIC". MOST OF US CAN REMEMBER WITH A SURGE OF PRIDE GEORGE M. COHAN's WORLD WAR ONE HIT "OVER THERE". EVEN THE MECHANIZED SCOPE OF WORLD WAR TWO COULD INSPIRE A SONG OR

TWO. THOSE IN THE PACIFIC REMEMBER — "PRAISE THE LORD AND PASS THE AMMUNITION". ON THE BEACH AT NORMANDY THE SONG WAS — "THE WHITE CLIFFS OF DOVER".

NO SONG CAME FROM THE WAR IN KOREA. THERE WAS NO TUNE APPROPRIATE TO AROUSE THIS NATION DURING THE CUBAN MISSILE CRISIS. IT SEEMS INCONGRUOUS TO ASSOCIATE MASSIVE NUCLEAR WEAPONS WITH A MUSICAL THEME. AND EVEN NOW WHEN THE UNITED STATES HAS OVER FOUR HUNDRED THOUSAND MILITARY ASHORE IN VIETNAM AND SOME SEVENTY-FIVE THOUSAND MORE IN THE FLEET SUPPORTING VIETNAM OPERATIONS, THERE IS NO WIDELY RECOGNIZED SONG IDENTIFIED WITH THIS CONFLICT.

SONGS ARE A SMALL POINT I KNOW — BUT THEY TELL A SIGNIFICANT STORY — THE NATURE OF CONFLICT TODAY IS UNLIKE THE ROMANTIC CONFLICTS OF CENTURIES PAST. SO, TOO, IS OUR DISPLAY OF PATRIOTIC EMOTION. THE CHALLENGES TO DEMOCRACY NOW ARE WORLD-WIDE, AGGRAVATING, FRUSTRATING AND CONTINUAL. AND ALTHOUGH THE SURGE OF PUBLIC EMOTION IS NOT AS APPARENT AS IT HAS BEEN BEFORE, IN MY VIEW, PATRIOTISM IN AMERICA TODAY IS GREATER THAN EVER. IT HAS TO BE, BECAUSE WE ARE FACING A CHALLENGE WHICH REQUIRES THE LARGEST PEACETIME ARMED FORCES IN OUR HISTORY. THESE FORCES REQUIRE OUR CONTINUING SUPPORT YEAR AFTER YEAR. THUS OUR PATRIOTISM HAS CHANGED FROM A PERIODIC demonstrative patriotism to quiet, patient patriotism, shared the world over by a greater number of Americans than ever before. Today's serviceman quietly serves all year in hardship, danger, and loneliness.

Within this background, then, let me report to you citizens of Seattle of the military capabilities of your nation. The United States today possesses the mightiest military power in the whole of human history. Statistics alone do not tell you the story of our military capabilities; but some statistics are meaningful. Right this minute more than three million three hundred thousand Americans are on active military duty. Seven out of every eight of these are

VOLUNTEERS. BEHIND THIS ACTIVE DUTY FORCE STANDS ANOTHER FOUR MILLION RESERVES ALL OF WHOM ARE VOLUNTEERS.

WITH THIS LARGE COMMITMENT, YOU MIGHT REASONABLY ASK IS THERE A SENSIBLE PLAN OR AN OBJECTIVE IN THE BUILDING OF U.S. MILITARY FORCE. I BELIEVE THERE ARE TWO PRINCIPLES WHICH GUIDE US. THE FIRST IS TO DEVELOP THAT FORCE STRUCTURE NECESSARY TO SUPPORT U.S. FOREIGN POLICY, AND THE SECOND, IS TO PROCURE AND OPERATE THIS FORCE AT THE LOWEST POSSIBLE COST. WE HAVE BEEN ATTENTIVE IN RECENT YEARS TO THESE TWO BASIC PRINCIPLES, AND OUR STRIDES FORWARD ARE WELL WORTH MENTIONING. FROM 1960 TO 1965 THE UNITED STATES ACHIEVED A FORTY-FIVE PER CENT INCREASE IN COMBAT READY

ARMY DIVISIONS; A ONE HUNDRED PER CENT INCREASE IN AIRLIFT CAPABILITY; A FIFTY-ONE PER CENT INCREASE IN AIR FORCE FIGHTER SQUADRONS; A ONE HUNDRED PER CENT INCREASE IN NAVAL SHIP CONSTRUCTION TO MODERNIZE OUR FLEET; A ONE THOUSAND PER CENT INCREASE IN THE SPECIAL FORCES TRAINED TO COMBAT WORLD-WIDE COUNTER INSURGENCY. THESE INCREASES YOU WILL NOTICE WERE IN OUR CONVENTIONAL FORCES. AT THE SAME TIME WE HAVE NOT NEGLECTED OUR NUCLEAR CAPABILITY. IN FACT, WE HAVE ACHIEVED A TWO HUNDRED PER CENT INCREASE IN THE NUMBER OF NUCLEAR WARHEADS AND THE TOTAL MEGATONNAGE OF OUR STRATEGIC ALERT FORCES. AND WE HAVE ACHIEVED A ONE HUNDRED PER CENT INCREASE IN THE NUMBER OF TACTICAL NUCLEAR

WEAPONS IN WESTERN EUROPE SINCE 1961.

WHAT I THINK WE ALL KNOW, IS THAT SINCE WORLD WAR TWO WE IN THIS COUNTRY HAVE TAKEN UPON OUR SHOULDERS THE MOST SERIOUS TASK OF GUARDING THE PRECIOUS CONCEPTS OF LIBERTY AND FREEDOM THROUGHOUT THE WORLD. WE ARE A STRONG NATION. AS A STRONG NATION IT IS OUR RESPONSIBILITY TO LEAD. WE MUST LEAD WILLINGLY AND WITHOUT COMPROMISE IN ORDER THAT THE THREATS POSED BY COMMUNISM TO SMALLER AND LESS AFFLUENT NATIONS WILL NOT BE SO GREAT AS TO FORCE THESE NATIONS TO GIVE UP THEIR FIGHT.

OUR WILLINGNESS TO DETER COMMUNISM HAS BEEN DEMONSTRATED IN BERLIN, THE MIDDLE EAST, LATIN AMERICA AND SOUTHEAST

ASIA, WHERE EACH CRISIS REQUIRED A DIFFERENT LEVEL OF FORCE. THEREFORE, EACH ATTESTS IN A DIFFERENT WAY TO THE WISDOM OF THE SYSTEM WHICH WE HAVE ADOPTED FOR THE MANAGEMENT OF OUR ARMED FORCES. I HAVE USED THE WORD MANAGEMENT ADVISEDLY SINCE AS I AM SURE THE BUSINESS LEADERS HERE TODAY KNOW, THE MANAGEMENT OF THE UNITED STATES ARMED FORCES REQUIRES EFFICIENCY, SKILL AND ECONOMY. IT IS IMPORTANT THAT WE HAVE THE PRODUCTIVE CAPACITY, COMMUNICATIONS AND TRANSPORTATION TO PERMIT US TO EMPLOY THE STRENGTH WHICH WE POSSESS AT THE RIGHT TIME, AT THE RIGHT PLACE - OFTEN WITH A MINIMUM OF WARNING. I THINK THAT AN ANALYSIS OF

OUR MILITARY AND QUASI MILITARY ENGAGEMENTS IN THE PAST TWO DECADES SHOWS CLEARLY THAT WE CAN SAY THAT WE ARE PREPARED. A CLOSER EXAMINATION WILL ALSO SHOW THAT THE FLEXIBILITY IN OUR RESPONSE IS INDICATIVE OF TECHNIQUES (SOME OF WHICH ARE OLD AND OTHERS WHICH ARE NEW) WHICH ARE APPROPRIATE TO THE SITUATION AND ARE SENSITIVE TO THE CHANGING REQUIREMENTS OF THE POLITICO-MILITARY SITUATION IN THE WORLD.

I CAN BEST ILLUSTRATE THIS FLEXIBILITY IF I DESCRIBE BRIEFLY THE ROLE OF YOUR NAVY IN VIETNAM. NAVAL OPERATIONS IN THOSE REMOTE WATERS ARE A CLASSIC EXAMPLE OF HOW THE UNITED STATES CAN AND HAS MADE THE SEAS WORK TO OUR

ADVANTAGE IN FIGHTING AGGRESSION SEVEN THOUSAND MILES FROM OUR SHORE.

OUR FORCES THERE OPERATE ON THE HIGH SEAS DAILY UTILIZING THEIR OWN "BUILT-IN" LOGISTIC SUPPORT. BY THIS I MEAN WE BRING THE "BEANS AND BULLETS" WITH US WHEN WE COME. WE ALSO BRING OUR OWN BLACK OIL WHICH PERMITS US TO STAY ON STATION NIGHT AND DAY OFF THE COAST. IN A MINUTE I'LL DESCRIBE SOME TYPICAL OPERATIONS. BUT WHILE I AM TALKING ABOUT BRINGING OUR OWN "BEANS AND BULLETS", LET ME POINT OUT THAT WE NOT ONLY BRING THE NAVY'S EQUIPMENT BUT, AS A MATTER OF FACT, MORE THAN NINETY-EIGHT PER CENT OF ALL SUPPLIES AND EQUIPMENT WHICH THIS NATION HAS SENT TO VIETNAM HAS COME BY SEA AND THE MAJORITY

OF THE MEN NOW IN VIETNAM HAVE BEEN PUT ASHORE FROM SHIPS.

IT DOES NOT APPEAR YET THAT THIS CAPABILITY TO MAINTAIN OUR PRESENCE FROM THE SEA HAS REQUIRED ANY GREAT CHANGES IN YOUR NAVY. BUT AS THE CHIEF OF NAVAL OPERATIONS, ADMIRAL DAVE McDONALD, HAS RECENTLY POINTED OUT TO THE SENATE ARMED SERVICES COMMITTEE, WE TOO HAVE PERSONNEL PROBLEMS. OUR SHIPS ARE GETTING OLD AND REQUIRE REPLACEMENT AND THESE REAL AND PRESSING NEEDS MUST BE FULFILLED IF WE ARE TO CONTINUE OPERATIONS AT THE CURRENT TEMPO AND AT THE SAME TIME BE FULLY RESPONSIVE TO THE UNKNOWN DEMANDS OF FUTURE COMMITMENTS.

WE HAVE BEEN IN SOUTHEAST ASIAN WATERS FOR A NUMBER OF YEARS AND YOU KNOW THAT WE HAVE HAD ADVISORS IN VIETNAM THROUGHOUT THE DECADE OF THE 1960s. IT WAS IN 1965, HOWEVER, THAT THE VIOLENCE AND FREQUENCY OF COMMUNIST ATTACKS INCREASED SHARPLY. OUR REACTION ON SHORE AND AT SEA WAS TO INCREASE OUR COMMITMENT. OF THE MORE THAN FOUR HUNDRED THOUSAND AMERICANS TODAY IN VIETNAM THERE ARE ABOUT TWENTY-FIVE THOUSAND NAVY AND COAST GUARD PEOPLE AND ABOUT SEVENTY-FIVE THOUSAND MARINES. IN ADDITION OFFSHORE STAND ABOUT ONE HUNDRED AND FORTY SHIPS AND, AS I MENTIONED, SEVENTY-FIVE THOUSAND NAVY MEN. IT IS INTERESTING TO NOTE THAT OF THIS NUMBER APPROXIMATELY FIFTEEN PER CENT

ARE RESERVISTS ON ACTIVE DUTY.

WE CHARACTERIZE NAVAL OPERATIONS IN VIETNAM IN TWO BROAD CATEGORIES - THE DEEP WATER OPERATIONS WHICH WE HAVE ALWAYS CONDUCTED, AND THE SECOND CATEGORY WHICH I WILL CALL COASTAL AND INLAND OPERATIONS OR "MUDDY WATER" OPERATIONS. OUR BLUE WATER PEOPLE OFFSHORE MAINTAIN CONTINUOUS AROUND-THE-CLOCK PRESSURE ON ENEMY LOGISTIC NETWORKS, COMMUNICATIONS AND INFILTRATION ROUTES. OUR PRINCIPAL WEAPON HERE IS TASK FORCE 77 (A NAME MADE FAMOUS DURING IDENTICAL OPERATIONS IN KOREA). THIS FORCE IS NORMALLY COMPRISED OF FIVE ATTACK AIRCRAFT CARRIERS. THE BRAVE YOUNG PILOTS FROM THESE CARRIERS TAKE THE

AIR WAR INTO NORTH VIETNAM AGAINST INTENSE OPPOSITION. THE NORTH VIETNAMESE ARE NOT CENTURIES BEHIND US, THEY ARE NOT ATTACKING OUR AIRCRAFT WITH CROSSBOWS AND RIFLES, THEY ARE USING MODERN ANTI-AIR WEAPONS AND SURFACE-TO-AIR MISSILES SUPPLIED BY THE SOVIETS AND THE CHINESE COMMUNISTS. BUT IT IS OUR NATIONAL POLICY THAT OUR RAIDS WILL BE PLANNED AND EXECUTED WITH PRECISION AND CARE AND THE NAVY PILOTS PARTICIPATING IN THESE RAIDS COMPLETE THEIR DANGEROUS MISSIONS WITH GREATER SKILL AND ACCURACY THAN AT ANY OTHER PERIOD IN THE HISTORY OF AIR WARFARE AND IT IS NOT UNCOMMON FOR A CARRIER BASED PILOT TO FLY ONE HUNDRED AND TWENTY-FIVE OF THESE DANGEROUS

COMBAT MISSIONS IN A SEVEN MONTH TOUR.

NATURALLY, OUR CARRIERS RECEIVE ANTI-SUBMARINE AND ANTI-AIR WARFARE PROTECTION FROM ACCOMPANYING CRUISERS AND DESTROYERS. THESE CRUISERS AND DESTROYERS ALSO PROVIDE GUNFIRE SUPPORT FOR THE FORCES ASHORE. DIRECT FIRE FROM THE SEA TO WITHIN ONE HUNDRED YARDS OF AN INFANTRYMAN IS ROUTINE AND THESE SHELLS COME FROM DESTROYERS AS FAR AS EIGHT OR NINE MILES AWAY. SEVENTH FLEET SHIPS ARE NOW AVERAGING THIRTY THOUSAND ROUNDS FIRED EACH MONTH. FINALLY, THE SHIPS OF OUR DEEP WATER STRIKE FORCE CARRY HELICOPTERS FOR THE PURPOSE OF SAVING OUR DOWNED AVIATORS. I SPOKE RECENTLY WITH THE CAPTAIN OF A

PACIFIC FLEET DESTROYER WHOSE YOUNG HELICOPTER PILOT HAD BEEN RECOMMENDED TWICE FOR THE SILVER STAR FOR RESCUE MISSIONS OVER NORTH VIETNAM TERRITORY UNDER CONDITIONS OF INTENSE GROUND FIRE AND LOW VISIBILITY. THIS DESTROYER CAPTAIN ASSURES ME THAT IF A PILOT OF A DAMAGED AIRCRAFT CAN MAKE HIS WAY TO THE SEA AND BAIL OUT OVER THE OCEAN HIS PROBABILITY OF RECOVERY IS PRACTICALLY ASSURED. OVER TWO HUNDRED AND FIFTY HAVE BEEN RESCUED FROM THE GULF OF TONKIN.

LET ME TURN NOW TO OUR OPERATIONS CLOSER TO THE SHORE. THIS SHORE INCIDENTALLY IS ELEVEN HUNDRED MILES LONG OR ROUGHLY TWICE THE DISTANCE BETWEEN DETROIT AND WASHINGTON, D.C.

IT IS FILLED WITH INLETS, BAYS, AND ESTUARIES WHICH OFFER PERFECT OPPORTUNITIES FOR COMMUNIST INFILTRATION AND RESUPPLY FROM THE SEA. HERE, IN COOPERATION WITH THE SOUTH VIETNAMESE NAVY, THE U.S. NAVY CONDUCTS AN OPERATION NICKNAMED "MARKET TIME". THIS IS A COOPERATIVE VENTURE WHERE AIRCRAFT CONDUCT SURVEILLANCE OF THE SEA APPROACHES, OUR DESTROYER ESCORTS AND MINESWEEPERS WORK IN THE OFFSHORE WATERS, AND COAST GUARD CUTTERS AND FAST PT BOATS WORK THE LAST GAP BETWEEN THE LARGER SHIPS AND THE SHORE. TO GIVE YOU SOME IDEA OF THE MAGNITUDE OF THIS OPERATION, SINCE AUGUST 1965 WHEN IT STARTED "MARKET TIME" FORCES HAVE

DETECTED SIX HUNDRED AND FIFTY THOUSAND SMALL JUNKS AND SAMPANS. ONE HUNDRED AND TEN THOUSAND OF THESE WERE SEARCHED. SOME WERE DEFINITELY VIETCONG.

OUR MARINES ASHORE IN VIETNAM ARE RESPONSIBLE FOR CONTROL OF THE NORTHEAST REGION JOINING THE DEMILITARIZED ZONE. THIS IS AN AREA OF SOME SEVENTEEN HUNDRED SQUARE MILES. WHEN I SAY CONTROL I MEAN THAT OUR MARINES WITH THE VIETNAMESE ARE RESPONSIBLE FOR PROVIDING SECURITY FOR THE CIVILIAN POPULATION IN THIS AREA. SECURITY IS IMPORTANT BECAUSE THE VIETCONG THRIVE ON MURDER, ASSASSINATION AND THREATS. IF WE ARE TO BE SUCCESSFUL, THIS INTIMIDATION MUST BE STOPPED AND SO OUR MARINES HAVE A PLAN.

THEY HAVE DIVIDED THEIR JOB INTO FOUR TASKS. FIRST, THEY WILL DEFEND THE KEY AREAS WHICH THEY HOLD. SECOND, THEY WILL FIGHT AND DESTROY COMBAT FORCES WHETHER GUERRILA OR NORTH VIETNAMESE REGULARS. THIRD, THEY WILL EXTEND THE AREAS WHICH THEY HOLD BEHIND A SECURITY SCREEN AND FINALLY TO COMPLETE THEIR CYCLE, BEHIND THE SCREEN, THEY WILL PROCEED WITH CONSTRUCTIVE PACIFICATION AND REBUILDING

NO STORY OF THE NAVY IN VIETNAM CAN BE TOLD WITHOUT MENTION OF THE SIX THOUSAND SEABEES NOW IN VIETNAM. THESE ARE YOUNG MEN WHO ARE PROFICIENT IN THE BUILDING AND CONSTRUCTION TRADES. THEY KNOW HOW TO BUILD A BASE OR A ROAD, OR TO DIG A TRENCH CANAL, OR TO

BUILD A LARGE JET AIRFIELD. AND THEY KNOW HOW TO DO THIS WITH A RIFLE NEARBY BECAUSE THEY MOVE INTO AREAS WHERE VIETCONG ATTACKS ARE REGULARLY EXPECTED. BECAUSE OF THIS EXTREME DANGER, IT IS NOT SURPRISING THAT THE NAVY'S FIRST MEDAL OF HONOR WINNER IN VIETNAM WAS A SEABEE (MARVIN SHIELDS) WHO WAS FROM WASHINGTON. HIS WIDOW RESIDES IN SEATTLE

I HAVE BEEN SPEAKING BRIEFLY OF THE FLEXIBILITY OF YOUR NAVY BECAUSE IT IS THE NAVY'S CAPABILITIES I KNOW BEST, BUT I CAN ASSURE YOU THAT THIS SAME FLEXIBILITY HAS BEEN WELL DEMONSTRATED BY ARMY AND AIR FORCE OPERATIONS IN VIET NAM. THERE IS EXCELLENT COOPERATION BETWEEN ALL OF OUR FORCES AND IT IS THIS COOPERATION WHICH WILL BRING ABOUT EVENTUAL

MILITARY SUCCESS.

I DO NOT BELIEVE THAT THERE IS GENERAL UNDERSTANDING OF THE ROLE OF OUR ALLIES IN VIETNAM. LET ME SAY SIMPLY THAT FIFTY-TWO THOUSAND TROOPS FROM FIVE ASIAN NATIONS ARE NOW FIGHTING ALONGSIDE THE UNITED STATES AND THE VIETNAMESE. I HAVE BEEN GRATIFIED BY RECENT RENEWED PLEDGES OF THESE ALLIES THAT IN ASIA AS ELSEWHERE IN THE WORLD THE AMERICAN FIGHTING MAN WILL BE STANDING SHOULDER TO SHOULDER WITH MEN OF THOSE COUNTRIES DIRECTLY BORDERING THE COMMUNISTS. THERE IS THEREFORE TANGIBLE SUPPORT FOR THE U.S. POSITION.

BUT I AM SPEAKING TODAY IN THE TERMS OF PRIMARY SOURCES OF THE POWER OF

THE UNITED STATES -- THE YOUTH OF OUR COUNTRY AND THE DEDICATION OF OUR CITIZENS. OUR FUTURE LIES IN A CONTINUATION OF THE PHILOSOPHIES WHICH HAVE PRODUCED OUR CURRENT CAPABILITIES. WE ARE, IN THE MILITARY, CONSTANTLY AWARE OF THE GREAT TECHNOLOGICAL CHANGE WHICH HAS ENGULFED OUR COUNTRY. BUT WE ARE EQUALLY AWARE THAT THE MOST COMPLEX PIECE OF EQUIPMENT REQUIRES A TRAINED TECHNICIAN WHO IS BOTH KNOWLEDGEABLE AND INTERESTED. MANY OF TODAY'S TECHNICIANS ARE STILL IN THEIR TEENS. THEY COME TO US FROM YOUR HOMES ENDOWED WITH THE KNOWLEDGE AND INTEREST WHICH YOU HAVE IN KEEPING THE CURRENT POSITION OF THE UNITED STATES

AS THE MIGHTIEST MILITARY POWER IN HISTORY. THUS IN A LARGE SENSE THE FUTURE GOALS OF OUR COUNTRY REMAIN IN THE HANDS OF YOUNG MEN AND YOUNG WOMEN WHOM YOU HAVE REARED, EDUCATED AND TAUGHT THE VALUE AND PRIDE IN BEING AN AMERICAN.

I AM SURE THAT MANY OF US, AT ONE TIME, QUESTIONED THE TOUGHNESS OF OUR YOUNG PEOPLE. WE WONDERED IF THE LONG HAIR, THE TIGHT BREECHES, THE BEATLE CRAZE REFLECTED A CHANGE IN THE FIBRE OF YOUNG AMERICANS. WE WONDERED, TOO, IF THE TROUBLE RAISERS, THE RECALCITRANTS AGAINST ANY DISCIPLINE AND EVEN AGAINST ACCEPTED RULES OF CONDUCT, IF THESE MALCONFORMISTS REPRESENTED A COMPLETELY NEW BREED OF MEN. WE NO LONGER HAVE TO

BE CONCERNED WITH YOUNG AMERICA. OUR YOUNG MEN HAVE BEEN TESTED AGAINST THE APPALLING TERRAIN IN VIETNAM, AGAINST A WAY OF LIVING COMPLETELY FOREIGN TO THEM, AGAINST OBSTACLES AND AGAINST ENEMIES WHO FIGHT SAVAGELY AND WITHOUT RESTRAINT. OUR YOUNG MEN HAVE PROVEN THEIR PHYSICAL AND MORAL STAMINA! WITHOUT HURRAH THEY HAVE STOOD THE TEST!

LAST MONTH I VISITED A MARINE CORPS RECRUIT GRADUATION AND THE NEXT DAY WENT ABOARD AN AIRCRAFT CARRIER WHERE YOUNG PILOTS WERE MAKING THEIR FIRST CARRIER LANDINGS. BOTH EVENTS MARKED A SIGNIFICANT TURNING POINT IN THE LIVES OF THESE YOUNG MEN. I CAN REPORT TO YOU THAT ON BOTH OCCASIONS THERE WAS A LOOK

OF COMPLETE DETERMINATION ON THEIR FACES. THE SEVENTEEN YEAR OLD MARINES AFTER ONLY EIGHT WEEKS TRAINING SHOWED THEIR PRIDE IN BEING MARINES AND IN SERVING THEIR COUNTRY. THE YOUNG JET PILOTS WHO, WHEN I SAW THEM, WERE MAKING THEIR FIRST LANDINGS ON A FAST MOVING CARRIER DECK ALSO SHOWED NOT ONLY THEIR TECHNICAL AND OPERATIONAL CAPABILITIES BUT THEIR DEDICATION AND THEIR PRIDE IN BEING AMERICANS. THESE MEN ARE PERFORMING AS AMERICAN MEN IN OUR ARMED FORCES HAVE PERFORMED THROUGHOUT OUR HISTORY, AND SO I CONTINUE TO BELIEVE THAT OUR MILITARY POSTURE RESTS ON A SOLID FOUNDATION IN OUR YOUTH. AND I COMMEND YOU AS PARENTS FOR THE EARLY TRAINING WHICH YOU HAVE GIVEN THESE YOUNG MEN.

THREE DAYS AGO I WAS DEEPLY HONORED TO PRESENT A NAVY CROSS TO THE PARENTS OF A YOUNG NAVY HOSPITALMAN WHO DIED WHILE ON DUTY WITH THE MARINES IN VIETNAM. I CAN THINK OF NO MORE APPROPRIATE WAY TO IMPRESS ON EACH OF YOU THE SENSE OF DEDICATION OF WHICH I HAVE BEEN SPEAKING THAN TO REPEAT THE WORDS OF THE MARINE OFFICER WHO WATCHED THIS YOUNG AMERICAN AS HE LEFT A COMPARATIVELY SAFE PLACE, AND RAN TWO HUNDRED YARDS IN HOSTILE FIRE TO ADMINISTER TO A WOUNDED MARINE. THE MARINE OFFICER WHO SAW THIS DESCRIBED IT IN A FEW SIMPLE AND POWERFUL WORDS:

"HOSPITALMAN SAMUEL ORLANDO WAS FOUND NEXT TO THE MAN HE WAS AIDING AND IT WAS CLEARLY APPARENT THAT HE HAD NO INTENTION OF LEAVING UNTIL HIS WORK WAS DONE. CONSEQUENTLY, HE DIED PERFORMING AN ACT OF EXTREME COURAGE".

LET ME REPEAT: "HE HAD NO INTENTION OF LEAVING UNTIL HIS WORK WAS DONE". THIS IS THE SAME DEDICATION WHICH SINCE 1776 HAS BEEN THE INSPIRATION WHICH HAS MADE AMERICA GREAT.

THE END

Remarks on occasion assuming duties as Headmaster
SEVERN SCHOOL.   Sept 21, 1968

"As a way of introduction to my new career in education, I would like to spend a few more minutes on my experiences in the Navy. I was relieved as commander of the amphibious forces very precipitously. One Thursday afternoon I had a phone call from a member of the staff of the Commander in Chief Atlantic Fleet telling me that I would be relieved of my duties as commander of the amphibious forces the next morning. I asked what my new duties would be and was told that he did not know. I asked why I was being relieved and was told he did not know. I then asked what I had done wrong to be relieved of such a splendid command and he said he did not know, but that I would be informed the next morning. I asked who my relief would be and he again reported he did not know. Sure enough the next morning the Admiral called me and told me that I would be relieved by my friend Admiral Rivero who is now Commander in Chief of all allied forces in Southern Europe and that the next morning I would be taking command of the fleet which consisted of all the combatant units in the Atlantic Fleet, therefore operating in the Atlantic. These events did transpire. When I assumed command of the fleet my Chief of Staff came up to me and told me that on this Saturday that we had orders to sail some ships and put them to sea and that we were ordered to send other ships to sea the next day - Sunday. This is against Navy regulations except in emergencies, so I called my boss Admiral Denison and asked him what he was doing with my fleet and asked if I could come to see him in his office. He replied that he wanted to see me but not in his office, for me to meet him in an airplane and we would be taking off for Washington within a few minutes. We spent the rest of that Saturday for the quarantine, or the blockade, or the invasion of Cuba. We were not cold of course, since we already had plans for the invasion of Cuba should that be needed but these plans needed updating to fit the actual forces in being and ready as of that date. I learned for the first time that the President would call a blockade on the following Wednesday and that my ships were to be at sea on the line at the time of the Presidential speech. I learned also that this was to be very closely held and that I would not be permitted to recall men from leave in order to fill out the crews, that no mention would be made in the press or the radio until after the Presidential speech on a Monday afternoon. I got my Captains together on Sunday afternoon and told them that we would be sailing the next day and gave them some orders for their initial provisions. The Fleet did sail. The Fleet was on the line on Wednesday when the Presidential proclamation became effective. We did do the job that had to be done. The President was successful in attaining the limited objectives he set forth and in my opinion the entire operation went flawlessly.

I have two general observations. First, we had the requisite force to accomplish the missions and tasks set forth and the American people showed the willpower to employ that force and Second, the men of the Fleet were superb. They accomplished long and difficult tasks and they did them well. The leaders in the Fleet were educated people. Their education and their knowledge paid off. The many examples of splendid initiative resulted from the self confidence possessed by educated people. My long experiences in the Navy have convinced me that the leaders in any endeavor will be people with knowledge. I have recently left the job as military advisor to the Embassador to NATO and to the Secretary of Defense and Secretary of State as regards the military affairs of the Alliance. Working with Harlan Cleveland, the U.S. Ambassador, was a real pleasure primarily because he is a smart, educated, knowledgeable, forceful, American diplomat. He is a road scholar, he has written books, he has been a key to our success in the U.S. leadership in NATO. He has been largely reponsible for U.S. policies as regard to this European Alliance. President Johnson on several occasions had him return to Washington and spend many weeks sitting in the offices of members of Congress explaining to Senators and Congressmen our objectives, our policies and our needs with regard to our Alliances. My conviction that education is vital to well being of this great country of ours and my wish to work with the youth of America, led me into the field of education. Now turning to the role of the Independent School. I believe there is general acceptance that Indepdndent Schools are needed now and will be needed in the future to fill voids in the achievements of the public schools. The majority of our public schools are doing a good job generally provided with superb physical plants, plants much better than many of the Independent Schools. There is all the education available in public schools that is needed by the majority of our youngsters. Outstanding youngsters particularly are able to get some good education. The private or Independent Schools have several advantages. First, the classes are smaller so that individualxinstruction can be given on an individual basis. Second, the student-teacher ratio relationships are closer with the resulting benefit not only to the education received but also to the accomplished feeling of accomplishment by both the teacher and the student. Third, these closer relationships result in development of maturity and of the whole man concept. That is, integrity, self discipline, self reliance. These advantages are evidenced by the fact that even though salaries paid by individual schools to teachess are much less than those in public school systems. Most teachers prefer to work in smaller classes and in independent schools.

-A.G.Ward

Ambassador Cleveland also left Government Service to join those in the field of Education He is now President University of Hawaii

www.ingramcontent.com/pod-product-compliance
Lightning Source LLC
Chambersburg PA
CBHW080621170426
43209CB00007B/1489